Reaching Students

Reaching Students

What Research Says About Effective Instruction in Undergraduate Science and Engineering

Nancy Kober

Based on the National Research Council Report
Discipline-Based Education Research:
Understanding and Improving Learning
in Undergraduate Science and Engineering

Board on Science Education

Division of Behavioral and Social Sciences and Education

NATIONAL RESEARCH COUNCIL
OF THE NATIONAL ACADEMIES

THE NATIONAL ACADEMIES PRESS
Washington, D.C.
www.nap.edu

THE NATIONAL ACADEMIES PRESS   500 Fifth Street, NW   Washington, DC 20001

NOTICE: The project that is the subject of this report was approved by the Governing Board of the National Research Council, whose members are drawn from the councils of the National Academy of Sciences, the National Academy of Engineering, and the Institute of Medicine. The members of the committee responsible for the report were chosen for their special competences and with regard for appropriate balance.

This study was supported by grant number DUE-0934453 between the National Academy of Sciences and the National Science Foundation and a grant from the Sloan Foundation. Any opinions, findings, conclusions, or recommendations expressed in this publication are those of the author and do not necessarily reflect the views of the National Science Foundation or the Sloan Foundation.

International Standard Book Number-13:   978-0-309-30043-8
International Standard Book Number-10:   0-309-30043-6
Library of Congress Control Number: 2014958653

All websites cited in this book were accessed and available as of December 4, 2014.

Additional copies of this report are available from the National Academies Press, 500 Fifth Street, NW, Keck 360, Washington, DC 20001; (800) 624-6242 or (202) 334-3313; http://www.nap.edu.

Suggested citation: Kober, N. (2015). *Reaching Students: What Research Says About Effective Instruction in Undergraduate Science and Engineering.* Board on Science Education, Division of Behavioral and Social Sciences and Education. Washington, DC: The National Academies Press.

THE NATIONAL ACADEMIES

Advisers to the Nation on Science, Engineering, and Medicine

The **National Academy of Sciences** is a private, nonprofit, self-perpetuating society of distinguished scholars engaged in scientific and engineering research, dedicated to the furtherance of science and technology and to their use for the general welfare. Upon the authority of the charter granted to it by the Congress in 1863, the Academy has a mandate that requires it to advise the federal government on scientific and technical matters. Dr. Ralph J. Cicerone is president of the National Academy of Sciences.

The **National Academy of Engineering** was established in 1964, under the charter of the National Academy of Sciences, as a parallel organization of outstanding engineers. It is autonomous in its administration and in the selection of its members, sharing with the National Academy of Sciences the responsibility for advising the federal government. The National Academy of Engineering also sponsors engineering programs aimed at meeting national needs, encourages education and research, and recognizes the superior achievements of engineers. Dr. C. D. Mote, Jr., is president of the National Academy of Engineering.

The **Institute of Medicine** was established in 1970 by the National Academy of Sciences to secure the services of eminent members of appropriate professions in the examination of policy matters pertaining to the health of the public. The Institute acts under the responsibility given to the National Academy of Sciences by its congressional charter to be an adviser to the federal government and, upon its own initiative, to identify issues of medical care, research, and education. Dr. Victor J. Dzau is president of the Institute of Medicine.

The **National Research Council** was organized by the National Academy of Sciences in 1916 to associate the broad community of science and technology with the Academy's purposes of furthering knowledge and advising the federal government. Functioning in accordance with general policies determined by the Academy, the Council has become the principal operating agency of both the National Academy of Sciences and the National Academy of Engineering in providing services to the government, the public, and the scientific and engineering communities. The Council is administered jointly by both Academies and the Institute of Medicine. Dr. Ralph J. Cicerone and Dr. C. D. Mote, Jr., are chair and vice chair, respectively, of the National Research Council.

www.national-academies.org

Contents

Acknowledgments

This book would not have been possible without the sponsorship of the Sloan Foundation and the National Science Foundation.

A group of experts in learning and teaching at the undergraduate level served as consultants and provided ongoing input in the development of this book. Special thanks are due to them for their invaluable guidance throughout the process. This group included Ann E. Austin, Professor of Higher, Adult, and Lifelong Education, Michigan State University; Melanie Cooper, Professor of Chemistry, Michigan State University; Heather MacDonald, Professor of Geology, College of William and Mary; Karl Smith, Cooperative Learning Professor of Engineering Education, School of Engineering Education, Purdue University, and Distinguished Teaching Professor and Professor of Civil Engineering, University of Minnesota; Carl Wieman, Professor of Physics and in the Graduate School of Education, Stanford University; and William B. Wood, Professor of Molecular, Cellular, and Developmental Biology, Emeritus, University of Colorado Boulder.

More than 70 individuals participated in the interviews conducted by the author. Their insights and experiences form the foundation for the many cases and examples in the book. A heartfelt thanks to them for the time and attention they gave to this project and their continued commitment to improving learning and teaching in undergraduate science, technology, engineering, and mathematics. (See List of Interviewees on p. 226.)

Deepest gratitude is owed to Heidi Schweingruber of the Board on Science Education, who played an essential role by developing, conceptualizing, and providing wise guidance on the content, organization, and writing of this book. Other Board staff who helped to produce this book include Rebecca Krone, Natalie Nielsen, and Joanna Roberts. Thank you as well to Stephen Mautner of the National Academies Press for his sound advice throughout the project.

This report has been reviewed in draft form by individuals chosen for their diverse perspectives and technical expertise, in accordance with procedures approved by the National Research Council. The purpose of this independent review is to provide candid and critical comments that will assist the institution in making its published report as sound as possible and to ensure that the report meets institutional standards for objectivity, evidence, and responsiveness to the charge. The review comments and draft manuscript remain confidential to protect the integrity of the process.

We thank the following individuals for their review of this report: Ken Bain, President, Best Teachers/Best Students Institute, South Orange, New Jersey; Teri Balser, Soil and Water Science Department, University of Florida; Diane Ebert-May, Department of Plant Biology, Michigan State University; Michael Klymkowsky, Molecular, Cellular, and Developmental Biology, Co-Director, CU Teach Science Teacher Recruitment and Certification Program, University of Colorado Boulder; David W. Mogk, Department of Earth Sciences, Montana State University; and Lorrie A. Shepard, School of Education, University of Colorado Boulder.

Although the reviewers listed above provided many constructive comments and suggestions, they were not asked to endorse the content of the report nor did they see the final draft of the report before its release. The review of this report was overseen by Joseph Krajcik, College of Education, Michigan State University. Appointed by the Division of Behavioral and Social Sciences and Education, he was responsible for making certain that an independent examination of this report was carried out in accordance with institutional procedures and that all review comments were carefully considered. Responsibility for the final content of this report rests entirely with the author and the institution.

Preface

If you teach science or engineering or have a strong interest in these disciplines, your undergraduate years were likely a turning point. Perhaps the initial excitement you felt as an adolescent when you observed the luminous clouds of the Orion Nebula through your new telescope grew into a desire for an astronomy career in an undergraduate course when you learned how and why this nebula is a place where stars are born. Or maybe a college field trip to a Paleozoic rock outcrop opened your mind to the immensity and longevity of the forces at work in Earth's formation and spurred you to pursue geosciences. Whatever the inspiration, you persisted through excellent courses and lackluster ones, through stimulating assignments and tedious ones, to complete an undergraduate major in science or engineering and go on to master a discipline.

Based on your own undergraduate experiences, you may assume that most students should be able to learn science the way you learned science, but that is not always the case. For too many students, the undergraduate years are the turnoff point. A single course with poorly designed instruction or curriculum can stop a student who was considering a science or engineering major in her tracks. More than half of the students who start out in science or engineering switch to other majors or do not finish college at all. Maybe they failed a crucial prerequisite course, or found little to engage their interest in their introductory courses, or failed to see the relevance of what they were being taught. For non-majors, an introductory course that confirms their preconception that they are "bad at science" may be the last science course they ever take.

Evidence from research on learning and teaching in science and engineering suggests that a large part of the problem lies in the way these courses are traditionally taught—through lectures and reading assignments, note-taking and memorization, and laboratories with specific instructions and a predetermined result.

A 2012 report by the President's Council of Advisors on Science and Technology, *Engage to Excel,* sizes up the issue in this way:

> Traditional teaching methods have trained many STEM [science, technology, engineering, and mathematics] professionals, including most of the current STEM workforce. But a large and growing body of research indicates that STEM education can be substantially improved through a diversification of teaching methods. These data show that evidence-based teaching methods are more effective in reaching all students—especially the "underrepresented majority"—the women and members of minority groups who now constitute approximately 70% of college students. (p. i)

To learn science and engineering well at the undergraduate level, students must understand in depth the fundamental concepts of a discipline. They must develop skills in solving problems and working with the tools of science and be able to apply these skills to new and somewhat different tasks. They must understand the nature and practices of science or engineering and be able to critically evaluate information.

How do students learn these crucial aspects of science and engineering? Are there ways of thinking that hinder or help these learning processes? Which kinds of teaching strategies are most effective in developing these types of knowledge and skills? How can instructors determine whether their students have met these learning goals? And how can instructors apply these strategies to their own courses or encourage them within their departments or institutions?

To inform these questions, this book offers evidence from an area of scholarship called discipline-based education research, or DBER, and related fields. DBER has arrived at insights about how students learn science and engineering and how to design instructional strategies that build on these insights to improve students' conceptual knowledge and attitudes about learning. The most comprehensive synthesis of findings from DBER and their potential to improve instruction can be found in a 2012 report by the National Research Council (NRC), *Discipline-Based Education Research: Understanding and Improving Learning in Undergraduate Science and Engineering.* The report was written by an NRC-convened committee of 15 experts from physics, astronomy, biology, chemistry, geosciences, engineering, cognitive psychology, educational psychology, and science education. Over the course of 13 months in 2010 and 2011, the committee members distilled the main findings from peer-reviewed DBER studies and examined the influence of this research on undergraduate instruction in the major science disciplines and engineering. They also identified issues for future research and considered the resources, incentives, and conditions needed to advance the field of DBER and enhance its impact on instruction. To help inform its work, the committee commissioned new papers and held four fact-finding meetings.

Along the way, the committee realized that its findings could have a far-reaching impact on those who teach undergraduate science and engineering or have an influence on instruction in these disciplines. This book for practitioners grew out of that realization.

This book is based on the 2012 NRC report on DBER, as well as on interviews with expert practitioners who have successfully applied findings from DBER and related research in their classrooms, departments, or institutions.[1] The goal is to summarize the most salient findings of the NRC committee and the experience of expert practitioners about how students learn undergraduate science and engineering and what this means for instruction. This book presents new ways of thinking about what to teach, how to teach it, and how to assess what students are learning. To encourage instructors and others to apply this information in their institutions, it also includes short examples and longer case studies of experienced practitioners who are implementing research-based strategies in undergraduate science and engineering courses or across departments or institutions. Although these findings could apply to a variety of disciplines, this book focuses on the disciplines addressed in the NRC study—physics, astronomy, biology, chemistry, geosciences, and engineering.

This book is intended for anyone who teaches or plans to teach undergraduate courses in science and engineering at any type of higher education institution or who is in a position to influence instruction at this level. Throughout the book, the term "instructor" is used broadly to refer to the full range of teaching staff— tenured, non-tenured, or adjunct faculty; lecturers and similar teaching positions; and postdoctoral scholars or graduate students with teaching responsibilities. Although many of the strategies and ideas in these pages are geared to instructors, others with an interest in science and engineering education will find suggestions for encouraging or supporting research-based instruction. These other audiences might include department heads; faculty development providers; provosts, deans, and other higher education administrators; leaders of professional societies and associations for science and engineering; and those with policy roles in higher education or science education.

---

[1] All of the interviews cited in this book were conducted by Nancy Kober between March 2013 and March 2014.

If you are a newcomer to research-based instruction, this book will introduce you to the main ideas about learning and teaching that are emerging from DBER, as well as strategies you might try in your classroom or institution. If you are already somewhat familiar with these ideas, you will find additional evidence-based approaches for addressing particular student needs, as well as advice for overcoming challenges that are bound to arise. If you are experienced in implementing this type of teaching, you may discover insights from other practitioners that could enrich your own practices.

Chapter 1 lays out the reasons why instructors and instructional leaders might consider evidence about how students learn science and engineering as they design their instruction. It introduces some of the main findings from DBER and gives examples of how instructors have applied these findings in a variety of settings. Chapter 2 shares suggestions from researchers and expert practitioners about how to get started with implementing research-based strategies and how to make the process less intimidating.

Chapter 3 summarizes general evidence from research on how people learn and specific findings about how undergraduates learn science and engineering. It also discusses how insights from these research fields have informed the design of instructional strategies that seek to improve students' conceptual understanding, problem-solving skills, and use of models and other visual and mathematical representations. Chapter 4 describes a range of research-based instructional strategies in science and engineering, including strategies to make lectures more interactive, use student group work to promote learning, and make learning more relevant, among other goals. Chapter 5 examines related aspects of effective instruction, including assessment, appropriate uses of technology, and changes in the learning environment.

Chapter 6 looks at some common challenges in implementing research-based instruction and ways to overcome these challenges. Chapter 7 discusses actions that departments, institutions, and outside groups can take to encourage and support effective undergraduate instruction in science and engineering. A concluding section recaps the main messages of the book.

Throughout the chapters you will find concrete examples and case studies that illustrate how skilled instructors and leaders from various disciplines and types of institutions have used findings from DBER and related research on learning to design and support instruction in their classrooms, departments, or institutions. These examples may inspire, intrigue, challenge, or provoke you. Whatever your reaction, the examples are intended to encourage reflection and discussion about effective ways to help students learn science and engineering.

This type of reflection is not always easy. Instructors may be unaware of this body of research. Even if they aware, they may be disinclined to change teaching methods that are familiar or ubiquitous in their departments and seem to be working, at least for some students. Departmental and institutional cultures may also present obstacles to changing practice, as discussed in later chapters.

On a positive note, however, as a scientist or an engineer you already have the intellectual tools and experience needed to examine students' learning and your own teaching from a research perspective. Every day, you tackle research problems in your discipline, consider various strategies to solve those problems, try out a strategy, and revise that strategy based on the results. Why not apply this same mindset to your teaching? The research is there, and so are a variety of curriculum materials, professional development opportunities, and other resources. With some effort, the rewards will be there, too—better educated students, greater professional satisfaction, and a brighter outlook for society.

Thinking About Learning and Teaching as a Researcher Would

If you're like many instructors of undergraduate science and engineering, you may be fairly satisfied with your teaching. You've made an effort to craft meaningful and interesting lectures that coherently present the content students should learn in your discipline. You may break up your lectures with questions that students answer anonymously on handheld devices. The students who work hard do well in your courses, and your evaluations are good, perhaps outstanding. While there are certainly things you could tweak, the other demands on your time—including, in many cases, your own research agenda—may make you hesitant to tamper with a solid course.

Or perhaps you're a department head, faculty development expert, or institutional leader who would like to invigorate instruction on a wider scale but must consider any reforms within a broader context of faculty autonomy, time and funding constraints, and other pressing priorities. Or maybe you're a graduate student or post-doc who would like to explore innovative teaching in your discipline but sees little incentive from your department or the competitive faculty job market to pursue those innovations.

So why take time to investigate effective approaches to teaching and learning? Why make the effort to redesign a course or program that on the whole seems to be working well? A short answer comes from the experiences of many instructors around the country—successful by standard criteria—who reviewed the research on learning, reflected on their teaching, and found it wanting. Drawing on this research base, they designed ways to help their students develop a better understanding of the fundamental concepts of a science or engineering discipline, become more engaged in their own learning, and begin to think and reason as scientists and engineers do. These instructors often started with modest changes and refined their techniques over time. And their results were often encouraging.

This chapter discusses the benefits of adopting a research-based approach to teaching and learning and introduces findings from research that are explored in greater depth in later chapters. The examples and case studies in this chapter describe the factors that motivated instructors to examine or conduct research on learning and make changes in their teaching. These cases also illustrate how research-based strategies can be feasible—exciting, even—in settings ranging from community colleges to large research institutions, and from small classes to big introductory lecture courses.

Research on Learning Spurs Changes in Teaching Practices

For Eric Mazur,[1] a professor of physics at Harvard University, the desire to change his teaching took shape in 1990, when he came across a series of papers by Ibrahim Halloun and David Hestenes (1985, 1987) showing that conventional physics instruction did little to alter students' misguided beliefs about common physical phenomena. Although, after a few months of physics instruction, most students could correctly recite Newton's third law and apply it in numerical problems, Halloun and Hestenes probed more deeply by administering an assessment they had developed called the Force Concept Inventory. The results suggested that many students did not truly understand basic Newtonian concepts. Mazur, who had been teaching introductory physics since 1984, doubted this was a problem for his Harvard students. But he was intrigued enough to try the test on his own science and engineering majors. "The results of the test came as a shock: the students fared hardly better on the [conceptual] test than on their midterm examination," Mazur writes. Yet, he notes, the midterm covered material of far greater difficulty—"or so I thought" (Mazur, 1997, p. 4).

Mazur's further research with his own students convinced him that although many could correctly solve conventional mathematics problems in physics, a sizable share continued to cling to alarming misconceptions. He concluded that many students do well on conventional problems "by memorizing algorithms without understanding the underlying physics." Moreover, he realized, even experienced teachers could be "completely misled into thinking that students have been taught effectively" (Mazur, 1997, p. 6).

---

[1] Except where noted, the information in this example comes from an interview with Eric Mazur, April 13, 2013.

Following this revelation, Mazur explored different strategies for teaching introductory physics. Over time, he developed an approach called Peer Instruction, described in more detail in Chapter 4. In Peer Instruction, brief lecture presentations are interspersed with short assessment questions, or ConcepTests, designed to expose common student difficulties in understanding a single concept. Students think about the question, come up with their own answers, and then discuss their responses for a few minutes with a small group of peers as they seek to reach consensus on the correct answer (Mazur, 1997).

A self-confessed "data junkie," Mazur analyzed years of statistics on his students' performance and continued to refine his teaching. His data show that students taught with Peer Instruction have greater mastery of conceptual reasoning and quantitative problem-solving skills than those in traditionally taught classes (Crouch and Mazur, 2001). More recent work by Lazry, Mazur, and Watkins (2008) found similar improvements in knowledge and skills, as well as decreased attrition in introductory physics courses, among community college students taught with Peer Instruction.

Eric Mazur working with students in his introductory physics class.

For Richard Yuretich,[2] a professor at the University of Massachusetts Amherst, the impetus to change grew out of his frustration with poor attendance and a lack of student engagement in his large oceanography course, which enrolled roughly 1,200 students. Most of the students were not science majors, and they were divided into four sections taught by different instructors. Although the course received high ratings on student evaluations, Yuretich, who at that point had been teaching for more than a decade, still felt that "the class was not being engaged on any level." He described the problem in this way (Yuretich et al., 2001):

---

[2] Except where noted, the information in this example comes from an interview with Richard Yuretich, April 4, 2013.

Despite our best efforts to deliver coherent, enthusiastic, and well-illustrated lectures, we questioned whether many students were learning as much as they could. Attendance on a typical day hovered at or below 50%, except just before exams when the class was packed. Students would routinely leave early or arrive late. Our attempts to engage the class in questioning and discussion resulted in the animated participation of a small cadre of motivated students, but the rest of the class was listless and disinterested.

Yuretich wanted to teach in a way that would convince students that "if they come to class, this is where learning is going to happen." A new center for learning on his campus had begun giving workshops on more interactive approaches to teaching, which inspired him to try something new. At that time, in the 1990s, research on geosciences education was quite limited, he notes, but he found enough to get started. He began encouraging more discussion by providing students with handheld microphones, interspersing his lectures with short videos, and doing demonstrations in class to illustrate basic principles.

A further breakthrough in Yuretich's thinking about instruction occurred when he served as a geology expert in a summer institute for K–12 teachers. As he worked with the teachers on developing hands-on learning activities, he kept thinking: "There's nothing here that can't work with undergrad students. So I started taking some of the things we were doing at the summer institutes and modifying them to work with the students in a lecture hall." He incorporated activities into his lectures that students could do in their seats in small groups, such as graphing, conducting short experiments, and classifying fossils, and this "seemed to get things moving," he says.

Yuretich and a group of colleagues received a National Science Foundation (NSF) grant to develop a systematic, campus-wide approach to improve science instruction for students who were preparing to become middle and high school teachers, and his oceanography class became the "test bed," he explains. He and his colleague Mark Leckie designed a series of in-class exercises that students could carry out with their peers sitting next to them after a brief lecture by the

> "Putting the toe in water is a better strategy than diving in and suddenly getting frozen. We started out just doing a few trial things ... and ultimately expanded to trying more. And then eventually the whole class changed over."
>
> —*Richard Yuretich,*
> *University of Massachusetts Amherst*

instructor. The exercises are intended to "help students think like scientific investigators" (Yuretich et al., 2001). To better understand the principle of density, for example, students work together to answer these questions:

1. List some ways that you could measure the density of water.

2. Is salt water more or less dense than fresh water? How could you tell?

3. Design an experiment that would allow you to measure the change in the density of water as temperature changes.

Evidence collected over several semesters showed a marked increase in student attendance and exam scores, compared with previous classes, and a positive impact on students' critical thinking skills as gauged by surveys and interviews (Yuretich, 2003). "Putting the toe in water is a better strategy than diving in and suddenly getting frozen," says Yuretich. "We started out just doing a few trial things . . . and ultimately expanded to trying more," he explains. "And then eventually the whole class changed over."

In the decades since Mazur and Yuretich began seeking out information, evidence has grown about how students learn in science and engineering disciplines and which instructional strategies are most effective. And an array of resources—including faculty development opportunities, curriculum websites, networks of colleagues, and institutional supports—are available to help instructors apply these techniques and overcome challenges.

These research-based strategies can be adopted or adapted by instructors, and by those in positions to influence instruction, in all types of public or private higher education institutions: research universities, comprehensive universities, liberal arts colleges, other undergraduate institutions, or community colleges. They can work in various kinds of courses: introductory and upper-level courses, small and large classes, lectures and labs, and courses for majors and non-majors. And these strategies are feasible not only for instructors who are interested in doing formal studies of teaching and learning in their discipline, but also for anyone who is open to incorporating ideas from existing research and reflecting on their teaching practices in a systematic way.

As the following case study illustrates, that's what Kaatje van der Hoeven Kraft did when she set out to improve her physical geology course at a community college with a large Hispanic enrollment.

Students Become Reflective Learners— and So Does the Instructor

In Kaatje Kraft's[a] geology classes at Mesa Community College in Arizona, the low-tech notebook is a tool for reflection—both for her students to reflect on what they are learning and for she herself to monitor students' understanding and adjust her teaching accordingly.

Investigating earthquakes using real data

"Why do we get different magnitude earthquakes?" Kraft poses this question to her students near the beginning of one class period in physical geology.

The 24 students, a diverse group that includes many Hispanic students, offer a variety of answers: *The depth of the earthquake. How much the plates move. Tension.*

After nudging students to consider the elastic rebound theory, which they had just learned, Kraft directs them to talk with their tablemates about the factors that might generate different size earthquakes.

For the next few minutes, the students, who are seated at tables in groups of four, discuss this question. Several pause occasionally to write in colorful course notebooks filled with assignments, worksheets, questions for reflection, and their own notes and drawings. Kraft circulates among the students, listening to their conversations and asking probing questions. "Ooh, intriguing!" she exclaims in response to one student's explanation.

Kraft moves to the front of the room, next to a large world map displaying the major plate boundaries. "Some of you are on the right track," she says. "But some of you are thinking about intensity versus magnitude. It's easy to confuse those."

As students from each group report their possible explanations to the whole class, Kraft writes their responses on a whiteboard and summarizes: "The rate of plate motion might actually influence how *often* you get an earthquake, whereas how much energy is built up determines how *big* it is. And so we go back to the elastic rebound theory—the more stress you build up, the bigger the earthquake is going to be," she says as she interlocks her fingers and pulls her hands in opposite directions until they release with a forceful jerk.

Kraft then preps students for the next task: each table of students will analyze one of six significant earthquakes that occurred between 2004 and 2011 in sites ranging from Chile to Sumatra. Each group will focus on four characteristics of their particular earthquake:

---

[a] Except where noted, the information in this example comes from an interview with Kaatje Kraft, April 13, 2013, and from a video of Kraft teaching a geology class. At the time of the interview, Kraft was teaching at Mesa Community College in Arizona. She has since moved to Whatcom Community College in Bellingham, Washington (as of September 2014).

1. Tectonic setting—whether the plate boundary is divergent (with plates moving away from each other) or convergent (with plates moving toward each other); and if it is convergent, whether it is a subduction zone, whereby one plate moves under the other and sinks into the Earth's mantle, or a non-subduction zone

2. Magnitude

3. Intensity at the epicenter and in other areas

4. Significant events such as loss of life, injury, or property destruction

Kraft encourages the students to consult data on the U.S. Geological Survey (USGS) website (every table has at least one laptop) and make sketches.

For the next 30 minutes, students talk animatedly. They look up information on the USGS website, consult their ubiquitous notebooks, and summarize what they found on small whiteboards. Kraft stops by each table to check on their progress and offer guidance. She tells them to write any remaining questions on a big whiteboard at the front of the room.

In the next segment of the class, students from each group present the highlights of their table's investigation to the whole class. As the other students listen to these presentations, Kraft asks them to think about the commonalities and differences among the six earthquakes. Their ideas come into play during a final class discussion about the characteristics that tend to produce earthquakes of large magnitude and the factors that could lead to differences in intensity and damage for earthquakes of similar magnitude.

Later in the semester, at the end of the earthquake unit, students apply what they've learned to an earthquake "case study" that extends over four class periods (Kraft, n.d.). Working with real data, each group of students analyzes a particular aspect of a significant earthquake, such as the Alaska earthquake of 1964 or the San Francisco Loma Prieta earthquake of 1989. One group develops an overview, another analyzes the resulting tsunami, a third studies the geologic maps and intensity, and a fourth looks at the hazards incurred. Using the "jigsaw" technique described in Chapter 4, students from each group reassemble into new teams to share what they learned from their initial group's analysis. These new teams come up with recommendations to government officials about the earthquake and its implications for future development, which they present to the whole class in a poster session. Next,

A group poster on a case study of the 1964 Alaska earthquake.

students write individual papers on the earthquake they studied, which are peer reviewed and revised. In a wrap-up activity, students reflect on their own strengths and weaknesses during the case study process and consider how they can be more successful learners in the future. This case study activity, which Kraft developed, has been rated as exemplary by On the Cutting Edge, a professional development program sponsored by the National Association of Geoscience Teachers.

Becoming a reflective practitioner

Kraft, who began teaching at Mesa in 1999, arrived at her current approach to teaching through what she describes as "a slow and gradual progression of learning more about the research and learning more about effective strategies." Although her graduate school experience had piqued her interest in geology education, some of the interactive strategies she tried in her early years of teaching did not go so well. "But as a novice teacher, things sometimes generally don't go so well. And as a novice teacher, I didn't actually know that," she explains. So she reverted to a more traditional way of teaching.

Her interest in trying new teaching strategies was rekindled in 2003, when she participated in a grant to develop curriculum in collaboration with middle and high school teachers. As a result of that experience, she began incorporating writing assignments into her courses in which students reflected on their learning. To expand her own knowledge of effective teaching strategies, she attended workshops offered by On the Cutting Edge. There she met faculty who were doing research on geology education. Kraft says the connections she made through these workshops have been "amazing" in helping her improve her teaching. "The more you have other people to bounce ideas off of and

support you, the more likely you are to take risks and try things." She has since led and presented at On the Cutting Edge workshops herself.

In 2007, Kraft took a sabbatical to collaborate on a project to study ways to improve student learning by engaging the affective domain—attitudes, motivation, beliefs, and other factors that can affect students' behavior and performance (van der Hoeven Kraft et al., 2011). The sabbatical altered how she viewed her role as an instructor and her students' roles as learners. "We really need to move away from that way of thinking that I just need to tell them everything I know. Rather, I have to help them negotiate content from the perspective of what I know," she explains. Typical of a community college, her students vary greatly in life experiences, prior preparation, and long-term goals, but most are taking an introductory geology course to meet a general science requirement. She wanted to teach in a way that would not only cover the required competencies, but also create an environment where students wanted to come to class and could develop skills that would serve them well no matter what they intended to pursue.

Reflecting on her own teaching has been an important part of her development as an instructor. "I started making notebooks, and I would reflect after every single lesson about what worked, what didn't work, what would I like to change for the future semester, and how I would approach that particular topic. . . . Every semester was a revisionary process."

Using notebooks to encourage student reflection

Student notebooks can be a valuable tool for encouraging students to "think about how they think," writes Kraft (2012). Everything students do in her classes is placed in their notebooks, including handouts, quizzes, records of data and procedures, drawings of geological concepts, written work, and "reflections" they write before, during, and after an activity. "I essentially tell them they're walking away having created their own personal textbook," says Kraft, who assigns online readings but does not use a formal textbook. Students are required to complete the notebook as part of their course grade, "which means they have to come to class to submit their notebook—that helps assure attendance," she explains.

Before class, students are required to do "reading reflections" in which they answer questions not only about the content of a reading assignment, but also about their prior knowledge and reaction to the reading. The reading reflection for a lesson on plate tectonics, for example, includes these questions:

- What were the main ideas from this reading?

- What questions do you still have from this reading?

- What surprised you most about this reading?

After each lesson, Kraft asks students to write down what they learned and how their ideas changed from their initial understanding. "So it's helping them recognize that they come in with prior understanding and knowledge and that their learning can change . . . or that some things have just been reinforced," she adds.

Periodically Kraft collects the notebooks; she grades students on whether they have completed the work and gives them feedback about their reflections. The information in the notebooks also helps Kraft reflect on her own teaching and modify her lessons to answer students' questions and clarify concepts that are not well understood.

As part of the national Geoscience Affective Research NETwork (GARNET) project, Kraft is collecting data on her students' attitudes and motivation. By the end of the semester, she reports, many students who initially felt they were "not very good at science" say they "love this science class." She attributes that to her focus on concepts and student inquiry rather than terminology and memorization.

Kraft uses several research-based strategies that are described in Chapters 3 and 4 of this book. These include learning exercises that require students to participate actively during class, collaborative activities in which students can learn from each other, tasks explicitly intended to promote metacognition, or "thinking about thinking," and opportunities for students to "practice" science using real data and tools of the discipline. And although community colleges do not generally require faculty to conduct research, a good way for faculty to maintain their scholarly practice is to participate in faculty development workshops, as Kraft has done. Her experience also shows the value of learning from the research of others, collaborating with a network of colleagues, and closely monitoring the impact of gradual changes in one's teaching practice.

The Importance of Improving Instruction

The reasons for exploring more effective approaches to science and engineering education go beyond the personal. The actions that you, as an instructor or an influential leader, take—or do not take—to improve undergraduate teaching and learning have an impact on the nation's future.

Consider, for example, the complex and worrisome challenges—new viruses, global climate change, nuclear terrorist threats, to list just a few—that will affect the quality of life for all of us, and for our children and grandchildren. Or consider the countless smaller decisions, from selecting health care to crafting food and land-use regulations, that citizens, consumers, parents, and political leaders make each day. Addressing these challenges and making these decisions will require a cadre of knowledgeable scientists and engineers and a scientifically literate public. College and university instructors and leaders play a critical role in preparing students to meet these challenges, whether as science and engineering professionals or as well-informed citizens.

In light of such challenges, instructors might ask themselves whether their courses are preparing science, technology, engineering, and mathematics (STEM) majors to solve new problems, communicate and collaborate effectively, and use their knowledge to contribute to society. Are their teaching approaches effectively helping students who are not headed toward a STEM career develop sufficient understanding of the "big ideas" of science and the ways of thinking about science to make good, rational choices?

During the past quarter-century, numerous national reports have emphasized the need to improve undergraduate education in STEM fields as an essential step in preparing a diverse technical workforce and a scientifically literate citizenry.[3] A 2012 report by the President's Council of Advisors on Science and Technology (PCAST) warns that the United States is "putting its future at risk by forfeiting its historical strengths in STEM education" (p. 1). If the United States is to retain its edge, it will need to prepare roughly 1 million more STEM professionals during the next decade than would be produced at current rates, the report concludes. But too many students abandon STEM majors during their first two years of college, citing such reasons as "uninspiring introductory courses," difficulty with the math required in introductory STEM courses, and an "unwelcoming atmosphere" from faculty who teach these courses (p. i). Increasing the retention rate of STEM majors from the current 40 percent to 50 percent would yield almost three-fourths of the 1 million additional STEM graduates needed during the next decade, the report estimates. (And even with such an increase, half of the students who start out pursuing a STEM major would not stick with it—still a disappointing attrition rate from most instructors' perspective.)

Completion rates are significantly lower in STEM disciplines than in other majors for all student groups and are a particular concern for students from underrepresented racial and ethnic groups, who have lower college completion rates in general. For example, Hispanic and African American students are as likely to start college with an interest in science and engineering as white and Asian students, but they are less likely to persist (National Academy of Sciences, National Academy of Engineering, and Institute of Medicine, 2011). Many of the reasons students give for switching out of a STEM major boil down to poor teaching in introductory courses (Seymour and Hewitt, 1997).

In light of these findings, you might ask: Is your style of teaching drawing students into science and engineering—or driving them away? Are you teaching in a way that motivates, engages, and supports the learning of *all* your students, including those with backgrounds or approaches to learning that differ from your own? Are your courses and your department's programs serving as gateways to learning science or engineering, or gatekeepers?

---

[3] These include *Undergraduate Science, Mathematics, and Engineering Education,* National Science Board (1986); *Science for All Americans,* American Association for the Advancement of Science (1989); *Shaping the Future: New Expectations for Undergraduate Education in Science, Mathematics, Engineering, and Technology,* National Science Foundation (1996); *Transforming Undergraduate Education in Science, Mathematics, Engineering, and Technology,* National Research Council (1999); and many others. A more complete list of major national reports calling for improvements in undergraduate science education can be found in *Vision and Change in Undergraduate Biology Education: A Call to Action,* American Association for the Advancement of Science (2011).

Instructors of undergraduate science and engineering affect the future of our society in another important way—by helping to prepare prospective K–12 teachers. These future teachers will need a solid base of scientific knowledge and positive attitudes about science to foster understanding and interest in science among the children they will teach. They also need to experience effective instruction that actively engages students as a model for how they might teach later. Are your undergraduate science courses, especially those for non-majors, accomplishing these goals?

If your answers to any of the questions posed above are "maybe," "I'm not sure," or a candid "no," then you may find ideas for energizing your instruction from an area of inquiry called *discipline-based education research,* or DBER, which emerged in the 1970s and has since gained momentum.

How Can DBER Help?

DBER combines the expertise of scientists and engineers about the challenges of learning a particular discipline with broader theories about teaching and learning. DBER investigates learning and teaching in a discipline using a range of methods

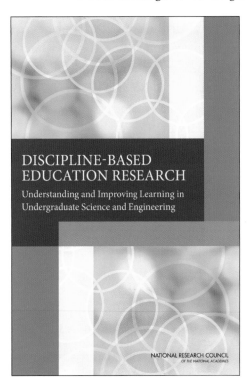

DISCIPLINE-BASED
EDUCATION RESEARCH
Understanding and Improving Learning in
Undergraduate Science and Engineering

NATIONAL RESEARCH COUNCIL
OF THE NATIONAL ACADEMIES

with deep grounding in that discipline's priorities, worldview, knowledge, and practices. It is informed by and complementary to more general research on human learning and cognition. DBER also helps to identify appropriate methods for investigating the learning and teaching processes. Thus, DBER scholarship has the practical goal of improving science and engineering education for all students.

DBER has generated insights that can be used to improve science and engineering education for all students. In particular, DBER sheds light on how students learn concepts and ways of thinking in a discipline and which types of teaching strategies can help students learn more effectively and retain what they have learned.

The major findings from peer-reviewed DBER studies, as well as the status of DBER as a research enterprise, are synthesized in a 2012 report by the National Research Council (NRC), *Discipline-Based*

Education Research: Understanding and Improving Learning in Undergraduate Science and Engineering. This NRC report is the source of much of the information in this book and includes a wealth of additional material for those who want to explore the research base in greater depth.

Theories of learning as a basis for instruction

The purpose of instruction is to help students learn. DBER starts from the premise that a more complete and nuanced understanding of how people learn science and engineering can lead to better instruction.

As described in Chapter 3, many findings about learning from DBER are heavily influenced by theories from cognitive research, which hold that learning involves much more than simply acquiring factual knowledge. Rather, students generate their own understandings and form meaning as a result of their experiences and ideas. Students' prior knowledge, including their mental models and preconceptions, may hinder or promote learning. Some DBER studies also draw from research on sociocultural theories of learning, which shows that students enrich their understanding by interacting with others who share a common interest.

DBER studies further reveal that undergraduates, as novices, have misunderstandings about a wide range of fundamental concepts in science and engineering. Such misunderstandings are common and even normal as many scientific explanations of the world run counter to our intuitive beliefs about how the world works (for example, the idea that everything around us—even a solid table—is made of tiny, moving particles can be tough to grasp at first). They also have difficulty mastering aspects of these disciplines that may seem easy or obvious to experts, such as solving problems or understanding graphs, models, and other visual and mathematical ways of representing important ideas.

These common student difficulties pose challenges to learning. Well-designed instruction recognizes and confronts these difficulties. It activates ways of thinking that can help novices integrate or replace their prior knowledge with new information to construct more expert-like understanding.

Evidence from DBER about student-centered instruction

Many DBER studies have looked at the effectiveness of "student-centered" instructional approaches, in which learners build their understanding by applying the methods and principles of a discipline and interacting with each other under the guidance of the instructor. Student-centered instruction can take a variety of forms,

> Studies clearly show that student-centered instructional strategies are more effective in improving students' conceptual understanding, knowledge retention, and attitudes about learning in a discipline than traditional lecture-based methods that do not include student participation.

as described in more detail in Chapters 3 and 4. Common elements often include actively engaging students in meaningful individual or group tasks, conducting frequent formative assessment, and encouraging students to think about and articulate their own understanding and reasoning, among others. Often DBER studies compare the effectiveness of a student-centered approach with the more traditional mode of an instructor transmitting factual information to a passive audience of students, predominantly through lectures.

In general, DBER scholarship and related studies clearly show that student-centered instructional strategies are more effective in improving students' conceptual understanding, knowledge retention, and attitudes about learning in a discipline than traditional lecture-based methods that do not include student participation. A limited amount of research suggests that making even incremental changes toward more student-centered approaches can enhance students' learning.[4]

The following excerpts from literature reviews, including several commissioned by the NRC to inform its DBER study, highlight the positive impacts of student-centered instruction in specific disciplines:

- In *physics,* results from conceptual and problem-solving tests administered to thousands of students "strongly suggest that the classroom use of [interactive engagement] methods can increase course effectiveness well beyond that obtained in traditional practice" (Hake, 1998, p. 1).

- Studies of *chemistry* education during the past decade demonstrate that various forms of socially mediated learning (in which students create meaning through interactions with others) produce positive outcomes, including "significantly higher test scores, higher final grades, better conceptual understanding, lower course withdrawal rates, and positive impacts on attitudes" (Towns and Kraft, 2011, p. 7).

---

[4] For a summary of this research and references to key studies, see Chapter 3 of this book. A more complete list of relevant studies can be found in Chapter 6 of the 2012 NRC report on DBER in the Overview section and the section on Instruction in the Classroom Setting.

- In *engineering,* actively engaging students "can be unquestionably confirmed as the best learning situation for learning the skills of both problem analysis and engineering design. It is also the most widely demonstrated key to deep conceptual understanding" (Svinicki, 2011, p. 15).

- Frequent assessment in combination with active student engagement has been shown to significantly improve student performance in *biology.* In addition, several analyses have shown that collaborative learning, particularly collaborative testing, improves student retention of content knowledge in biology (Dirks, 2011).

- To produce significant gains in learning in *geosciences,* "it is necessary to use instructional strategies that minimize lecture and maximize other teaching methods. We know that students learn best when they are engaged with real objects or phenomena, working in cooperative groups, solving complex problems, and interested in what they are learning" (Piburn, Kraft, and Pacheco, 2011, p. 19).

This is not how most faculty members teach undergraduate science and engineering. Traditional lecture is still the most common mode of instruction. Science and engineering faculty are more likely, on average, to rely primarily on lectures than instructors in other fields and are the least likely to use student-centered or collaborative instruction (Fairweather, 2005; Schuster and Finkelstein, 2006).

A scientific or engineering mindset

Applying findings from research on teaching and learning to improve your instruction involves the same type of thinking you would use to solve a scientific or an engineering problem in your discipline, whether it is studying how fungi adapt to cold temperatures or developing new construction materials from industrial waste. Jo Handelsman, a Yale University biology professor, uses the phrase "scientific teaching" to refer to the process "in which teaching is approached with the same rigor as science at its best" (Handelsman et al., 2004, pp. 521–522).

Paula Heron, a physics professor and education scholar at the University of Washington, describes it as "both brilliant and obvious to take the perspective of an experimental scientist and apply it to teaching and learning in the discipline."[5]

Others see similarities between instructional redesign and engineering design, in that both seek to improve complex systems (such as human learning) within the constraints of available resources. In both endeavors, write Purdue University engineering professors Ruth Streveler, Karl Smith, and Mary Pilotte (2012), "we start with requirements or specifications, emphasize metrics, and then prepare prototypes that meet the requirements" (p. 1).

In 2003, Beth Simon[6] was in her second year as a professor in computer science at the University of San Diego when she "began to think about my teaching with the same sort of brain that I use in doing my computer science research," she says. "My previous computer science research was in optimization, which is about making computer programs go faster. So I would always wonder, where are the inefficient parts?" When she would create a new lecture, she would wonder, "Did that go better than the old one? How would I know? How would I measure it? How can I figure out if I'm producing a better, more efficient, and optimal learning experience for students?"

This insight led Simon on a quest to learn more about effective instructional practices. She participated in a three-year NSF-funded project where she learned how to do qualitative research on instruction. She later took a sabbatical to become a Science Teaching and Learning Fellow in the Carl Wieman Science Education Initiative at the University of British Columbia. When she took a teaching position at the University of California, San Diego (UCSD), she implemented Mazur's Peer Instruction approach in her courses as a means to improve students' learning and retention and to attract more women and students from

---

[5] Interview, April 12, 2013.
[6] Interview, August 20, 2013.

underrepresented groups to the computer science major. Simon has since collaborated with faculty at other institutions to study the impact of more interactive approaches to teaching computer science. Their research shows a dramatic decrease in failure rates among students taught with Peer Instruction (Porter, Bailey-Lee, and Simon, 2013). In her current role as senior associate director of UCSD's Center for Teaching Development, Simon continues to apply a researcher's mindset to improving instructional practice across the computer science and engineering department.

Does This Mean the End of Lecturing?

Findings from DBER and related research do not mean that lecturing is inherently ineffective and should be eliminated. Lectures can be student-centered if they are carefully crafted to consider student needs, background, and understanding and are implemented with opportunities for student responses. Nor do these findings mean that student-centered approaches are automatically more effective. Good instruction involves more than just asking students questions or putting them to work on activities; it also means helping to move students toward the types of expert thinking that characterize the knowledge and practices of a discipline. The point is that any instructional approach should be used in a thoughtful way that promotes student learning.

Research has identified a variety of instructional strategies that can enhance student learning, including several discussed in more detail in Chapter 4. These strategies range in scope and complexity from increasing student interaction within a basic lecture format to devoting the bulk of class time to activities in which students work together to solve complex problems.

Peer-Led Team Learning (PLTL) is an example of a research-based approach that requires only modest changes in a lecture course and can be implemented with materials developed by others. As explained in the following case study of the PLTL model developed by David Gosser at the City College of New York, a portion of a lecture course is replaced with a workshop, led by trained undergraduates, in which students collaborate in small groups to solve problems or complete other exercises that reinforce the concepts taught in the lecture.

Peer-Led Team Learning

MODEST CHANGES IN COURSE STRUCTURE YIELD MAJOR CHANGES IN STUDENT LEARNING

In 1990, David Gosser[a] was a junior faculty member in the chemistry department at the City College of New York (CCNY), an institution he describes as "basically the UN [United Nations]" in terms of student diversity. The department had a problem with student attrition. The general chemistry introductory course enrolled several hundred students, including many who did not plan to major in the subject. Just 45 percent received a passing grade.

To tackle this problem, Gosser investigated a model that had been used successfully by Uri

Treisman at the University of California, Berkeley, in which students reinforced what they were learning in lectures by working on problems in study groups led by graduate students. At CCNY, however, hundreds of students took General Chemistry, and the graduate student population was too small to provide a sufficient number of peer leaders for the study groups; about 12 such leaders would be needed every semester for each section of 100 General Chemistry students. Therefore, CCNY recruited undergraduate students who had done well in chemistry in the first semester to serve as "peer facilitators" in the second semester, explains Gosser,

---

[a] Except where noted, the information in this case study comes from an interview with David Gosser, July 3, 2013.

who currently directs the Center for Peer-Led Team Learning at CCNY. One hour of a four-hour lecture course was replaced with a weekly two-hour workshop. The class was divided into numerous workshop sections of six to eight students, each led by a peer facilitator.

"Even starting from a simple idea and using off-the-shelf problems, [the model] was very robust," says Gosser. "It was clear that students enjoyed the structure." Gosser received a National Science Foundation grant that provided a major stimulus for the program and met with faculty from his college's School of Education to incorporate research on collaborative learning.

A critical component of this model, called Peer-Led Team Learning (PLTL), is the training provided to peer facilitators, who are paid a stipend. At CCNY, these students participate in an orientation session before the semester starts, are overseen by a faculty member throughout the semester, and attend weekly meetings to practice and discuss the material they will cover that week. Faculty make an effort to ensure that the problems studied in the peer-led sessions are well matched to the topics covered in the lecture.

In the training sessions, facilitators practice strategies to elicit students' reasoning, says Roland Maio,[b] who was a peer facilitator in spring 2013. "You want [the students in your section] to work through the problem. You don't want them to just sit there if they're stuck, but you don't want to throw the answer at them. That sort of teaching style is part of PLTL," he says. When most of the students seem unsure about how to approach a problem, "then I fall back on a Socratic method, asking questions to bring out their own reasoning and see what they are thinking."

In the peer-led sessions, students collaborate on problems that are slightly more difficult than standard end-of-chapter textbook questions. Often these problems require students to record their observations and carefully outline the logic used to arrive at a solution. For example, one such problem asks students to draw the structure of several molecules and determine the molecular geometry of each structure. In another problem, students simulate chemical reactions using pennies, nickels, and dimes and discuss their conclusions before writing out formulas. Manipulating objects helps students understand the role of particles, Gosser explains, a concept that is not obvious by simply learning a formula.

The workshop sessions can be particularly empowering for introverted students, says Ashea West,[c] who served as a peer facilitator in spring 2013. "You can be intimidated by professors in a big lecture hall with big classes. Students who are really shy and not outspoken were better after the workshop. It is an easier way for students to learn more and make friends for study groups."

One barrier to many reform models is that they require faculty to "turn upside down their whole approach," says Gosser. "With PLTL, the faculty have a much bigger comfort zone because they can start from where they are. . . . It's a lot less disruptive to their approach. You can still lecture pretty much the way you want, but you have to think about integrating it with this workshop."

The PLTL model has been widely replicated in science and engineering disciplines at more than 100 sites nationally, and a large number of appropriate PLTL problems are readily available for instructors who want to try this approach. A review of studies of PLTL at several institutions found a higher percentage of A, B, or C grades and higher test performance among students participating in PLTL workshops compared with nonparticipants (Gosser, 2011).

---

[b] Interview, August 13, 2013.

[c] Interview, August 14, 2013.

PLTL illustrates how strategies of collaborative learning and problem solving can be imported into a large lecture course. The small-group sessions provide students with extra exercises to help them master difficult concepts, as well as additional opportunities to receive answers to their questions. These sessions also engender a sense of community and encourage students to learn from each other and take responsibility for their own learning. Students gain experience with working in teams and communicating better, while peer leaders hone their teaching and group management skills and strengthen their self-confidence.

Scaling Up Research-Based Instruction

So if research-based instruction works, why aren't more people doing it?

Handelsman and her colleagues (2004) put this question another way: "So why do outstanding scientists who demand rigorous proof for scientific assertions in their research continue to use and, indeed, defend on the basis of their intuition alone, teaching methods that are not the most effective?" (p. 521).

Efforts to encourage undergraduate STEM faculty to adopt research-based teaching approaches are often beset by challenges. For example, in a national survey of physics faculty, Henderson, Dancy, and Niewiadomska-Bugaj (2012) found that nearly all faculty were familiar with one or more research-based practices, and approximately half were using at least one such practice. At the same time, however, many faculty had modified the research-based practices, and they frequently discontinued a practice after trying it for one semester. The researchers surmised that faculty who abandon research-based practices either lack the knowledge needed to customize the practice to their local situation or underestimate the other factors that tend to discourage innovation in teaching.

Rogers' (2003) seminal theory of the diffusion of innovation proposes that the decision to adopt and sustain an innovation begins only when an individual has knowledge or awareness of the innovation. The next step is persuasion, as the individual evaluates the innovation, a process strongly influenced by the views of close peers. If the individual decides to adopt the innovation, possibly with some modifications, he or she often remains uncertain of its benefits. The final step is confirmation, when the individual looks for support for his or her decision. At this stage, the individual may decide to discontinue the innovation.

Instructors who are resistant to or skeptical about adopting research-based teaching strategies often emphasize practical challenges. For example, they may

Good instruction involves more than just asking students questions or putting them to work on activities; it also means helping to move students toward the types of expert thinking that characterize the knowledge and practices of a discipline. The point is that any instructional approach should be used in a thoughtful way that promotes student learning.

express concerns about possible negative reactions from students accustomed to traditional types of teaching, the time involved in redesigning a course, the challenge of learning new teaching methods, the feasibility of supporting active student engagement in a large lecture hall, or the need to drop important content to make time for student interaction.

Other research on factors that influence faculty decisions about teaching practices points to challenges in the areas of institutional leadership, departmental peers, tenure and reward systems, and the beliefs and values of the individual faculty members themselves (Austin, 2011; Fairweather, 2008). These challenges, along with ways to surmount them, are discussed in Chapters 6 and 7.

While you may cringe at the prospect of having to dramatically revamp an entire course all at once, you may be heartened to know that most effective instructors did not attempt such a feat. Even instructors who have thoroughly embraced student-centered instruction, like Scott Freeman at the University of Washington, often started with modest changes. In his early years of teaching introductory biology, Freeman mostly lectured. But as he became more familiar with the research on science instruction, he added more and more strategies to actively engage students and began collaborating with colleagues to study the impact of these changes. Eventually, as the following case study shows, Freeman did away with formal lectures, even as enrollments soared to several hundred students. Instead he structures his course around "clicker" questions that students answer anonymously using handheld devices and group exercises that probe students' understanding of biology concepts. The closest he comes to lecturing is when he introduces an activity, answers a question that could benefit the whole class, or clarifies a confusing point.

Six Hundred Students, One Big Auditorium, and Minimal Lecture?

THE EVOLUTION OF AN INTRODUCTORY BIOLOGY COURSE

Scott Freeman[a] cues up his slides, adjusts his remote mic, and walks casually to center stage of the largest lecture hall at the University of Washington. Most of the auditorium's 700 seats are filled with students talking, laughing, and flipping through notebooks. This scene could be the prelude to any traditional lecture at any large university. But as the class unfolds, it becomes clear that the Biology 180 course taught by Freeman is far from traditional.

In this highly structured course, students are responsible for learning basic information on their own time through assigned readings, daily online quizzes, and weekly practice exams. This frees up class time for active learning exercises that challenge students to apply concepts, analyze data, and reflect on their reasoning with expert guidance and feedback from the instructor. But the course, which focuses on evolution, Mendelian genetics, and ecology, did not start out this way. Rather, it evolved, so to speak, as Freeman gradually introduced research-based instructional strategies and as he and his colleagues studied the year-by-year impact of these changes on student performance.

Clicker questions challenge students' thinking

"Clickers out, cellphones off," says Freeman, signaling the official start of the 50-minute class. Several students fiddle with their clickers—handheld response devices that resemble small TV remotes. "In our last adventure yesterday," Freeman begins, "you

were figuring out that inbreeding and other forms of nonrandom mating are going to increase the percentage of homozygotes in a population. So it's clicker time—think about this one please." The large screen at the back of the stage displays this clicker question, which is based on the previous day's reading assignment:

Q: Why do small populations become inbred?

1. They are usually stable or declining in size.

2. Population bottlenecks cause large changes in allele frequencies.

3. Founder events establish small populations in isolated habitats (low likelihood of gene flow, after the founder event).

4. Eventually, all individuals are closely related.

---

[a] Except where noted, the information in this case study comes from an interview with Scott Freeman, May 24, 2013, and from an unpublished video of Freeman teaching a class provided by L. Tong and P. Liggit, Eastern Michigan University.

The students have less than one minute to consider the question individually and record their initial responses with the clickers. "Ten more seconds . . . five seconds," says Freeman. "Okay, start talking it over, please."

The room fills with chatter as students turn to their neighbors to discuss their answers and the reasoning behind them. Freeman chooses clicker questions that are difficult enough to stimulate students' thinking and include common student misconceptions among the possible answers. "You're shooting for student responses of 40 to 60 percent [correct] the first time they look at the question," he says in a later interview, adding that it is important to use clickers in ways supported by evidence. "There's a tremendous amount of clicker abuse going on," he asserts, citing the example of instructors who use clicker questions that are too easy. "We have tons of people saying, 'Oh, yeah, I do active learning; I use clickers.' And they're seeing no changes in student responses because they're not using them right."

After a few minutes, Freeman closes out the peer discussion and asks for volunteers to share their answer with the whole class. "Remember to explain

your logic," he reminds them. A student in the middle of the auditorium confidently lays out her reasons for choosing answer 4. Two more students chime in with additional arguments on behalf of choice 4.

"Actually, a lot of people answered 3," says Freeman. "So you think 4 is a true statement. Then you have to parse: first, is it true, and then, is it addressing the issue you're raising now? Is it causative—would that be a mechanism why small populations become inbred?"

The discussion continues for a few more minutes, as more students explain why they think a particular answer is correct. Freeman asks for a show of hands from the students who agree that 4 is the correct answer. Hundreds of hands shoot up. Next a smaller number of students raise their hands to indicate they disagree. "The correct answer is 4," Freeman reveals, adding that students who are still uncertain or have questions can see him during office hours, email him, or talk more about this topic during an exam review session scheduled for the next day.

For the next 15 minutes, the students work through three more clicker questions using the same

model of thinking and responding individually, talking with their neighbors, and discussing responses with the whole class. At this point, however, Freeman switches to "randomized calling"—using a randomly generated class roster to pick which students will explain their answers. (Students have the option of passing or putting themselves on a "do not call" list.) Randomized calling helps ensure that students are prepared for class, Freeman later explains. In one end-of-course evaluation, he asked students what they thought of this approach to calling on students: "the overwhelming majority said they absolutely hated it—but make sure you do it all the time."

From lecture to highly structured active learning

"What motivated me was failure," says Freeman about the evolution of his introductory biology course. When he first started teaching the course in 2001, he used a modified Socratic style in which he mostly lectured but stopped occasionally to ask questions of students. But he soon became discouraged by the high percentage of students who dropped the class or received a final grade of less than 1.5 on a 4.0 scale. (More than 18 percent of students fell into this latter category in spring 2002, which meant they could not advance to the 200-level biology course.) About 40 percent of all University of Washington undergraduates take Biology 180, mostly as sophomores, and the five-credit course is a prerequisite for biology majors. The class meets four times a week, plus a two-hour lab session.

To address the failure rate and improve student learning, Freeman reviewed the developing research literature on active learning and attended a National Science Foundation workshop with some of his colleagues. He also began collecting data on his own class. "I wanted to convince myself, and eventually my colleagues, that if I changed what I was doing in my classroom and saw changes in student performance, I could actually have the data to show that something real was going on."

Spurred by research suggesting that active learning can help reduce student failure rates without compromising the rigor of a course, Freeman began to incorporate more active strategies into his teaching. In 2003, he added ungraded active learning exercises to his Socratic lectures. These included Think-Pair-Share activities (see Chapter 4) in which students individually consider a question posed by the instructor, discuss their ideas with a neighbor, and arrive at a final answer, which is then discussed by the whole class. These ungraded additions didn't work very well, says Freeman. "I didn't see any change in student performance."

Starting in 2005, when technology made it practical to use clickers in a large class, Freeman made time during his lectures for daily clicker questions with peer discussion. (A grant from the university provost paid for the initial purchase of the clicker technology.) He also added online weekly practice exams consisting of five short-answer questions that were graded by peers. As he had done in the past, he gave two midterm exams and a final. As different strategies were tried in the course, Freeman and his colleagues David Haak and Mary Pat Wenderoth documented the impact. With the addition of clicker questions, the percentage of students who received failing final grades decreased (Freeman et al., 2011).

In fall 2007, Freeman stopped giving formal lectures altogether—an approach he has maintained even as enrollments soared from 340 to a high of 700 in 2009. He began using clicker questions and worksheet problems to drive the entire discussion of a given topic, and he introduced randomized calling and daily quizzes on reading assignments in addition to the practice exams. "Essentially, I

was flipping the classroom," he says, referring to a model in which students learn basic information outside of class and work on collaborative projects and problems during class time that are designed to deepen their understanding. "If the students have done the reading, they have the basic information to be prepared to work on problems before they come to class." He still gives what might be called mini-lectures in class, but primarily to answer questions, guide the discussion, or provide a brief introduction to worksheet problems.

The active learning elements "made the class size of 500 seem a bit smaller," says Hyunsoo Bak,[b] who took the class as a sophomore in fall 2012. "It was fun." In her view, the main benefit of the class

was that "it put more weight on how I think . . . and why I think that way."

The class redesign did not require more money, smaller class sizes, or more class time (Haak et al., 2011). In fact, during the period studied (2002–2009), class size increased, the number of graduate teaching assistants decreased, and the hours devoted to labs were reduced.

Group worksheets elicit students' understanding

Students in the Biology 180 class also collaborate on longer worksheet problems. Some of these problems are intended to "show students that their intuition doesn't work and get them to start thinking about the problem," says Freeman. Others are

---

[b] Interview, June 28, 2013.

designed to confront common student misconceptions in biology, such as the notion that genetic mutations arise in response to the environment rather than randomly.

One such worksheet asks students to create a section of a "tree-of-life" diagram showing the evolutionary relationships among six groups of animals: lizards, ray-finned fish, mammals, snakes, amphibians, and sharks and rays. To set up this activity, Freeman provides a two-minute explanation of the role and history of these phylogenetic trees. Working in groups of three for about 20 minutes, students create their trees, using a data table that shows whether a specific group has a particular trait, such as internal bones, limbs, and amniotic eggs. To get students thinking about traits that distinguish one species as an outgrowth of another, Freeman sings a snippet from an old Sesame Street song: "One of these things is not like the other!"

As the students work, Freeman and his teaching assistants circulate among the groups, monitoring students' discussions and using questions to subtly guide those who seem confused. Often he stops to praise a student for a correct answer or a useful contribution to the group's discussion.

Kaitlyn Lestak,[c] a biology major, recalls in a later interview that when she was stumped by something in the worksheets, Freeman "wouldn't really give you the answer to any question, but he would talk you through it in a way that could help you solve it. Or he would ask, 'What do you think the answer is?' And you would give him your answer, and he would say, 'You're on the right track, but think about this instead.' He would ask you questions to help you get the right answer eventually." Although the course was challenging, says Lestak, she believes the level of challenge helped her to learn. "I've never taken a class so engaging."

---

[c] Interview, June 27, 2013.

Evidence of effectiveness

From 2003, when Freeman began revamping the Biology 180 course, to 2009, when he had fully implemented the highly structured version, the percentage of students who received failing final grades decreased from 18 percent to 6 percent (Freeman et al., 2011). Freeman and his colleagues did special analyses to control for student ability and ensure that the test questions had not become easier. They concluded that the class itself was consistent, if not slightly more difficult, across the years of the study.

Particularly encouraging was the disproportionate drop in the failure rate for students from educationally or economically disadvantaged backgrounds (Haak et al., 2011). (About 45 percent of students enrolled in the course are Asian American, about 45 percent are white, and roughly 10 percent to 12 percent are from minority groups underrepresented in science; altogether, about 15 percent of the students are from disadvantaged backgrounds.) The researchers attribute these improvements in performance to the many opportunities students have in class to apply scientific thinking by solving problems, reflecting on and articulating their reasoning, and considering other points of view.

To his colleagues who resist using evidence to change their teaching, Freeman points out that they would readily adapt a powerful new technology that makes it easier for them to do biological research. "If they just brought that same mindset to their teaching, I think things would change in a hurry."

Freeman's experience addresses some common concerns about the feasibility of implementing research-based strategies and contains guidance for others who are interested in trying similar approaches:

- The evolution of Freeman's Biology 180 course illustrates how an energetic instructor with a strong commitment to improving student learning can introduce active learning strategies—and revise, discontinue, or add to these strategies based on classroom data about their impact.

- The later, more highly structured version of the course shifts more responsibility to the students to learn basic content and vocabulary outside of class through assigned reading, quizzes, and practice exams. This partly addresses a common concern among instructors that if they increase student interaction, they will not be able to cover important content. Just because content is covered does not mean students will learn it.

- Even in a class of up to 700 students taught in a traditional lecture hall, it is possible to reduce lectures to a minimum and shift the instructor's role from delivering information to guiding student learning. Rather than directly telling students who are stuck on a problem what to do, the instructor asks probing questions that nudge students to think in a different direction.

- Simply injecting clicker questions into a lecture does not mean an instructor is implementing a research-based practice. As discussed at more length in Chapter 5, it matters a great deal whether the questions are appropriate in their level of difficulty, address common student misconceptions, are nested within a larger research-based course design, and, most importantly, are presented in a format that allows students to discuss their ideas with their peers.

Conclusion

The ideas and examples described in this book are not meant to be a "bag of tricks" from which you can whip out a slick activity for tomorrow's chemistry class. Rather, they are intended to encourage you to reflect on your teaching and consider trying new approaches that are compatible with the learning goals for your course.

Many instructors who have gone down this path not only say it was worth the effort, but also declare they can no longer imagine teaching any other way.

Their students are more enthusiastic and motivated and have better attendance. Often their students have higher performance as a group than those in their previous classes or in traditionally taught sections of the same course. Through activities that encourage student reflection and various forms of assessment, instructors can better grasp how well their students understand fundamental concepts.

Although students may balk at first when they are asked to assume greater responsibility for their learning, they often become enthusiastic supporters of active learning strategies. According to Karen Kortz,[7] a geology professor at the Community College of Rhode Island, many of her students tell her, "I love this class; it makes me feel like I'm not afraid of science." She elaborates: "One of my goals is to have students enjoy the class. I don't mean make it easy for them. I mean make it so they're not afraid of it, and they like attending and doing the work."

Changing your teaching can also be rewarding and intellectually stimulating for you as an instructor. Beth Simon[8] at the University of California, San Diego, tells the story of a colleague in the computer science and engineering department who adopted some of Simon's Peer Instruction materials. Midway through the term, Simon asked the colleague how the course was going. "He said, 'I haven't had so much fun teaching in a long time. This is why I wanted to go into education. I didn't want to stand up and talk at students. I wanted to have interesting discussions with them.'" Simon adds: "And that's something we've seen frequently."

Resources and Further Reading

Center for Peer-Led Team Learning
    https://sites.google.com/site/quickpltl

Discipline-Based Education Research: Understanding and Improving Learning in
    Undergraduate Science and Engineering (National Research Council, 2012)
        Chapter 2: The Emergence and Current State of Discipline-Based Education Research

Engage to Excel: Producing One Million Additional College Graduates with Degrees in
    Science, Technology, Engineering, and Mathematics. Report of the President's Council
    of Advisors on Science and Technology (February 2012)

---

[7] Interview, April 5, 2013.
[8] Interview, August 20, 2013.

Getting Started

Based on decades of research, we now know more than ever about how students learn science and engineering disciplines. We also know more about the effectiveness of innovative instructional approaches based on these findings about learning. Yet these innovations have not spread widely. The problem, writes James Fairweather (2008), a Michigan State University professor who has studied faculty rewards and strategies to improve student learning, "lies less in not knowing what works and more in getting people to use proven techniques." There are many understandable reasons why instructors or administrators may be daunted by the prospect of reorienting their courses or programs around research on learning.

This chapter offers suggestions for how to get started, drawn from studies of instructional transformation and the experience of practitioners who have successfully incorporated research-based strategies into their own undergraduate teaching.

Taking the First Step

In the mid-1990s, Deborah Allen[1] was asked by a group of biology colleagues at the University of Delaware to join them in implementing problem-based learning, an instructional strategy in which students learn by working in small groups to solve challenging problems. "I was a skeptic," says Allen. At that time she was, by her own description, a bench scientist who knew little about pedagogy. She was wary of the philosophy underlying problem-based learning—that students can construct their own knowledge by working actively on complex problems. "It's really saying that learning begins with a problem and that what you learn is what you need to

---

[1] Except where noted, the information in this example comes from an interview with Deborah Allen, April 11, 2014.

resolve the problem," she explains. "Of course, that's how you learn in real life, but for a school, it's very radical to have faith that students can do that."

Nevertheless, Allen decided to plunge ahead because of concerns about her students' lack of engagement during her lectures. She suspected that her lecture-based approach to teaching was "reinforcing passive behaviors" among her students. "It seemed like a vicious and futile cycle—the more we tried to help students, the more we inadvertently were not helping them," she recalls. Problem-based learning, described in more detail in Chapter 4, appeared to offer a way out of that cycle. Allen took workshops on this strategy through her campus center for learning, which she now directs. She collaborated with a core group of faculty to develop biology curriculum around problem-based learning and assess the effects. "I could not have survived without that group of people I could go to," she says.

This experience "led me to rethink teaching and learning," says Allen, who in 2013 received the Bruce Alberts Award for Excellence in Science Education. She now uses a range of research-based strategies in her classes depending on which is best suited to a particular learning need. "Problem-based learning was my only option when I was a 'reformed lecturer,' but now I feel like I have more options," she says. Others who are dubious about whether it's worth the effort to try a new approach to instruction might find encouragement in Allen's advice to simply "get involved and try it out."

Considering New Ways of Thinking About Teaching and Learning

As the Allen example suggests, the process of changing your approach to teaching and learning begins with a willingness to look at your practices from a new perspective or with a new understanding. "A shift in attitude is really profound in terms of underpinning change in practice," says Cathy Manduca,[2] director of the Science Education Resource Center (SERC) at Carleton College, a national network for professional development, curriculum, research on learning, and community building.

Noah Finkelstein,[3] a physics professor at the University of Colorado Boulder, views a shift in mindset as "the first and most important prerequisite for any kind of transition." In particular, he says, you must be willing to move away from "the idea that teaching is the transmission of information, and learning is the acquisition of information, to the notion that teaching and learning are about enculturating people to think, to talk, to act, to do, to participate in certain ways."

---

[2] Interview, May 13, 2013.
[3] Interview, April 23, 2013.

> "You must be willing to move away from the idea that teaching is the transmission of information and learning is the acquisition of information, to the notion that teaching and learning are about enculturating people to think, to talk, to act, to do, to participate in certain ways."
>
> *—Noah Finkelstein,*
> *University of Colorado Boulder*

For many instructors, this change in mindset begins with an awareness that their students are not really learning as well as expected. "It takes an effort to change," says David Sokoloff,[4] a physics professor at the University of Oregon. "The first thing is for people to convince themselves that it's worth the effort." What convinced him to make the effort was mounting evidence that students who completed introductory physics courses did not understand key concepts.

As part of this shift in attitude, faculty members may need to recognize that many of their students do not learn in the same ways that they did or are not motivated by the same things. Faculty often went into academia because they were good at learning through a traditional lecture model, says Rebecca Bates,[5] the chair of integrated engineering at Minnesota State University, Mankato, but "that's not always the best way for others to learn." Most undergraduates will not get advanced engineering or science degrees or become academics. "If we think about our students not being like us, not learning like us, not having the same motivations as us, then we start to imagine where they could be, and we can actually reach them more easily," she notes.

Sara Brownell and Kimberly Tanner (2012) propose that scientists' professional identities may be "an invisible and underappreciated barrier to undergraduate science teaching reform" (p. 339). These identities are forged by training that emphasizes research over teaching and a culture that views teaching as lower in status than research. Steeped in this culture, some scientists may have qualms about "coming out" as teachers lest they lose an identity they value. Scientists who are grounded in a research identity "may view pedagogical training with skepticism, considering it to be a waste of time and effort, in particular if the training tries to promote teaching methods that depart from the cultural teaching

---

[4] Interview, July 8, 2013.
[5] Interview, July 8, 2013.

norm in science: lecturing," the authors write (p. 343). In this situation, changing one's mindset involves recasting one's professional identity to include a focus on effective teaching in training, disciplinary meetings, and scientific journals.

Approaching Instructional Improvement as a Research Problem

One way to begin reorienting instruction around findings about how students learn is the "teaching as research" model developed by the Center for the Integration of Research, Teaching, and Learning (CIRTL), which is dedicated to advancing effective science, technology, engineering, and mathematics (STEM) teaching practices in higher education and funded by the National Science Foundation (NSF). This model frames instructional improvement as "a research problem, to which STEM instructors can effectively apply their research skills and ways of knowing" (Center for the Integration of Research, Teaching, and Learning, n.d.a, p. 2). The steps of the model include reviewing existing research on teaching and learning; creating student learning goals; developing a hypothesis about ways to achieve these goals; defining measures of success; developing and implementing teaching practices within an experimental design; collecting and analyzing data; and reflecting, evaluating, and adjusting based on the evidence collected.

"Almost every grad student knows how to perform research, because that's what you do, but this method applies it to teaching," says Chris Richardson,[6] a former participant in a CIRTL fellowship program at Michigan State and an early career faculty member in the physics department at Elon University. "You have a hypothesis. And in teaching, you have a goal for your students—what you want them to learn. You decide, just as in research, what you're going to accept as proof that that hypothesis is correct. And in teaching you say, how am I going to assess this?"

Another prominent model designed to guide practitioners through the process of instructional change grew out of research on course transformation across 12 departments participating in the Science Education Initiative (SEI) at the University of Colorado Boulder (Colorado) and the University of British Columbia (UBC). (More information about the SEI appears in Chapter 7.) This model, which has measurably improved learning in several courses and has been adapted by other institutions, aims to bring instructional practices in line with research

---

[6] Interview, May 2, 2013.

about how students learn science. Key steps of the model include the "development of learning goals, instructional materials based on student difficulties, and assessment to see whether the approach worked" (Chasteen et al., 2011, p. 70).

An approach for revising undergraduate biology courses suggested by the American Association for the Advancement of Science (2011) blends the "scientific teaching" principles of Handelsman and colleagues (2004) and the "backward design" paradigm articulated by Wiggins and McTighe (2005). (Backward design recommends first setting goals for student learning and then choosing instructional strategies and assessment methods aligned to these goals.)

In geosciences, a process for designing effective and innovative teaching methods is available through workshops and an online tutorial[7] sponsored by On the Cutting Edge (Tewksbury and Macdonald, 2007). This process encourages instructors to set goals for courses that focus on developing students' abilities to think for themselves and solve problems while they master important course content.

While these and other models for transforming instruction differ in their specifics, they generally emphasize certain key steps:

- Establish learning goals that define what students should know and be able to do by the end of a unit or a course.

- Design, adopt, or adapt curriculum materials and instructional strategies that will help students achieve these goals.

- Administer assessments to determine how well these goals are being met.

- Use the results of the assessments to guide subsequent improvements to the course.

The step of assessing the impact of instructional changes is an important one. Although many of the experts highlighted in this book have published formal discipline-based education research (DBER) studies of learning and teaching approaches, you do not have to become a DBER scholar to improve your instruction. Evidence to inform teaching can be collected through less formal means than published research—for example, by administering a standardized assessment of students' conceptual understanding (see Chapter 5), giving exams specifically tailored to your course, and conducting pre- and post-instruction surveys of students. In addition, it can be helpful for faculty who are trying new instructional strategies to "take notes after class each day on what worked and

---

[7] See http://serc.carleton.edu/NAGTWorkshops/coursedesign/tutorial/index.html.

what didn't—it takes six minutes," suggests Eric Brewe,[8] a physicist and professor of science education at Florida International University (FIU).

Setting Learning Goals to Drive Instruction

From the outset, decisions about revising instruction should focus on how students learn in a discipline and what they need to learn well. The how part is discussed in detail in Chapter 3. The what part is addressed by establishing learning goals, also called learning objectives or performance expectations, that define the knowledge and skills students are expected to master by the end of a unit, course, or program of study. These goals will then shape which teaching strategies and assessments you choose.

Before writing learning goals, you will need to consider the context of your course, such as whether it is a prerequisite for later courses; whether your students are mostly majors in the your discipline, non-majors, or both; and whether the course includes a lab component (Tewksbury and Macdonald, 2007). Expert instructors recommend that learning goals focus on the kinds of deeper conceptual knowledge and more complex skills that are consistent with modern practices in a discipline and will help move students toward more expert-like understanding. In addition to addressing concepts and content knowledge, learning goals might also focus on students' mastery of technical skills in a discipline; "soft skills" such as writing and communication; and affective qualities such as curiosity, motivation to learn a subject, and retention in a discipline.

Learning goals should also "explicitly communicate the key ideas and the level at which students should understand them in operational terms," according to Michelle Smith, a biology professor at the University of Maine, and Kathy Perkins, a physics professor at Colorado (2010). Based on their experience writing learning goals for Colorado's SEI, Smith and Perkins recommend that learning goals take this form: "'At the end of this course/lecture/unit, students will be able to . . .' followed by a specific action verb and a task" (p. 32).

These learning goals can pair knowledge of a specific concept in a discipline with a scientific practice, such as creating a model or formulating an argument (Cooper and Klymkowsky, 2013). A performance expectation in cell biology might look like this (Klymkowsky and Cooper, n.d.):

---

[8] Interview, April 16, 2013.

Make a model for how organisms could control membrane fluidity in the face of changing environmental temperatures; identify the factors that would limit the cell's response.

Faculty often find it useful to consider both course-level and topic-level goals. A typical set of learning goals might include 5 to 10 course-level goals that convey the major learning themes and concepts, along with more specific topic-level goals aligned with the course-level learning goals (Smith and Perkins, 2010). Because courses and disciplines differ in their goals, the learning goals will be different for each course. Box 2.1 shows examples of a general course goal and specific content goals in physics developed by the Carl Wieman SEI at UBC (2009).

BOX 2.1 LEARNING GOALS FROM AN INTRODUCTION TO MODERN PHYSICS COURSE

Course learning goal
Background: A bunch of old curmudgeon engineers complain to the engineering curriculum committee that quantum mechanics is a waste of time for any engineering student to take, claiming that regular engineers only work on things that use classical (non-quantum) physics, and quantum physics is so weird it makes no sense and it is probably wrong anyway.

Goal: You will be able to convince the engineering curriculum committee that the ideas of quantum physics are true and that it is useful for engineers to know about them.

Specific content goals (related to emission and absorption of light by isolated atoms)
Be able to . . .

- Explain how the discrete colors produced by neon signs, mercury and sodium streetlights, and other discharge lamps rule out Rutherford's model of the atom as like a miniature solar system with electrons orbiting the nucleus.

- Relate the colors of light produced by a hydrogen discharge lamp to energy levels of the electrons in the atoms in the lamp.

- Explain why such light sources are so much more efficient than incandescent lightbulbs.

- List the basic assumptions of the Bohr model of the atom and explain how those assumptions are consistent with the light emitted by a hydrogen discharge lamp.

- Provide a basic design for a gas laser, giving the basic components and qualitative requirements for it to operate.

The goal-setting process can be particularly effective if a group of faculty can reach consensus about a minimum set of learning goals for a particular course, while leaving flexibility for individual instructors to add their own goals. To transform a junior-level course in electricity and magnetism at Colorado, for example, a group of several faculty, including many who had previously taught the course, met several times to discuss and review learning goals for the course. Analyses of the SEI suggest that faculty can often agree on about 75 percent of course goals, which allows individuals sufficient flexibility and creativity to put their own stamp on the remaining goals (Chasteen et al., 2011).

Instructors use different means, and often more than one means, to communicate learning goals to students. The goals might be included in the course syllabus or written on the board at the beginning of class. Homework and in-class activities might include the appropriate goals targeted by an assignment or an exercise.

Research shows that the use of learning goals can have a positive impact on both students and instructors (Simon and Taylor, 2009). Nearly all of the students in three classes analyzed by Simon and Taylor saw learning goals as very valuable, particularly in helping them "know what to know." Students also frequently reported that learning goals helped them study, get more out of lectures, and determine the most important material to learn. Faculty indicated that learning goals were useful in communicating course material to students and other faculty and creating course assessments.

The value of learning goals depends not only on how well they have been developed, but also on how effectively they are used. The experience of David McConnell, a professor of geology at North Carolina State University and a science education researcher, shows how well-chosen learning goals can guide efforts to make instruction more effective and engaging in a course with an enrollment of nearly 100.

> "If we think about our students not being like us, not learning like us, not having the same motivations as us, then we start to imagine where they could be and we can actually reach them more easily."
>
> —*Rebecca Bates,*
> *Minnesota State University, Mankato*

DESIGNING LEARNING

Learning Goals "Drive Everything"

When students walk into David McConnell's[a] introductory course in physical geology at North Carolina State University, the first thing they see on the lecture room screen is a slide with the day's learning goals. For a lesson devoted to volcanoes and volcanic eruptions, they find these goals:

- I can compare and contrast the features of a shield volcano and a composite volcano.

- I can define viscosity and give examples of everyday materials with high and low viscosity.

- I can explain the relationship of gas content, viscosity, magma type, and plate tectonic setting in volcanic eruptions.

- I can list the features and processes that geologists study when trying to predict an eruption.

Students can also access a complete list of the course learning goals online to help them do homework or prepare for exams. "Think of this as your study guide," McConnell tells his students.

These goals not only signal to the students what they should understand by the end of the lesson, but also shape how McConnell, a science education researcher as well as a geology professor, designs his curriculum, teaching strategies, and assessments.

The central role of learning goals

McConnell's main advice for instructors who want to improve their teaching? "Have and assess learning goals—that drives everything." The first step to redesigning one's teaching is to think about what you want students to learn. From there, he says, you think about what tasks will help students meet that goal and what questions you need to ask to determine whether they have met it. "Have a clear objective matched with a clear assessment."

McConnell recommends that learning goals be more challenging than just requiring students to memorize facts. They should aim for students to comprehend and apply important concepts and analyze information. When instructors write these kinds of learning goals, he says, "it makes you think about your instruction, and you're much more intentional." It leads the instructor to ask what kinds of activities will help students achieve a particular goal.

In each class, McConnell presents several ConcepTests—multiple-choice questions that focus on one key concept of the major learning goals for a lesson (McConnell et al., 2006). Students use clickers to give their individual response, then discuss their answers with their peers and vote again. A typical class may also include short lectures with photographs, video clips, and animation; open-ended questions that require students to collaborate on analyzing information and applying their learning to real-world situations; and a "minute paper" in which students reflect on the most important thing they learned that day. "It's never just me standing up and talking for the whole time," he says. "We're always jumping back and forth."

McConnell did not always teach this way. He started out by recognizing room for improvement in his teaching, researching various strategies to address the problem, and attending workshops to learn more.

---

[a] Except where noted, the information in this case study comes from an interview with David McConnell, June 8, 2013.

From skeptic to advocate

About 10 years into his teaching career, McConnell, who was then at the University of Akron, realized that although he still enjoyed teaching and was getting decent results, "something was missing." He had not changed his lecture-based teaching strategies in a decade, and he felt his classes lacked the

David McConnell discussing a ConcepTest with his class.

kind of interaction that occurs in a lively seminar. He reviewed the research on various active learning strategies and decided to try ConcepTests. At that time, in the late 1990s, published DBER research was limited, especially in geology, but ConcepTests had been shown to improve student learning and increase student engagement in physics (Mazur, 1997). To stimulate student discussion of ConcepTest questions, McConnell chose the Think-Pair-Share approach, in which students first consider their

answer on their own and then discuss it with a neighbor before settling on a final answer (see Chapter 4 for a fuller explanation).

Around the same time, two faculty members from the biology department persuaded him to accompany them to a workshop held in Kentucky and sponsored by the Faculty Institutes for Reforming Science Teaching (FIRST) at Michigan State. "We were a little skeptical when we went," says McConnell. "We thought it was going to be this old touchy-feely, self-esteem kind of stuff, but it turned out to be very different from what we had anticipated. We all left as rabid reformers, but we didn't really know enough to do anything at that point."

It took a few years of trial-and-error and additional workshops for McConnell and David Steer, a fellow geologist at Akron, to hone their approach. Initially, the biggest challenge for McConnell was giving up some classroom control to allow for student discussion. "One of the things about controlling the classroom is that you know what's going to happen, and you can dictate the process and the timing and everything else. Once you let that go, you have to be ready to do almost anything. . . . Chaos could ensue if you have not planned well."

McConnell and Steer applied for and received a grant to buy clickers and began developing their own ConcepTests because these materials were not readily available in geosciences at that time. Along the way they hit a few snags. "The first half of the ConcepTests we made, we tried in class and they didn't go well. So we made new ones," says McConnell. At first the students were surprised that they were being encouraged to talk to each other in class, but they soon adapted and seemed to enjoy the new approach. "When you have 160 kids in an enclosed space and they turn and start talking, it's a real adrenalin rush," says McConnell. "The noise goes up, and it's like, yeah, that's learning right there—that is what it looks like."

McConnell also stresses the value of connecting with disciplinary colleagues who are pursuing research-based reforms. "Working with others who are teaching similar classes gives you someone to bounce ideas off of and compare notes with," he says. The collaborations that McConnell forged with Steer and other colleagues benefited his teaching and research and led to the creation of a textbook (McConnell and Steer, 2014) with learning objectives, ConcepTests, and exercises for active learning, many of which McConnell uses in his own class.

Learning activities inside and outside of class

During a class on plate tectonics, students consider this sample ConcepTest:

Examine the map and answer the question that follows. How many plates are present?

 a. *3*
 b. *4*
 c. *5*
 d. *6*

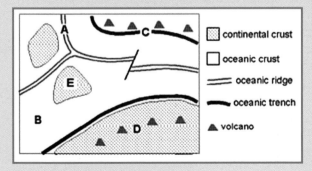

Sample ConcepTest.

In their initial individual responses to this question, 44 percent of students in a small environmental geology class chose the correct response, C. After discussion, the percentage of students who chose this answer increased to 75 percent (McConnell et al., 2006).

McConnell alternates among delivering short lectures on a particular topic, posing more ConcepTests, and making time for students to work on other problems. In a unit on volcanoes, for example, students fill in a Venn diagram showing which characteristics are common to both composite volcanoes and shield volcanos and which are distinct to one type. In another task, students compare and contrast the perceptions of risk among four constituencies—scientists, government agencies, businesses, and the general public—in the weeks preceding the Mount St. Helens eruption. Later, working in groups, they try to figure out why one city near a volcano is devastated by an eruption while another city of similar size near a different volcano suffers only light damage when its local volcano erupts. McConnell addresses any student misconceptions before moving on to the next segment.

He emphasizes to students that it's okay to make mistakes in class; the activities done in class do not count toward their grade. "I encourage them to fail brazenly in class and not worry about it—it's part of the learning process," he says. "The point is to recognize when you don't know something so you can fix it."

Other important learning activities take place outside of class. Students complete "learning journals" that encourage them to reflect on what they learned from the assigned readings. For example, after reading portions of textbook chapters on earthquakes and a news article about Italian scientists being put on trial for failing to predict a deadly earthquake in the town of L'Aquila, students must answer three questions:

1. In your own words (and using complete sentences), what is this trial about?

2. What would be the biggest challenge associated with making predictions about the potential for a future earthquake?

3. L'Aquila has many buildings that are hundreds of years old and a history of past earthquakes. If Raleigh were in a similar situation, who would you think should be responsible for determining a possible course of action following a series of small-to-moderate-sized earthquakes? (Rank the responsibility level of the citizens, the scientists of the state's geological survey, city and state government officials, and local news media.)

As part of their learning journals, students also take short online quizzes consisting of questions about the content of reading assignments, as well as questions that ask them to reflect on their learning, such as describing the most interesting thing they learned from the reading. The quizzes are graded automatically online while short-answer questions (like those above) are graded by teaching assistants. McConnell reviews the results before the next class to determine how well students understand the material.

As part of his research for the Geoscience Affective Research NETwork (GARNET) project, which is studying the impact of student attitudes and motivation on learning, McConnell asked his students whether they would do the out-of-class assignments if they were optional. Almost all of them said, "No, we would probably not do it on our own, but keep making us do it," he reports. This led him to conclude that students recognized the benefit of these assignments to their learning. He shares the results of his research with his students so they can see that those who complete the assignments do better in the course.

Course assessments and evidence of effectiveness

In addition to obtaining feedback on students' learning from the ConcepTests and learning journals, McConnell administers "two-part" exams that count toward students' grades. All but a few of the simplest questions on these exams are tied to the course learning goals. Students first do a version of the exam in a group with their neighbors and hand it in; the group exam accounts for roughly 25 percent of their grade on the test. In the next class period, they take a different, longer version of the exam individually and hand it in to determine the other 75 percent of their exam grade. "Because they have to do the group exam a day before the regular exam, they are actually studying twice, which is good because they are hopefully retaining the information better," McConnell explains. If a student does better on the individual exam, the score on the group exam is ignored; otherwise, the student will gain a small benefit from the group exam grade. Students like the group exams, McConnell says, and often have animated discussions about what they have learned.

McConnell, Steer, and several other colleagues have studied the impact of using ConcepTests in a range of geosciences courses at different types of institutions by examining pre- and post-test data from the Geoscience Concept Inventory (GCI) and qualitative feedback from students and instructors (McConnell et al., 2006). Students in classes that used ConcepTests did better on the GCI than students nationally or in two "control" sections of a course taught by the same instructor. Attendance and student satisfaction also improved according to qualitative evidence.

In McConnell's course he combines several research-supported practices, such as clearly defined learning goals, ConcepTests with peer discussion, collaborative activities, assignments that encourage students to reflect on their learning, and frequent assessment that provides feedback to the instructor and the students. Here are some particular points from his experience that may be helpful to instructors at the early stages of implementing student-centered instruction:

- Establishing learning goals at the outset will guide decisions about the best instructional strategies to help students reach these goals and assessments to measure effectively how well they have met them.

- Telling students explicitly what the learning goals are and reminding them often can reinforce what they need to study and make them more likely to buy into new ways of teaching.

- The first steps of applying a scientific or engineering mindset to your teaching often include identifying any problems with your teaching, reviewing prior research on effective strategies, attending workshops or other developmental opportunities, and collaborating with colleagues who have similar educational interests.

- Even if you are initially dubious about these new instructional approaches, it is worth attending a workshop to learn more about them.

- You may find it difficult at first to develop and incorporate student-centered activities, but the result can be exciting and rewarding for both you and your students.

- Many effective instructors use a mix of research-based strategies. The specific strategies may evolve over time as you gain more experience, analyze their impact, and discover which options work best for you.

Starting Small

Many instructors who have effectively used research-based pedagogies began by implementing one idea on a small scale, such as adding thoughtful clicker questions or tutorials to their lectures or setting aside time during one class period a week for a group activity. Others have piloted a new research-based approach with one section of a large class. By phasing in reforms, these instructors gained the confidence needed to make greater changes. "The biggest help for me was recognizing that students still need to learn content," says Christopher Swan,[9] a Tufts University professor who incorporates small-group work on projects, often with a sustainability focus, into his engineering courses. Swan still maintains some traditional assignments and exams but incorporates shorter projects throughout a course and a longer project near the end that are designed to help students learn important content.

Many instructors who would like to try out active learning strategies are intimidated by what Robin Wright,[10] an associate dean in the College of Biological Sciences at the University of Minnesota, calls a "big misconception"— namely, that faculty who have effectively taught a well-designed lecture course for several years "think they've got to throw all of that away and start from scratch." But that is not the approach she and her colleagues took when preparing to teach in a new building with classrooms designed especially to facilitate active student engagement. Rather, says Wright, they started by making students responsible for learning through homework some of the less demanding content that was previously included in lectures. This freed up a portion of class time for activities designed to help students discover the more challenging content. "Most of the activities we do in class are derivative of lectures. . . . I call it starting where you are," Wright says. "Don't lose the content, but cover it by giving students a quiz at the beginning of class. Then have students wrestle with data instead of having you explain how to wrestle with data."

Several experienced practitioners interviewed for this book reported that after they tried one or two research-based strategies and saw what a difference they made, they became excited about doing more. "You don't even have to go all the way in. Even a little bit is good. And then you get addicted and you keep doing more," says Elizabeth Derryberry,[11] a biology professor at Tulane University.

Collaborating with Like-Minded Colleagues

Taking those first steps toward research-based instruction can be easier with the encouragement, guidance, and support of colleagues. "Often teachers feel they are working alone in the dark. If they can instead work with a team, it can enhance their motivation and the quality of the outcome," says Cynthia Brame[12] of Vanderbilt University's Center for Teaching.

---

[9] Interview, August 27, 2013.
[10] Interview, April 12, 2013.
[11] Interview, May 1, 2013.
[12] Interview, April 29, 2013.

Many expert instructors started out by collaborating with faculty who already had some experience in or passion for implementing new teaching strategies. Relationships formed in this way may last for years and lead to further refinements in course design and teaching techniques. Several instructors began by doing graduate work with or being mentored by senior colleagues who were leaders in research-based instruction; many of these graduate students or junior faculty went on to become leaders in the field themselves and to serve as mentors to others.

The forms and benefits of these collaborative relationships vary. Several instructors interviewed for this book found inspiration from sitting in on a colleague's class. Eric Brewe of FIU maintains that having faculty observe research-based classes is a good way of getting buy-in from those who may otherwise be hesitant to change. At the University of Minnesota, the first teaching assignment for newly hired, tenure-track professors in biology is to team teach an existing course aligned with their interests, explains Wright. "We hope that this will help change the 'secret' culture that teaching often has—that people would be threatened by someone else there watching. We've got to get over that," she says.

Many expert instructors have arranged to co-teach one or more courses with like-minded colleagues. As discussed in Chapter 6, this approach enables them to share the workload involved in developing materials and redesigning a course and makes it easier to address implementation challenges. Team teaching has been enormously valuable to the College of Biological Sciences at Minnesota, says Wright. "You've got somebody right there to help you trouble-shoot based on student performance."

And, as emphasized in Chapter 7, various types of support from a department or institution can be extremely helpful for instructors who are just getting started with revising their instruction around research.

Joining a Learning Community

If you are itching to try out new strategies but sense you will need encouragement and additional knowledge in the process, or if you feel that you require a more structured, collegial relationship to follow through on your intent to change your teaching methods, then you may find what you need in a formal or an informal learning community or similar network. Learning communities are an effective form of ongoing professional development that bring together instructors—and in some cases, graduate students, post-docs, and others—to learn about and try out new instructional approaches and generate new knowledge (Austin, 2009; Beach and Cox, 2009). They can be important forces in promoting instructional reform (Fairweather, 2005). These communities may be live or virtual. They can exist within a department or an institution or through an external network, such as a disciplinary society, online resource center, or other professional organization. Some learning communities are forged by people who met at an initial professional development workshop and then made a commitment to help each other implement and expand on what they learned.

Within an institution, even a few interested colleagues can create an informal learning community to support and learn from each other, share materials, and provide momentum for reform. In some institutions, faculty interested in research-based teaching meet periodically for informal lunches or "journal clubs."

If others in your department do not share your interest in research-based instruction, external learning communities can help fill this void. The On the Cutting Edge program, for example, supports virtual communities of learners in geosciences through online journal clubs, webinars, and active listservs. Sometimes the disciplinary affiliation is as strong as the departmental affiliation. The point is to build community either live or virtually.

Allison Rober,[13] a biology professor who began teaching at Ball State University in 2013, is an example of an instructor who has found ideas and support through an online community forged with mentors and colleagues who met through the Future Academic Scholars in Teaching (FAST) fellows program at Michigan State. "One of the things I valued most from FAST and similar programs is the community," she says.

To be effective, the members of a learning community must engage in meaningful interactions that are focused on accomplishing particular goals within a course or learning activities. Within a community, all participants take responsibility for achieving the learning goals. Members support each other, but also may challenge each other's ideas (Center for the Integration of Research, Teaching, and Learning, n.d.b).

Taking Advantage of Existing Resources

Instructors who want to implement reforms rooted in research on how students learn their discipline do not have to develop curricula from scratch, as their predecessors had to do several years ago. A variety of resources to support this type of instructional reform are available in published form or on the Web through cen-

---

[13] Interview, April 29, 2013.

ters like the Science Education Resource Center (SERC); through projects devoted to specific instructional strategies, such as The Process Oriented Guided Inquiry Learning (POGIL) Project or Student-Centered Active Learning Environment with Upside-down Pedagogies (SCALE-UP) (described in Chapters 4 and 5, respectively); and through professional organizations and networks. These resources include curricula and learning activities, tutorials, assessments, videos, and other materials. Many of these materials have been validated by research studies or cited as exemplary through peer reviews.

Several of the instructors interviewed for this book started out by using curriculum materials developed by others, an approach that is time-efficient and cost-effective. "Stand on the shoulders of giants," emphasizes Noah Finkelstein, a professor of physics at Colorado. He offers this analogy: Although lasers are used in his physics classes, he does not build a laser system from scratch. "I build on the work that others have done on that system. . . . I go to the laser expert; I don't want to have to become the laser expert."

At the same time, instructors often adapt existing materials or modify implementation of an approach to suit their particular students, learning goals, context, and resources. Although the learning materials developed for The POGIL Project have been carefully constructed, says Rick Moog, a chemistry instructor at Franklin & Marshall College and the Project's executive director, users are encouraged to modify the implementation of the pedagogy to suit their own needs. "The [POGIL] approach is philosophical and pedagogical; it's not a set of directions on what to do," says Moog. "You have to figure out what works for you."

When adapting materials, however, one must be careful to recognize and maintain the elements that research has shown to be critical to realize the improvements in student learning that others have achieved.

Participating in Professional Development

Most instructors who use research-based strategies in their courses participated in professional development about these strategies at some point in their careers, and some went on to lead professional development activities themselves. Attending a workshop or institute was often the catalyst for practitioners to adopt research-based strategies. It is only a first step, to be sure; implementing meaningful change in practice requires sustained opportunities for faculty development, access to resources, and a supportive community, as discussed later in this book.

Stephen Krause,[14] an engineering professor at Arizona State University, calls his initial participation in an NSF-funded workshop on rigorous research in engineering education a "transformative experience." Krause now conducts workshops on evidence-based approaches to engineering education.

Alex Rudolph,[15] a professor of physics and astronomy at California State Polytechnic University, Pomona, and a frequent workshop leader, says he was "won over" after first participating in a workshop on research-based teaching and learning offered by the Center for Astronomy Education. "I went ahead and incorporated the entire set of pedagogical strategies they had developed—lock, stock, and barrel." Rudolph encourages instructors with an interest in trying new strategies to first attend a workshop. "Those two days of immersion make all the difference in the world," he says. "It gives you a basis on which to start, without feeling like you're picking up a hammer when you've never been a carpenter and you're being told to build a house."

Professional development activities vary considerably in their focus, duration, delivery methods, extent of follow-up, and other characteristics. They also vary in their effectiveness, as discussed below.

A wide array of professional development opportunities—ranging from daylong workshops to fellowships extending over one year or more, and from efforts on one's local campus to large-scale national programs—are available to instructors who want to learn more about research-based approaches to teaching and learning. These programs are sponsored by individual institutions, disciplinary societies and professional organizations, networks of practitioners using a particular instructional approach, and other entities. Some professional development efforts are geared to instructors with little or no experience in research-based approaches, while others are aimed at more seasoned innovators and alumni of previous workshops who want to go into more depth.

Several professional development initiatives are described in Chapters 6 and 7. The example below of the Summer Institute for Undergraduate Education in Biology sponsored by the National Academies and the Howard Hughes Medical Institute gives a taste of the experiences available to instructors through a multi-day workshop in research-based teaching approaches.

---

[14] Interview, July 9, 2013.
[15] Interview, August 20, 2013.

Bringing the Rigor of Research to Science Teaching at the National Academies Summer Institute

At the annual National Academies Summer Institute for Undergraduate Education in Biology, faculty and other instructional staff from around the country spend an intensive week learning about and gaining experience in "scientific teaching." This approach encourages instructors to improve their undergraduate science classes by applying the same rigor, creativity, critical thinking, and scientific spirit that they use in their biology lab work (Center for Scientific Teaching, 2014).

First offered in 2004 and currently sponsored by the National Academies and the Howard Hughes Medical Institute, the Summer Institute (SI) was the first major national professional development program for life sciences faculty. The SI emphasizes active learning, methods for assessment of student learning and teaching effectiveness, and instructional strategies that engage a diverse group of students. Participants work in small groups to develop instructional materials with clearly defined learning goals, which they can take back to their home campuses and use right away. In addition, they learn how to lead workshops on scientific teaching (National Academies, n.d.).

"One difference between the SI and many other professional development workshops is that we model scientific teaching rather than simply telling participants about it. So, for example, participants in an active learning session actually experience what it's like to be a student in an active learning classroom," says Bill Wood,[a] a University of Colorado Boulder biologist and a co-founder and former co-director of the SI. With this type of preparation, par-

ticipants "are better able to implement active learning later in their own teaching," explains Wood.

For the first several years, the SI was limited to biology faculty and offered at a single site, the University of Wisconsin–Madison. In order to reach a greater number of faculty, the sponsors expanded the program in 2011 to include workshops at several regional sites (Howard Hughes Medical Institute, 2011). While biology remains the main focus, some regional workshops have recently included multidisciplinary or interdisciplinary activities.

"Teaching in the light"

When Michelle Withers, now a biology professor at West Virginia University, arrived at the first SI in 2004, she knew she needed to improve her teaching methods. "I was still rewriting the book on PowerPoint slides. I was still the talking head," she says (Howard Hughes Medical Institute, 2011). Attending the Institute "was sort of like someone flipped the light switch for me, and I went, 'Oh, okay, this is what it's like to teach in the light, and I've been teaching in the dark and didn't realize it,'" she says (Mazella, 2013). Withers not only implemented the strategies she learned at the SI in her own classes, but also set up workshops on scientific teaching for the faculty and teaching assistants at her home campus. She now runs one of the regional SI workshops at her home institution.

Clarissa Dirks,[b] a biologist at The Evergreen State College in Washington State and leader of a regional SI workshop, describes her experience in

---

[a] Email from Bill Wood to Nancy Kober, March 23, 2014.

[b] Interview, March 24, 2014.

the first SI cohort as "life-changing." Although she had previously used some active learning strategies in her courses, the SI workshop helped her realize "there are all these tools for doing things differently in the classroom, and the literature shows they're more effective." For example, she says, the SI experience helped her design better curriculum and instruction for a workshop for students from underrepresented groups. By examining assessment data, she determined that weak-

nesses in science processing and reasoning skills were a major stumbling block for many of these students. "I designed an entire program to teach these kinds of skills, and as a result, they went on to become incredibly successful in introductory biology," Dirks explains. Currently Dirks is designing a national assessment to measure scientific process and reasoning skills in biology.

Changing practices and influencing others

Since 2004, roughly 1,000 biology instructors have participated in the SI, notes Wood.[c] All but a few of the major research universities, as well as other types of institutions, have sent instructors to the SI. Typically, two or three instructors from the same institution attend together so they can support each other in implementation after they return home.

To encourage SI participants to become agents for change at their home campuses, the program asks them to make a commitment to use and evaluate the impact of the materials they developed at the workshop and to coordinate a workshop on scientific teaching at their own institution for faculty, post-docs, or graduate students.

The SI has had several "spinoff" effects, says Dirks. She and several other alumni have gone on to engage in DBER scholarship, publish their findings in journals, and assume leadership roles in efforts to improve science education.

Evaluations of impact

Surveys of the first five SI cohorts conducted before, shortly after, one year after, and two years after their participation show a substantial increase in scientific teaching practices over time (Pfund et al., 2009). For example, two years after participating in an SI, more than 68 percent of alumni reported using three main strategies emphasized during the

[c] Email from Bill Wood to Nancy Kober, March 23, 2014.

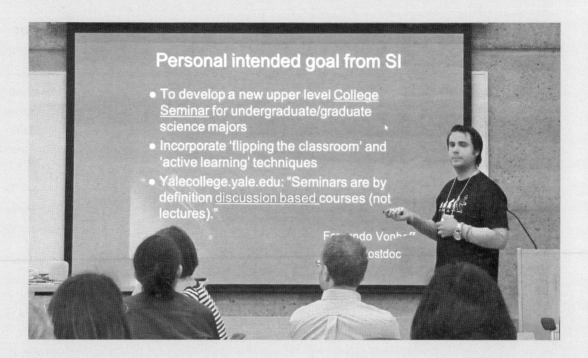

workshops—active learning, assessments of learning and teaching effectiveness, and diversity strategies— in at least half of their class sessions. A large majority of SI alumni also reported that they had mentored a colleague in teaching and presented a seminar or workshop about teaching, according to self-reported survey data (Pfund et al., 2009).

A study of the impact of professional development on participants in the National Academies SI and a related professional development effort, the NSF-funded Faculty Institutes for Reforming Science Teaching (FIRST II), used videotaped observations of classes in addition to participant surveys to address some of the limitations inherent in self-reported data (Ebert-May et al., 2011). Findings from this study were mixed. Although more than 75 percent of participants reported frequent use of learner-centered and cooperative learning on the surveys, the observational data, which were analyzed using an established protocol, found that up to 18 months after the workshop, the majority of study partici-

pants still used mainly lecture-based instruction.

In addition to the obvious differences between self-reported survey data and observational data, these two evaluations also differed somewhat in the cohorts of participants studied and the time elapsed after the workshop. The design and delivery of the workshop continued to be refined over time, says Dirks.[d] It is also noteworthy that SI alumni often say that it took them three or more years of experimenting before they felt they could effectively use learner-centered teaching strategies (Pfund et al., 2009). As the National Research Center (NRC) report on DBER concludes, "These results suggest that measuring the influence of DBER and related research on teaching requires a nuanced, longitudinal model of individual behavior rather than a traditional 'cause and effect' model using a workshop or other delivery mechanism as the intervention" (National Research Council, 2012, p. 173).

_____
[d] Interview, March 24, 2014.

Professional development can take forms other than attending traditional workshops, institutes, and seminars. Obtaining regular and timely feedback from experts on how one is implementing changes in instruction is a powerful form of professional development (Henderson, Beach, and Finkelstein, 2011). Prather and Brissenden (2008) suggest a model of "situated apprenticeships" in which instructors actively practice teaching strategies and critique each other's implementation through an ongoing peer-review process.[16] Other options include reviewing videos of skilled instructors teaching in their classrooms with expert commentary, or reviewing videos of one's own teaching with feedback from a mentor.

Evidence of the effectiveness of different types of professional development comes largely from self-reports from participants, which must be interpreted with caution, and in a few cases from more detailed types of follow-up and observations of instructional practices of former participants. In general, this evidence suggests that professional development activities have been more successful in increasing instructors' awareness about research-based strategies than in changing teaching practice. A limited amount of evidence suggests, however, that professional development efforts can have a positive impact on practice, particularly if the professional development program is longer in duration and incorporates the components described in the next paragraph. (For a more detailed discussion of studies of professional development, see Chapter 8 of the 2012 NRC report on DBER.)

How do you go about choosing an effective professional program? You can start by looking for programs focused on research-based approaches in your discipline, because they will be more likely to address principles of teaching and learning that are specific to the courses you teach. Although additional research needs to be done on the relative effectiveness of different kinds of professional development, programs with some evidence of success in changing faculty practices generally include more than one of the following components (Henderson, Beach, and Finkelstein, 2011; Loucks-Horsley et al., 2009; Wilson, 2011):

- A duration of four weeks or more (although not necessarily all at the same time)

- A focus on making participants aware of the learning principles underlying an innovation and changing their conceptions about teaching and learning, through opportunities for self-reflection or other means

---

[16] Connecting with like-minded colleagues, discussed above, facilitates the process of obtaining feedback from experts.

- Modeling of the instructional practices that participants are expected to use—for example, by teaching the workshop through active learning and engaging participants in the types of activities students would do

- Expert leaders with a strong grounding in the discipline and experience in implementing the specific strategies they are teaching to participants

- Opportunities for participants to practice new instructional approaches in the workshop and receive expert feedback as they do this

- Use of research-validated techniques to motivate adult learners, such as relevant content, opportunities for reflection, and group work (Wlodkowski, 1999)

- Activities that encourage participants to articulate clearly how they will put what they have learned into action after the workshop (Hilborn, 2012)

- Follow-up activities for workshop alumni, such as peer mentoring, Web networks, and gatherings

Conclusion

The trajectory of Karen Kortz,[17] a geology professor at the Community College of Rhode Island (CCRI), illustrates how an instructor with a strong desire to increase her students' learning and engagement but with little previous exposure to DBER relied on several of the suggestions described in this chapter.

As a new faculty member at CCRI in 2001, Kortz wanted to be a great teacher, but she was not certain what that entailed. Many of her students were working or raising families while attending college, and most were taking her course primarily to meet a laboratory science requirement. She hoped to be able to dispel her students' fears about science and give them a compelling reason to attend class. "I knew courses should be interactive, but I didn't know how to do that," she says.

Kortz began by attending a workshop for early career geosciences faculty offered by On the Cutting Edge, a professional development project of the National Association of Geoscience Teachers. "That really opened my eyes," she says. There she learned more about how to design interactive instruction and was inspired by people who were doing DBER. ("I had no idea there was such a thing," she adds.)

---

[17] Except where noted, the information in this example comes from an interview with Karen Kortz, April 5, 2013.

After that workshop, Kortz started changing her courses a little at a time. One of the first things she did was develop worksheets that students would do in small groups between lecture segments. At another workshop on interactive teaching of astronomy, Kortz learned about lecture tutorials, which are designed explicitly to tease out students' inaccurate ideas about science concepts and lead them to deeper understanding (Prather et al., 2007). "I thought, this is what we need in geology," she says.

Kortz and her colleague Jessica Smay of San Jose City College began turning their initial set of informal worksheets into a more formal series of lecture tutorials that targeted common student misconceptions in geosciences identified by research. Their tutorials have been made available on the SERC website[18] and have also been used by other instructors and published as a book (Kortz and Smay, 2012). One study across multiple institutions revealed that the use of these lecture tutorials improved students' test scores in introductory geosciences courses (Kortz, Smay, and Murray, 2008).

In the meantime, Kortz introduced other interactive techniques into her classes, including clicker questions, Think-Pair-Share, and the jigsaw approach (all explained in Chapter 4). In a few cases, she abandoned techniques that were not worth the class time they required. Eventually, she completed a Ph.D. in geosciences education while continuing to teach. Acknowledging that in her early career she sometimes spent unnecessary effort trying to "reinvent the wheel," she also advises instructors to "build on the work that's already out there."

Kortz, who has won awards for her teaching, now leads On the Cutting Edge workshops herself. "So it's come full circle," she says. Her students show higher-than-average improvement in their scores on the GCI, a standardized assessment designed to diagnose students' conceptual understanding and learning in entry-level Earth science courses. Kortz tells instructors who want to improve their teaching: "Don't give up."

Resources and Further Reading

The Center for the Integration of Research, Teaching, and Learning (CIRTL) Network
www.cirtl.net

Discipline-Based Education Research: Understanding and Improving Learning in Undergraduate Science and Engineering (National Research Council, 2012)
Chapter 8: Translating Research into Teaching Practice: The Influence of Discipline-Based Education Research on Undergraduate Science and Engineering Instruction

The Science Education Resource Center (SERC) at Carleton College
www.serc.carleton.edu

---

[18] See http://serc.carleton.edu/NAGTWorkshops/teaching_methods/lecture_tutorials/index.html.

3

Using Insights About Learning to Inform Teaching

"I think it's about putting yourself in the students' shoes and seeing how a first-time student, maybe someone who hasn't even taken chemistry before, is looking at it."

—*Valerie Taraborelli, undergraduate chemistry student, University of Arizona*[1]

"In some ways, I think the people who are the most successful as teachers are the ones who are able to remember what it was like being uncertain and not knowing. When you become an expert, things are easy. So the idea is to try and see where [students] are coming from and why they've developed this misconception and what you can do to specifically address it."

—*Dee Silverthorn, biology professor, University of Texas*[2]

These two quotations underscore a point made by research—that effective science and engineering instruction involves much more than conveying to students what you, as an expert, already know and what you think they should know. Rather, effective teaching in these disciplines involves ascertaining what students know, what they don't know, and what they think they know but do not really understand accurately or fully. Using that information, you can help students establish a solid framework of understanding that can better support new knowledge.

While teaching and learning are often seen as distinct processes—one controlled by the teacher and the other by the student—they are really intertwined aspects of a complex process shaped by both teacher and student. Understanding

---

[1] Interview, April 24, 2013.
[2] Interview, June 25, 2013.

how students learn is a key aspect of good teaching.

This chapter describes some of the main insights from research on how people learn in general and how undergraduate students learn science and engineering in particular. Rather than being a comprehensive review of evidence from discipline-based education research (DBER), the findings and examples highlighted in this chapter are intended to illustrate how an understanding of learning can lead you to think differently about instruction and design more effective approaches. Additional information from research on how undergraduate students learn science and engineering is available in the 2012 National Research Council (NRC) report on DBER.

General Insights About How Students Learn

Karl Wirth, a geosciences professor at Macalester College, is one of many instructors who have been strongly influenced by research on how people learn.

In designing new instructional strategies, Wirth and others have drawn on four decades of findings from cognitive sciences, neurosciences, and related fields. This body of scholarship comprises "an extraordinary outpouring of scientific work on the mind and brain, on the processes of thinking and learning, on the neural processes that occur during thought and learning, and on the development of competence" (National Research Council, 2000, p. 3).

DESIGNING LEARNING

Helping Students Become Intentional Learners

In the 1990s, Macalester College professor Karl Wirth[a] realized that although he thought he had been teaching his geosciences students effectively, "when they did senior capstone projects, they really weren't very well prepared. That came as sort of a shock to me." This realization led him to seek out ways to help his students develop deeper under-standing and critical-thinking skills and become more strategic, self-motivated learners. He attended workshops and read the research literature on learning, including *How People Learn: Brain, Mind, Experience, and School,* a seminal study by the National Research Council (2000).

Drawing on this body of research, Wirth incor-porated activities into all of his courses to develop students' skills in metacognition, or thinking about their own thinking and learning. The first reading assignment in his courses is a paper called *Learning to Learn,* prepared by Wirth and University of North Dakota professor Dexter Perkins (2008), which high-lights research on learning and metacognition and signals his expectation that students will learn in ways that go far beyond memorizing content.

Each time Wirth's students complete an out-of-class reading assignment, for example, they do a short writing assignment, or "reading reflection," in which they answer questions like these: *What is the main point of this reading? What information did you find surprising and why? What did you find confusing and why?* Similarly, after completing an in-class activity, students write a brief "learning reflec-tion," in which they respond to questions like these:

What are the three most important things you have learned? Why? Describe the learning strategies that you are using. How might they be adapted for more effective learning? How does learning in this course relate to other courses?

These reflection exercises prompt students to monitor their own understanding and progress and motivate them to come to class better prepared, says Wirth. In addition, the exercises provide the instruc-tor with frequent feedback about students' learning that can be used to guide improvements in instruc-tion, a function known as formative assessment. "They give me a sense of where the sticky points are in their content learning," he says. "More than anything, it puts me in touch with what's going on in their brains." Often Wirth shows students graphs of the positive correlation between completion of the reading reflection assignments and their course grades. "When they see that, they begin to realize that the people who are doing well are doing all the reading reflections." The reflection process "not only leads to deeper and more effective learning, but also lays the groundwork for being a self-directing learner" (Wirth and Perkins, 2008).

Spurred by research on the value of active stu-dent engagement and student collaboration, Wirth has adopted a so-called studio format in his classes that makes no distinction between lecture and lab. Students spend the better part of each two-hour class period conducting hands-on lab activities and solving problems.

One such activity is the M&M® magma chamber, which Wirth designed to help students better under-stand how magma changes in composition through the effects of crystallization and gravitational settling.

---

[a] Except where noted, the information in this example comes from an interview with Karl Wirth, July 8, 2013.

This is one of the most important processes in geology, and one that students often have difficulty understanding, says Wirth. The activity is also intended to provide students with an opportunity to use and reinforce concepts learned in a mineralogy or petrology course, such as stoichiometry or classification and chemical variation diagrams, and to give them practical experience in designing and using spreadsheets (Wirth, n.d.).

Using different colors of M&Ms to represent different elements, students work through a 10-step simulation of the crystallization process, in which they remove the M&Ms in specific proportions to create representations of rock layers formed by the accumulation of crystals at the bottom of a "magma chamber" drawn on butcher paper. After each step, they calculate and record on spreadsheets the relative percentages of each element remaining, as well as the proportion of magma remaining as a fraction of the original magma. They graph the changing composition in the layers. The diagram below shows the M&M magma chamber at four stages of evolution (Wirth, 2003, p. 4).

As a wrap-up, students apply and reflect on what they have learned from the activity by answering a series of questions about changes in minerals and the composition of the magma at various stages, the reasons why certain transformations occur, and which aspects of the simulation are realistic and which are not. They apply their understanding of magma differentiation by crystal fractionation to predict what would happen if certain circumstances were changed and to determine the approximate volume of basaltic magmas needed to produce the lavas of the Yellowstone Plateau.

"It's fun, it's colorful, it's kinesthetic, they're moving things around—it's chaos," says Wirth of the exercise, which has been widely disseminated as part of the Science Education Resource Center (SERC) collection of exemplary teaching activities.[b] This exercise also uses a familiar analogy of sorting candies by color as a "bridge" to help students understand a complex concept—a strategy consistent with research on learning. After students work through the M&M model, says Wirth, they understand and remember the underlying concept much better than they did when he taught it by lecturing for 20 minutes and drawing with colored markers on the board. Since he incorporated this exercise into the curriculum, "student knowledge of fractional crystallization and magmatic differentiation, as indicated by exam results and course projects, has increased significantly," he reports (Wirth, 2003, p. 1).

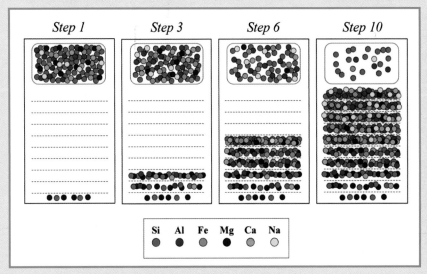

The M&M magma chamber at four stages of evolution.
SOURCE: Wirth, 2003, p. 4.

[b] See http://serc.carleton.edu/NAGTWorkshops/petrology/teaching_examples/24646.html.

Following is a summary of general findings about learning with the greatest relevance to undergraduate science and engineering education. This information is drawn mainly from *How People Learn: Brain, Mind, Experience, and School: Expanded Edition* (National Research Council, 2000); a companion volume, *How People Learn: Bridging Research and Practice* (National Research Council, 1999); and the sections on metacognition and knowledge transfer in Chapter 7 of the 2012 NRC report on DBER.

Prior knowledge shapes learning

Learners do not come to a new topic knowing nothing, particularly by the time they are undergraduates. Learners of all ages possess understandings, skills, and beliefs that significantly influence how they remember, reason, solve problems, and acquire new knowledge.

Prior knowledge can either facilitate or interfere with new learning. When students' prior knowledge is accurate, it can provide a foundation for constructing new knowledge. When students' existing ideas, or preconceptions, are basically correct but incomplete, instructors can use what students do know as a bridge to help them fill in gaps in understanding. But when students have misconceptions—ideas, beliefs, and understandings that differ from accepted scientific and engineering explanations—they may have difficulty integrating new knowledge with their inaccurate notions. Misconceptions can persist through the undergraduate years, even when students have been taught accurate explanations in their earlier science classes. In your own courses, you may have encountered students who cling to misconceptions like these: *Individuals can evolve during a single lifespan. Chemical bonds store energy that is used to make them.* As discussed later in this chapter, DBER has identified prevalent misconceptions in specific science and engineering disciplines.

Rather than simply telling students the right explanation, good instructors make an effort to elicit students' prior knowledge and use it to help students construct a more complete and accurate understanding.

Learning is a process of actively constructing knowledge

Learning is not simply the accrual of information; rather, it involves a process of conceptual reorganization. The brain is a "dynamic organ"; even a mature brain is structurally altered during learning (NRC, 2000, p. 235). The brain actively seeks to make sense of new knowledge by connecting it with prior knowledge and experience. Through this process, the learner "constructs" new understanding and meaning.

Constructing new knowledge is easier when a student has a strong foundation of sufficient, well-organized, and accurate knowledge on which to build. It becomes more difficult, however, when it requires an upending or complete restructuring of students' current understanding. In this case, instructors will need to address inaccurate or incomplete preconceptions and guide students in reorganizing their thinking in more fruitful ways, as discussed later in this chapter.

A related idea from research on cognition emphasizes that meaningful learning occurs when students select, organize, and integrate information, either independently or in groups, and take control of their own learning (National Research Council, 2000, 2012). This principle of "active learning" has strongly influenced many DBER scholars and studies and undergirds many research-based strategies for teaching science and engineering.

This view of a student as an active constructor of knowledge does not mean that instructors should never tell students anything directly. In some situations, "teaching by telling" can be an effective part of a broader instructional design, but only after students have been primed for this "telling" process by grappling with the ideas on their own in a carefully structured way (Schwartz and Bransford, 1998). Even during "times for telling," instructors still need to attend to students' interpretations and provide guidance when necessary.

Experts organize knowledge and approach problems differently from novices

The work of a science or engineering instructor might be seen as a process of moving students from novice toward more expert-like understanding in a discipline. Undergraduates cannot be expected to develop the expertise that it has taken you, as a professional, many years of dedicated practice to attain. Your goal, then, is to help move students farther along this continuum. Instructors sometimes have difficulty with this process because of blind spots—for instance, they fail to see that a step in problem solving that is automatic to them as an expert may be a substantial challenge for novices.

Research provides insights about differences between how novices and experts think and perform. Acquiring a rich body of knowledge in a discipline is a necessary starting point for developing expertise. To become an expert, one must spend enough time studying and working in a discipline to master its content. The more one knows about a subject, the easier it is to learn still more.

But expertise consists of more than just knowing an impressive array of facts. What truly distinguishes experts from novices is experts' deep understanding of the concepts, principles, and procedures of inquiry in their field, and their framework for *organizing* this knowledge. Experts also know when and how to apply particular aspects of their knowledge, and their mental organizations make it easier for them to remember and access relevant knowledge. This depth and organization of knowledge enables experts to notice patterns, relationships, and discrepancies that elude novices. It allows them to quickly identify the relevant aspects of a complex problem or situation, make inferences, and draw conclusions.

> Meaningful learning occurs when students select, organize, and integrate information, either independently or in groups, and take control of their own learning.

The knowledge that novices possess, by contrast, is often disconnected, unorganized, and therefore less usable. Novices do not always connect the relevant knowledge they do have to new tasks. And they may focus on aspects of a problem, such as superficial details, that make it more difficult rather than easier to solve.

Thus, while students need to acquire a foundation of knowledge in a discipline, this is not enough to become competent. Students also need to be able to affix their knowledge to a coherent mental framework. Instructors can help students develop more expert-like understanding by emphasizing organized bodies of knowledge and embedding specific ideas, principles, and concepts within these structures. Because knowledge is organized differently for different disciplines, attaining expertise in an area requires knowledge of both its content and its broader structural organization. More detailed findings from DBER about how novices and experts solve problems and approach other aspects of learning science and engineering are discussed in a later section of this chapter.

Metacognition can help students learn

Metacognition—the mind's ability to monitor and control its own activities—is an essential competency for learning. Students who have greater metacognitive capacity are better learners overall. They monitor their comprehension as they learn: for example, by asking themselves when they encounter a new concept whether they truly understand it, or by pausing to consider whether their strategy is working when they tackle a problem. If they find they do not understand or are not making headway, they can take corrective steps.

Although relatively few students report using metacognitive strategies when studying on their own (Karpicke, Butler, and Roediger, 2009), research suggests that students can develop metacognition over time when metacognitive strategies are embedded into instruction (Weinstein, Husman, and Dierking, 2000). The reflection exercises in Wirth's classroom, described above, are one way to build metacognitive activities into science teaching.

In chemistry, students who took laboratories designed specifically to prompt metacognitive activity showed significant gains on the Metacognitive Activities Inventory, which measures students' monitoring of their own thinking during problem solving (Sandi-Urena, Cooper, and Stevens, 2011). Consistent gains on this inventory were also found among students who participated in a workshop designed to promote metacognition (Sandi-Urena, Cooper, and Stevens, 2011). Studies in engineering education have found that incorporating reflection steps and self-explanation prompts into instruction can improve students' problem solving (Svinicki, 2011).

Activities that require students to generate their own explanations of concepts or explain a concept to another person also have a metacognitive element. Studies indicate that these "self-explanation" strategies can enhance learning more than just having students read a passage or examine the diagrams in a textbook (National Research Council, 2012).

Students who can transfer their knowledge to new situations learn more readily

If students can apply what they have learned only in conditions that are exactly the same as those in which they learned it, their education will have little practical value. The ability to "transfer" knowledge to new contexts inside and outside the classroom helps students learn related information more quickly. Knowledge transfer is a mark of a well-educated person and an ultimate goal of education—but it is often an elusive goal.

There are different degrees of transfer. "Near transfer" occurs among highly similar tasks in the same setting, such as using knowledge learned from one type of problem to solve similar problems in the same course or a sequential course in the same discipline. For example, physics students who have learned to apply Newton's second law of motion to a problem involving a block on an inclined plane should be able to recognize that they can apply the same law to understanding the data collected in a physics lab experiment.

"Far transfer" takes place when knowledge learned in one setting is applied in a distinctly different setting, such as transferring what has been learned in one course to a course in a different discipline or using what has been learned in the classroom in a new professional context or everyday situation outside of school. Far transfer is more challenging for students to master.

Students often have difficulty applying their knowledge in a new context, according to DBER studies. Research in chemistry, for example, has demonstrated that while students can memorize how to solve problems that require them to manipulate symbols and chemical formulas, they typically cannot transfer these skills to a similar problem involving drawings of atoms and molecules (see, for example, Nakhleh and Mitchell, 1993). As discussed later in this chapter, students' difficulties in transferring knowledge across various types of problems are often related to their inability to distinguish the critical features of a problem.

Findings from *How People Learn* and the 2012 NRC report on DBER shed light on the kinds of learning that support knowledge transfer. Students must have a body of sufficient knowledge about a particular topic, but this should consist of more than a collection of facts. For students to be able to transfer what they have learned, they need to understand the core concepts related to that topic that can serve as a structure for organizing their knowledge. In biology, for example, students would be expected to know the facts that arteries are thicker and more elastic than veins and carry blood away from the heart, while veins carry blood back to the heart. But to be able to apply their knowledge of the circulatory system to a new problem, students must also understand why arteries and veins have these different properties and how these properties are integral to their distinct functions (National Research Council, 2000, p. 9).

Spending a lot of time studying material and practicing its application is not sufficient to promote transfer of knowledge; what matters is *how* this time is spent. The goal is to spend time on activities that promote deeper learning. Students are more likely to develop the kind of flexible understanding that supports transfer if they learn how to extract themes and principles from their learning activities. Some instructors address this by calling attention to underlying principles and designing activities in which students explicitly practice transfer.

Moreover, if students learn a concept mostly by working on problems and examples that are similar in context—such as problems involving balls that are thrown upward or dropped from buildings—their knowledge can become "context-bound" (National Research Council, 2000, p. 236). This can be addressed by using different kinds of problems and examples that encourage students to extract the relevant features of a concept—to think in terms of problems of gravitational force and energy rather than problems involving balls. Giving students complex, realistic problems can also provide them with practice in transferring their knowledge to a new situation.

Interactions with others can promote learning

Much in the way that children learn to talk by hearing the people around them converse or that adults acquire new skills by working alongside colleagues, students construct understanding through social interactions, such as talking about and collaborating on meaningful learning activities (Vygotsky, 1978). The evidence is very strong that collaborative activities enhance the effectiveness of student-centered

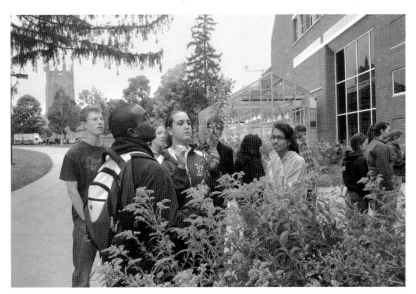

learning over traditional instruction and improve retention of content knowledge (see, for example, the meta-analyses by Johnson, Johnson, and Smith, 1998, 2007, and numerous other studies cited in Chapter 6 of the 2012 NRC report on DBER).

When students work together on well-designed learning activities, they establish a community of learners that provides cognitive and social support for the efforts of its individual members. In such a community, students share the responsibility for thinking and doing.

They can help each other solve problems by building on each other's knowledge, asking each other questions, and suggesting ideas that an individual working alone might not have considered (Brown and Campione, 1994). By challenging each other's thoughts and beliefs, they compel the members of the group to be explicit about what they mean and to negotiate any conflicts that arise, which in turn fosters metacognition. Social interactions also have a positive effect on motivation by making individuals feel they are contributing something to others (Schwartz et al., 1999).

Much in the way that children learn to talk by hearing the people around them converse or that adults acquire new skills by working alongside colleagues, students construct understanding through social interactions, such as . . . collaborating on meaningful learning activities.

Instructors can help create this sense of community by designing learning activities that encourage this type of intellectual camaraderie and by creating classroom environments in which all students, including those from groups underrepresented in science, feel safe about sharing their ideas. To be effective, these approaches must be carefully selected and implemented and well aligned with student learning outcomes and assessment procedures. Chapter 4 gives some examples of effective collaborative approaches.

Many DBER studies are grounded in general findings about learning from cognitive science and related fields. But DBER goes deeper by looking at how students learn the knowledge, practices, and ways of thinking in a science or engineering discipline. Much of this body of work focuses on three aspects of learning that are central to developing competency in these disciplines at the undergraduate level:

1. Understanding and applying the fundamental concepts of a discipline

2. Framing and solving problems with greater expertise

3. Using visual and mathematical representations, such as graphs, models, and equations, of important ideas and situations in a discipline

While other aspects of learning science and engineering have also received scholarly attention, these three have been studied the most extensively. Across disciplines, DBER has identified common challenges in these three areas that can impede students' learning, as well as approaches that can further learning. The core findings in these three areas, which are discussed in the sections that follow, are a good entry point for science and engineering instructors who want to use research to improve their teaching.

Understanding and Applying the Fundamental Concepts of a Discipline

Each of the disciplines discussed in this book is built on a set of fundamental concepts—ideas that can be applied in multiple contexts to explain and predict scientific phenomena. To become competent in biology, for example, students need to understand the concept that *species arise, change, and become extinct over time*. Students of chemistry must comprehend that *the atoms of a compound are held together by chemical bonds formed by the interaction of electrons from each atom*.

Students often have difficulty mastering the fundamental concepts of a discipline. These concepts tend to be abstract, and students may fail to recognize their value as keys to thinking about the discipline.

DBER has helped to elucidate how students develop an understanding of central science and engineering concepts and where they run into difficulty. An extensive body of DBER scholarship has identified and analyzed common student misconceptions in specific disciplines. DBER studies have also examined the effectiveness of strategies for promoting conceptual change. This research is reviewed at length in Chapter 4 of the 2012 NRC report on DBER; the major findings are summarized below.

Misconceptions

In every science and engineering discipline, undergraduates harbor misconceptions. These misconceptions are often derived from what students have observed in their own experience or what seems to be common sense. In physics, for example, students may think that denser objects fall more quickly than lighter objects in a vacuum because they have seen a rock plummet to the ground while a leaf wafts slowly downward. In biology, many students have an inaccurate "round-trip" notion of the human circulatory system in which they envision blood flowing in a continuous circle from the heart around the body before returning to the heart (Pelaez et al., 2005). Incorrect ideas may also arise from inaccurate instruction in the K–12 grades or be influenced by cultural or religious beliefs.

Across disciplines, some of the most difficult concepts for students to grasp are those for which they have no frame of reference, especially those that involve very large or very small scales of space or time. In chemistry, for example, the idea that all matter is composed of particles too small to be seen with a microscope—molecules, atoms, and subatomic particles—is one of three main domains of knowledge students are expected to master. This "particulate" domain is often represented as one corner of "Johnstone's triangle"; the other two corners are the macroscopic domain, or entities and properties that can be perceived with the human senses, and the symbolic domain, such as the letters and numbers used to represent compounds (Johnstone, 1991). While students struggle to comprehend all three domains, understanding the particulate nature of matter is one of their greatest barriers to learning chemistry (Gabel, Samuel, and Hunn, 1987; Yezierski and Birk, 2006).

In geosciences, biology, and astronomy, the concept of "deep time" often confounds students. Deep time refers to the age of Earth or the universe and involves time scales spanning billions of years (see Box 3.1).

Misconceptions about scientific and engineering concepts do not always surface during traditional instruction. Moreover, deeply rooted misconceptions can be hard to change. For example, even some students who have completed undergraduate chemistry

---

BOX 3.1 HOW LONG IS 4.5 BILLION YEARS, REALLY?: COMPREHENDING DEEP TIME

Most of us have seen a chart in the form of a metaphorical calendar that compresses the entire history of Earth into the scale of one single year and places the first appearance of humans in the final minutes of the last day of that year. This notion of "deep time," or geologic time—the well-established concept that Earth is billions of years old—is one of the revolutionary ideas in geology and a framework for understanding evolutionary biology (Catley and Novick, 2008). In astronomy, deep time extends back even further, across several billion years to the Big Bang and the origin of the universe. In all three disciplines, the very large scales make deep time a difficult concept for students to grasp.

Research has found that although most undergraduate students place significant events in geologic history—such as the formation of Earth, the first appearance of life, and the arrival of dinosaurs—in the right order, they misunderstand the scale of time between events (Libarkin, Kurdziel, and Anderson, 2007). Very few students produce estimates that are close to the scientifically accepted timeline. Students also sometimes conflate events that are far apart, such as the age of the dinosaurs and the age of humans. While the majority of students recognize that Earth is very old, some hold a "young Earth" perspective, including some who explicitly embrace creationist beliefs (Cervato and Frodeman, 2012; Libarkin, Kurdziel, and Anderson, 2007).

An analysis of 79 peer-reviewed studies of geosciences misconceptions (Cheek, 2010) notes that a poor understanding of large numbers could partially account for students' difficulty in understanding geologic time. In some of these studies, participants seemed to pick the largest number they could think of but showed no real sense of how much time it represented.

Students' problems with the concept of deep time have wide-ranging implications for learning because so many areas of geology, as well as biology and astronomy, are premised on this idea. Concepts such as plate tectonics, rock layering, and sedimentation, among others, all depend to some extent on an understanding of geologic time. Libarkin, Kurdziel, and Anderson (2007) suggest that instructors incorporate a thorough discussion of the basic concept of deep time early in their introductory courses and reiterate its effects on other aspects of geology throughout the course. Dodick (2012) proposes that instead of simply focusing on the raw numbers in the chronology of deep time, instructors direct students' attention to the significance of the numbers by anchoring a specific time period with key events they can visualize, much in the way that people might associate a particular month with their birthday.

courses still stand by the misconception that chemical bonds release energy when they break (Sözbilir, 2004). If instruction does not address misconceptions like these, students may fail to grasp new concepts and information. Or, they may learn them well enough to pass a test but go back their old, inaccurate ways of thinking outside the classroom.

It's especially important to probe the reasoning that underlies misconceptions, says Lillian McDermott,[3] a physics professor at the University of Washington who has designed tutorials and other interventions to facilitate conceptual change. "The problem with the term 'misconceptions research' is that it seems to imply that all that needs to be done is to identify a mistaken interpretation of a concept and replace it with a correct one. It is the reasoning in physics, however, that distinguishes related concepts from one another, identifies their relationship, and makes possible their correct application," writes McDermott in a forthcoming manuscript.[4] "Our emphasis has therefore not been on the *eradication* of misconceptions, but rather on the *development of reasoning skills* necessary for the proper application of concepts."

Assessing students' conceptual understanding

To improve conceptual understanding, instructors first need to determine what students know, what they understand incompletely, and where they have misconceptions. With this information in hand, instructors can then help students replace or refine misconceptions and use what they already know as a framework for building a more complete and accurate understanding.

As discussed in more detail in Chapter 5, scholars have designed various tools to assess students' conceptual understanding. These range from formal instruments like concept inventories to everyday classroom methods like ConcepTests in the form of clicker questions. It is often necessary to use more than one type of assessment. Pelaez and colleagues (2005) found that their essay exams were insufficient to expose the extent of common student misconceptions about the circulatory system and that other assessment methods, including drawings and individual interviews, were required to discover how and what students thought.

A relatively simple way of regularly assessing how well students understand the concepts being taught is to have them reflect in writing on the concepts that confuse them—soliciting the "muddiest points," as Patricia Cross and Thomas Angelo (1988) called them in their widely used handbook on classroom assessment techniques. Stephen Krause, an engineering professor at Arizona State University, has adapted this approach in his courses.

---

[3] Interview, April 13, 2013.
[4] Unpublished manuscript by Lillian McDermott titled *A View from Physics: Discipline-Based Education Research in a University Physics Department, 1973–2013.*

Clarifying the Muddiest Points in an Engineering Class

How do instructors know which ideas in their courses are misunderstood by or confusing to students? And once they know, how do they address that?

One quick and simple way of obtaining feedback is to ask students to reflect anonymously on what they found to be the "muddiest points" discussed during each class—the concepts or other issues that remain unclear to them or that they feel uncertain about. Stephen Krause[a] uses this approach in his introductory engineering courses at Arizona State and is part of a group of engineering faculty members who have studied the impact. While the idea of soliciting muddiest points from students was first

mentioned by Cross and Angelo (1988), Krause and others have refined the approach in various ways, such as using Web software to collect and display students' reflections and adding YouTube tutorials that explain difficult concepts.

At the conclusion of each class, Krause's students take a few minutes to fill out a worksheet that asks them to identify the concepts and topics they had trouble understanding and to rate the degree of difficulty they experienced with a particular concept. Their responses are catalogued in a spreadsheet that the instructor and assistants review. This direct feedback enables Krause to readily gauge how well

COVALENT CERAMICS POLYMERS
IONIC BONDSTRENGTH
VANDERWAALS
ENERGYWELLS METALLIC BONDENERGY

Word cloud in which the size of type reflects the degree of students' confusion about the term.

---

[a] Except where noted, the information in this case study comes from an interview with Stephen Krause, July 9, 2013.

students understand the course content and address misunderstandings in the next class. In addition, students can anonymously access a running catalogue of their own responses to see how their thinking has progressed during the semester.

At the beginning of each class, Krause displays a selection of the muddiest points from the previous session using the students' own words. (Krause employs a slide or the online Blackboard® software to display the results; some other instructors use the online Concept Warehouse system to generate a word cloud of the muddiest points.) For example, after a lesson on crystallographic planes—geometric planes linking the nodes (atoms, ions, molecules) of a crystal—one student raised this question: *Why are the crystallographic planes important?* Following a lesson on phase diagrams, which represent the various phases of a substance under different pressure and temperature conditions, a student was confused about this point: *How do I find chemical composition and phase fractions from a phase diagram?* Bethany Smith,[b] who served as Krause's undergraduate assistant in her junior year of 2012–2013, admits that she herself was initially confused by phase diagrams when she took the course as a sophomore.

Krause uses the first 5 or 10 minutes of class to address the most common muddiest points. Smith says this type of review discussion helped her to better understand phase diagrams. In fact, she adds, much of what she learned in the sophomore materials class has proved to be "definitely useful" in later classes in the materials science sequence.

_____
[b] Interview, July 11, 2013.

After clarifying the muddiest points, Krause moves on to a mini-lecture to prepare students for the activities they will do that day. "The nice thing about the muddiest points is that they activate the knowledge from the previous class and provide a connection to the current class," he says. "They can provide segues into that day's mini-lecture."

Krause and Smith have also produced a series of YouTube tutorials (https://www.youtube.com/user/MaterialsConcepts) that list a few of the muddiest points cited by students for a particular topic and explain each one using voiceover narration and visual aids. Students view the videos to clarify difficult

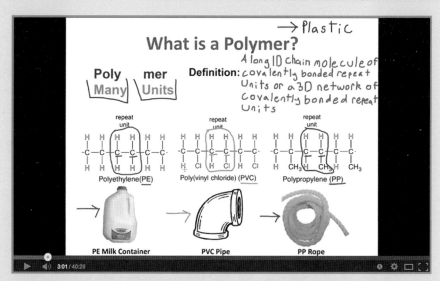

Screen capture from a YouTube tutorial.

concepts and help them with homework. Preliminary results have found significant gains in achievement on the content included in the YouTube tutorials, compared with test results for previous classes (Krause et al., 2013a).

The muddiest point reflections are just one part of Krause's student-centered instructional approach, which he calls Just-in-Time Teaching with Interactive Learning (JiTTIL). This approach is described in Chapter 4.

Teaching for conceptual understanding

DBER has identified various instructional strategies that can help students develop a deeper and more accurate understanding of important concepts and, where necessary, promote conceptual change. This type of change depends on students recognizing that their preconceptions are not facts but hypotheses or models that must be evaluated in light of empirical evidence (National Academy of Sciences, National Academy of Engineering, and Institute of Medicine, 2005). Many of these strategies seek to create situations in which students realize that their preconceptions conflict with new evidence and that they must change their thinking to fit with new knowledge.

To adapt their thinking to new evidence, students may need to add, remove, or revise elements of an existing mental model; create a new model where there was none before; or replace a preconception with a different and better one—or make each of these changes at different times (Clement, 2008). Because students' preconceptions are nonscientific in different ways, instructors may need to use a variety of approaches, possibly even in the same class, to help students refine or replace these nonscientific ideas and beliefs. And students will need multiple exposures to the same concept in different contexts before they begin to really understand it.

David Sokoloff[5] has seen these kinds of change occur in students' conceptual understanding in his physics lecture and laboratory courses at the University of Oregon. To foster conceptual change and increase student participation in a lecture course, Sokoloff and Ron Thornton, a physics professor at Tufts University, developed a curriculum built around Interactive Lecture Demonstrations (ILDs)—physical demonstrations of scientific phenomena that the instructor conducts in class. In the approach used by Sokoloff and Thornton, students first predict what will happen before the instructor does the demonstration. Students next discuss their predictions in small peer groups and explain their predictions to the whole class. Then the class observes the instructor conducting the demonstration. In the final stage, students compare their observations to their predictions (Sokoloff and Thornton, 2004).

Sokoloff, Thornton, and Priscilla Laws at Dickinson College have also developed a related curriculum for active learning laboratories called Real Time Physics. In these labs, students do experiments supported by real-time, computer-based tools. But before conducting an experiment, students make predictions about the outcome and discuss their predictions in small groups.

---

[5] Except where noted, the information in this example comes from an interview with David Sokoloff, July 10, 2013.

In both the ILDs and the lab activities, the prediction and discussion phases are essential to the process of conceptual change, says Sokoloff. In many cases, "students are confronted with the fact that the predictions don't describe the situation," he explains. This creates a moment of "psychological disequilibrium" in which students recognize they have to restructure their thinking to integrate new information. "For many years, the majority of physics instructors did demonstrations in their classes," says Sokoloff. "They would do some kind of physics experiment at the front of the room—hopefully as dramatic as possible, because they thought that the more dramatic it is, the more likely that students will learn from it. There's now some very significant research that shows that unless you do demonstrations in the context of asking students to make predictions about them before you do them, they won't learn anything from them." Research by Sokoloff and Thornton (1997) indicates that ILDs can improve students' understanding of foundational physics concepts as measured by the Force and Motion Conceptual Evaluation. For example, after physics students experienced a sequence of ILDs related to Newton's third law, they retained an appropriate understanding of the law months later.

The ILDs developed by Sokoloff and Thornton are also sequenced in a way that gradually leads students toward a better understanding of concepts like Newton's laws. In lessons on kinematics and dynamics, for example, the initial demonstrations are designed to solidify students' understanding of very basic concepts. Later demonstrations introduce more complex concepts (Sokoloff and Thornton, 1997). (See Box 3.2.)

This progression of ILDs is an example of "scaffolding"—a term first used by Wood, Bruner, and Ross (1976) to describe the process of starting with what students know and providing them with carefully structured support to move them toward more accurate understanding. Scaffolding provides successive levels of temporary support that allow learners to accomplish a task and reach a level of understanding that they would otherwise be unable to achieve without assistance. The idea is that eventually the instructor will systematically remove the scaffolding supports so that students will use the newly acquired concepts and skills on their own.

Another example of scaffolding is the use of "bridging analogies" that connect a situation that students understand correctly with another situation about which they harbor a misconception. For example, students in a physics class may realize that when they hold a book, both the book and their hands are exerting forces, and that the forces are balanced if the book does not move. But if a book is placed on a table, many students fail to understand that an upward force from the table is balancing the downward force of the book. To help students understand

Demonstration #1:

The cart (with very small friction) is pulled with a constant force so that it moves away from the motion detector, speeding up at a steady rate.

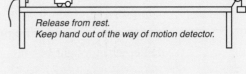

Release from rest.
Keep hand out of the way of motion detector.

Demonstration #2:

The cart with larger friction (friction pad in contact with ramp) is pulled with a constant force so that it still moves away from the motion detector, speeding up at a steady rate.

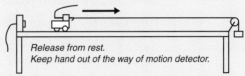

Release from rest.
Keep hand out of the way of motion detector.

Demonstration #3:

Show that cart accelerates in either direction when only one fan unit is on (as seen in previous demos). With both fans on (balanced), the cart does not move. Now push and release and observe velocity and acceleration.

Push cart to the right.
Keep hand out of the way of motion detector.

Demonstration #4:

Cart with very small frictional force is given a brief pull away from the motion detector and released.

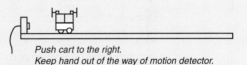

*Pull **on force probe** and release.*
Keep hand out of the way of motion detector.

Demonstration #5:

The cart (with very small friction) is given a push toward the motion detector and released. A constant force acts in the direction away from the motion detector. The cart moves toward the motion detector, slowing down at a steady rate.

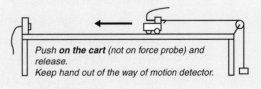

*Push **on the cart** (not on force probe) and release.*
Keep hand out of the way of motion detector.

Demonstration #6:

The cart (with very small friction) is given a push toward the motion detector and released. A constant force acts in the direction away from the motion detector. The cart moves toward the motion detector, slowing down at a steady rate, comes to rest momentarily, and then moves away from the motion detector.

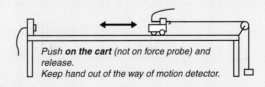

*Push **on the cart** (not on force probe) and release.*
Keep hand out of the way of motion detector.

that the table is applying a force, an instructor might take students through a series of bridging situations—putting their hand on a spring, placing a book on a foam pad, setting a book on a flexible board—and ask them to discuss similarities and differences with the earlier situations. As part of this lesson about force, the instructor might show students a microscopic model of a rigid object (like a table) that is composed of atoms connected by spring-like bonds. The lesson might conclude with an experiment in which a mirror is placed on the table and someone stands on the table; when a light beam is reflected off the mirror and onto the wall, the beam is deflected downward, indicating that the table has been compressed ever so slightly (Clement, 1993).

In geosciences, evidence on the effectiveness of instructional strategies in fostering conceptual change is derived mostly from studies of individual courses during brief periods. One such study by Rebich and Gautier (2005) found large increases in knowledge and a decrease in misconceptions among students who had participated in a three-week mock summit on climate change; this approach used role-playing, debate, and discussion to heighten awareness of the concepts underlying climate change.

Changing students' conceptual understanding can be difficult. An example comes from a study of a two-semester sequence of introductory geology in which researchers examined students' concept maps—diagrams that typically use words or phrases, along with boxes and lines, to connect and show the relationships among a list of concepts (Englebrecht et al., 2005). Although students were able to identify more geological concepts after a sequence of instruction, they showed only small improvement in their ability to integrate those concepts into a framework of understanding.

In sum, improving students' conceptual understanding takes time and a range of instructional techniques. Chapter 4 describes additional approaches in a variety of disciplines that hold promise for accomplishing this goal.

Framing and Solving Problems with Greater Expertise

Learning how to solve problems is an important part of developing competency in science and engineering. Whether in an educational or a professional setting, the ability to solve problems is central to the practice of science and engineering. Problem solving also comes into play in other areas of everyday life when one needs to reach a goal but is uncertain how to attain it. To solve problems effectively, students must not only have the types of conceptual understanding discussed above, but they must be able to apply those concepts correctly. They must also bring to bear other sophisticated thinking skills that go beyond rote memory.

Problem solving is a significant focus of DBER in physics, chemistry, and engineering, and it is an emerging area of study in biology and geosciences. This line of research has found that students, as novices, tend to approach, organize, and go about solving problems differently than experts. DBER studies have identified the particular difficulties students experience with various aspects of problem solving. In addition, the research literature offers insights about instructional approaches that can help students develop greater expertise with problem solving. The sections that follow summarize the main findings about problem solving from DBER; a more complete treatment of this topic can be found in Chapter 5 of the 2012 NRC report on DBER.

Focusing on superficial features instead of underlying principles

When people set about solving a problem, they construct a model of how they might approach the problem—in their minds and sometimes in a tangible form like a drawing. These models, whether arrived at deliberately or with little forethought, will guide the steps people take to solve it.

As novices, students approach problems in ways that are consistently and identifiably different from those used by experts. Students typically focus unduly on the superficial features of a problem, such as the specific objects, terms, and phrasing used in a question. Experts, by contrast, look at the deeper structure of the problem—the underlying principles that are required to solve it. In one interview study, for example, undergraduate biology students grouped classical genetics problems according to their surface features, such as whether the problem concerned humans or fruit flies and how it was worded, whereas biology professors grouped them according to key underlying concepts, such as the mechanism of genetic inheritance (Smith, 1992).

When confronted with two problems that have the same underlying structure, experts easily recognize these as the same kind of problem "deep down." This understanding of the essential features of a problem leads to better reasoning and problem solving. Students, however, may assume the problems are distinctly different due to superficial variations and may construct very different models of the two problems. For example, students may not recognize that a problem involving discs of different sizes stacked on a peg has the same structure as a problem involving acrobats of different sizes standing on one another's shoulders.

Research from physics, and to a lesser extent from chemistry and biology, supports this finding. When asked to categorize physics problems according to how they are solved, experts grouped them according to the major concepts or principles that could be applied to solve them, such as determining that a problem relates to Newton's second law. Novices relied much more on surface features, such as whether the problem mentions pulleys versus inclined planes versus springs (de Jong and Ferguson-Hessler, 1986). A study in biology (Kindfield, 1993/1994) compared the diagrams of chromosomes drawn during problem solving by two groups: a group with more knowledge of meiosis and chromosomes and a group with less knowledge. The drawings of the less knowledgeable participants often more literally resembled the way chromosomes looked under a light microscope and included features like dimensionality and shape that were irrelevant to the solution. The more knowledgeable participants included chromosome features that were biologically relevant to the problem.

> As novices, students approach problems in ways that are consistently and identifiably different from those used by experts. Students typically focus unduly on the superficial features of a problem, such as the specific objects, terms, and phrasing used in a question. Experts, by contrast, look at the deeper structure of the problem—the underlying principles that are required to solve it.

Research on human cognition (see, for example, Bassok and Novick, 2012) has found that for some problems, getting the right mental model of the problem is a key to finding a solution. Neither the model nor the process is fixed; each influences the other. A process for solving a problem may change as the solver's model of the problem changes, which in turn may lead to changes in the solutions one tries. However, students need to acquire sufficient expertise before they can recognize when they need to change their strategy instead of moving down the same dead ends, as novices tend to do.

By focusing on superficial aspects, students miss the essence of a problem, which makes it much harder to solve. This approach is also less efficient. Because experts can recognize structural relationships and patterns, they can tap into their long-term memory about what to do when certain patterns are present and can readily see solutions.

A failure to recognize the most salient features of a problem also makes it difficult for students to apply what they have learned from one problem to new problems that are similar in structure but different in context. This type of knowledge transfer is crucial to becoming a more expert-like problem solver.

These findings also suggest that students need a solid grounding in the core principles of a science or engineering discipline—the kind of conceptual understanding discussed above—in order to determine the "deep structure" of a problem. Research in engineering education, for example, indicates that a lack of understanding of fundamental concepts impedes students' ability to solve problems (see, for example, Baillie, Goodhew, and Skryabina, 2006).

Working "backward" instead of working "forward"

Another difference between novices and experts relates to how much time they spend creating a model of the problem versus working to find a solution. Novices often jump immediately to the end goal of a problem and start looking for an equation that might help them solve it. Then they must use another equation to calculate an unknown quantity in the first equation, and so on, until they find an equation that includes all the necessary quantities. This "working backward" strategy puts a heavy load on their working memory—their ability to hold key information in mind temporarily while they do the work of problem solving. This burden leaves little room for them to learn general strategies for solving similar problems. It also makes it easy for them to forget crucial elements of the problem at hand. And when they get stuck, they lack strategies to proceed.

Experts spend more time analyzing the nature of a problem from the outset and creating a coherent solution strategy. Experts go on to enrich their model of the problem with information from what they know and remember, such as procedures they have used to solve similar problems in the past. In this "working forward" approach, they start with the information given, make inferences based on that information, and continue refining their inferences until they have reached their goal. Experts monitor their progress as they solve a problem and evaluate whether an answer is reasonable.

This difference between the working backward approach of novices and the working forward approach of experts has been documented in numerous studies. In physics, for example, research has shown that expert problem solvers typically begin by considering the *qualitative* aspects of a problem and using that information to decide on a solution strategy before taking the *quantitative* step of writing down equations. Beginning physics students typically start by writing down equations that match the quantities provided in the problem statement and then work backward to find an equation for which the unknowns are supplied directly in the problem (see, for example, Larkin et al., 1980).

Research in chemistry education has found that students tend to rely more on algorithms to solve problems—stuffing numbers into a formula that worked with a very similar problem or applying memorized chemical reactions—than on a logical problem-solving process (Bhattacharyya and Bodner, 2005). Sometimes students can solve problems with these less skillful approaches, even though they have a shallow understanding of the underlying concept (see, for example, Gabel and Bunce, 1994). But these methods will fail when students are confronted with problems that don't fit the mold.

In order to work forward, problem solvers must have an organized framework of disciplinary knowledge, as well as experience in solving problems in that discipline. A command of basic facts and conceptual knowledge is a necessary part of this framework, but other elements are also critical. The framework should include discipline-specific models for approaching problems, as well as criteria for selecting the model appropriate to a context, determining which information in the problem is relevant and which is not, and evaluating whether an answer makes sense (Mayer and Wittrock, 2006).

Helping students to improve problem-solving skills

Taken together, these findings suggest that it is important for science and engineering instructors to help students recognize the need for both a good mental model of a problem and a sound method to solve it. When students run into difficulties in solving problems, they first need to consider alternate ways of representing the problem and then contemplate possible methods for figuring out an answer. Some instructors ask students to justify why their proposed procedures for solving a problem are reasonable. Toward this end, instructors might provide examples of how a good model can make it easier to find a solution, while a flawed one can make it harder.

A body of research indicates that problem-solving skills can be taught and that carefully designed forms of scaffolding appear to benefit students. The learning gains from any one type of support appear to be small and difficult to measure, however. These findings point to the wisdom of using multiple forms of scaffolding within a systematic approach to improving students' problem-solving skills.

Research has investigated a variety of strategies for moving students from novice toward expert problem-solving approaches. Promising strategies include the following (for specific references, see Chapter 5 of the 2012 NRC report on DBER):

- Teaching specific, organized methods for solving problems

- Explaining the different problem types

- Providing examples of problems with the solutions worked out

- Providing guidance and greater classroom interaction

- Having students solve problems in collaborative groups

- Making symbols more transparent to students by using more explicit labeling

- Assigning authentic (real-world) problems

- Assigning open-ended problems that encourage students to invent and test various models to solve them

- Incorporating prompts for students to reflect on and explain their approaches to solving problems

Chapter 4 of this book discusses several broader instructional approaches aimed at improving problem solving and other aspects of science and engineering learning.

Using Visual and Mathematical Representations

In every science or engineering discipline, visual, spatial, and mathematical representations are essential tools for communicating and remembering ideas and solving problems. A map of a rock outcrop; the formula for determining frictional force; a graph of the density of different species in a habitat; a chemical structure that shows the shape of a molecule and the bonding between its atoms; an engineer's free-body diagram that depicts all of the forces acting on an object—these are just a few of the myriad representations that are common in science and engineering disciplines.

Representations serve several purposes. They enable people to communicate ideas within a discipline in a shorthand way. By storing information succinctly, they free up working memory that can be devoted to other thinking processes. In some cases, representations can simplify the nature of a task. Consider, for example, how most people can estimate proportions more easily by looking at a pie chart than by studying a numerical table. Representations also assist in problem solving and other types of critical thinking. Some representations are created to analyze a phenomenon in research; these may be quite complicated and targeted mainly at other researchers in the same field. Other representations are intended to convey information to someone else; these may omit the complexities in order to better communicate the central idea (Dutrow, 2007).

Each discipline has its own common ways of representing key concepts that are easily recognizable to experts. For students to communicate conversantly in a

discipline, they need to be able to interpret and use the major types of representations for that discipline. Just as importantly, they need to understand the concept a particular representation is intended to convey and know why both the representation and the underlying concept are important.

Research suggests that when students construct their own representations, in addition to interpreting those produced by experts, they are often more engaged and learn better (Ainsworth, Prain, and Tytler, 2011). When instructors observe how their students interpret, use, create, and translate among different types of representations, they can gain insights about how well students understand important concepts. When modeling—a pervasive but infrequently taught aspect of engineering—is taught explicitly, students gain a better understanding of how to use models and why they are important (Carberry and McKenna, 2014).

Representations that instructors and other experts can easily interpret may completely befuddle undergraduates, however. DBER studies and cognitive science research highlight the challenges students face in mastering representations. Findings from this body of research are described in Chapter 5 of the 2012 NRC report on DBER; the main points are summarized below.

Interpreting and constructing representations

Across disciplines, students often have difficulty interpreting representations and constructing their own from existing information. In physics, a field with a strong research base on this topic, students struggle to interpret representations that are common in introductory courses (Rosengrant, Etkina, and Van Heuvelen, 2007). Students often misunderstand the quantities and concepts being represented in diagrams, according to some research, and they shy away from using them because they have few opportunities to practice the skills needed to construct diagrams (Van Heuvelen, 1991).

A good example of the difficulties students confront in interpreting and creating representations comes from chemistry, another discipline with a considerable research base on representations. As an initial step toward understanding the relationships between the molecular structure of a material and its properties, chemistry students are often taught to draw and manipulate diagrams called Lewis structures. Many students struggle with this task (see Box 3.3).

In a related vein, many students have difficulty extracting the most salient information from representations. As in problem solving, novices often have trouble seeing beyond superficial but irrelevant features of a representation to grasp the abstract idea being represented (Hegarty, 2011). Even when students know the conventions for how a diagram is meant to represent reality, they tend to miss important patterns that experts pick up.

Students also have difficulty processing diagrams that violate familiar conventions. For example, students often try to process visual representations from left to right because that's the direction in which they read text (Nachshon, 1985). In diagrams where this left-to-right processing makes it difficult to interpret relationships, simply shifting the diagram 180 degrees above the vertical axis can improve comprehension (Novick, Stull, and Catley, 2012). Similarly, circles and

To understand chemistry, students must understand that matter is made up of atoms bonded together into molecules and that the properties of a material can be predicted from its molecular structure (and vice versa). As an initial step toward comprehending the relationships between molecular structure and properties, students are often taught to draw and manipulate Lewis structures. These diagrams, which are common in chemistry, use atomic symbols, lines, and dots to show the arrangement of atoms and electrons in a molecule and the bonds between atoms. While concise in design, Lewis structures are packed with important information that can be used to predict and explain the physical and chemical structure of a substance (Cooper et al., 2010). Knowing how to construct them is an essential skill in chemistry.

For chemists, drawing a Lewis structure is second nature. Rules for how to do this are found in most chemistry textbooks. Yet many students struggle with this task—they get "lost in Lewis structures," as Melanie Cooper and her colleagues have described the problem (Cooper et al., 2010). "What may appear to the expert to be a simple task is, in fact, inherently difficult, complex, counterintuitive, and all too often meaningless to many students" (p. 869).

Cooper and her colleagues (2010) tracked the processes used by undergraduate students in general and organic chemistry, as well as by graduate students and faculty members, as they drew Lewis structures. Many students, and even a few faculty members, were confused about how to draw valid Lewis structures. As the number of atoms in the diagram increased from six to seven or more, the percentage of students who drew accurate representations plummeted. The increase from six to seven atoms represents a shift to a molecular structure with more than one carbon atom. Indeed, students had difficulty drawing even one-carbon compounds if they were not given structural clues. Students' success in producing the correct representation depended a great deal on how the formula was initially presented to them, "suggesting that they were relying on memorized cues rather than an understanding of the rules involved" (Cooper et al., 2010, p. 871).

Students often assume, incorrectly, that all Lewis structures must be symmetrical, or "balanced." Many Lewis structures are symmetrical, such as the correct structure of dimethyl ether shown on the left in the figure in this box. But this misconception about symmetry may lead students to produce incorrect structures, such as the one for methanethiol on the right in the figure in this box (Cooper et al., 2010, p. 871).

A reason for students' confusion, note Cooper and colleagues, is that conventional approaches to teaching Lewis structures conflict with findings about how people learn. The rules for drawing

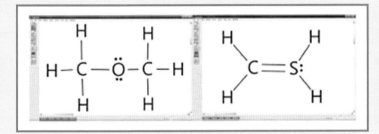

Examples of symmetrical Lewis structures produced by students. The structure on the left for C_2H_6O is correct; the one on the right for CH_4S is incorrect.

these structures are presented to students without connecting them to concepts that students already understand, which makes them seem mysterious. The rules also include numerous exceptions, but students are not given meaningful criteria for deciding when they apply.

Interviews conducted for the study revealed that most students did not understand the kinds of chemical information that can be inferred from Lewis structures. Many students emerge from chemistry courses with a "fractured and muddled" understanding of not only how they should create Lewis structures, but also *why* they should do it (Cooper et al., 2010, p. 872).

Based on this research, Cooper and colleagues (2012) have developed and evaluated a chemistry curriculum that emphasizes the critical connection between energy changes and atomic interactions as a core concept. Within this curriculum, students learn about key concepts, such as the properties of materials and the different models of bonding, *before* they are asked to draw Lewis structures. To gain familiarity with the structures involved, students work with physical and computer-based three-dimensional models of simple molecules. At that point, students are introduced to Lewis structures as convenient two-dimensional "cartoons" that represent three-dimensional structures rather than as an end in themselves (p. 1,352). After students have practiced going back and forth between two- and three-dimensional representations, more complex structures are introduced. Once students are able to draw simple structures from a given molecular formula, they move on to the task of decoding the information contained in the formula.

Students taught with this curriculum show marked improvements in their ability to create structures, compared with a control group of students (Cooper et al., 2012). They also do significantly better at decoding the information contained in these structures.

lines seem more naturally suited to representing physical objects or locations than relationships or motion (Tversky et al., 2000). When diagrammatic representations are consistent with these conventions, college students are able to make appropriate inferences more quickly and accurately (Hurley and Novick, 2010).

Translating among different representations of the same thing

Undergraduates also struggle to see similarities among different representations that describe the same phenomenon. In chemistry, for example, students have difficulty translating among alternative ways of representing the same set of relationships, such as videos, graphs, animations, equations, and verbal descriptions (Kozma and Russell, 1997).

Take, for example, the diagrams used in biology to represent the evolutionary relationships among groups of organisms. These diagrams, called cladograms, typically take the form of a tree or a ladder, or in some cases circles nested within larger circles. Biology students have trouble understanding these diagrams and translating among alternative formats that show the same set of relationships (see, for example, Novick, Stull, and Catley, 2012).

A study by Novick and Catley (2007) asked students who had taken at least one semester of an introductory biology class for majors to transfer a hierarchy of relationships from the nested circles format to the tree and ladder formats, and from the tree format to the ladder format and vice versa. Students' diagrams were less accurate whenever the ladder format was involved. One factor that appeared to confuse students was the use of the long, slanted "backbone" line of the ladders. Consistent with a principle from psychology known as "good continuation," students interpret this continuous line as a single entity—in this case, a single level in the hierarchy. In follow-up work, students were given ladder diagrams that departed from the traditional format by "breaking" good continuation at exactly the points in the diagram that mark a new hierarchical level, and their performance improved greatly (Novick, Catley, and Funk, 2010).

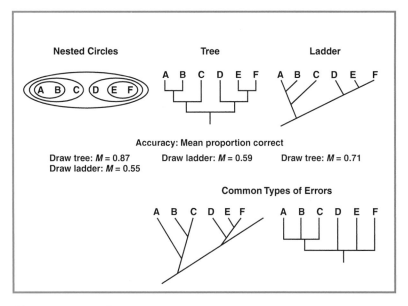

Diagrams representing evolutionary relationships.

Spatial ability

Using representations effectively requires a reasonable level of spatial ability; that is, competence in mentally manipulating two- and three-dimensional objects. In engineering design, for example, the abilities to visualize a three-dimensional image from a two-dimensional representation and to mentally rotate three-dimensional objects are important to success. Spatial ability is also an essential skill in geosciences: practitioners and students must envision what lies behind, beneath, or between rock outcrops and make inferences about rock deformation, temperature trends, and other events from the shape of natural objects like minerals and fossils. To understand chemistry, students must learn how to create visual representations of the unseen molecular level and translate those representations into the format of an equation.

Students often have difficulties with spatial thinking. In geosciences, some students find it challenging to visualize what a three-dimensional volume would look like when they are presented with information in one or two dimensions. In one study (Kali and Orion, 1996), students were given a two-dimensional drawing that depicted three sides of a block of Earth's crust and were asked to draw a slice, or vertical cross-section, of the block. Students who gave incorrect answers had difficulty "penetrating" the block, as shown in the figure below; some simply copied a pattern from one side of the block. Students who were more successful with this task used specific strategies to visually penetrate the block, such as continuing a pattern vertically or horizontally.

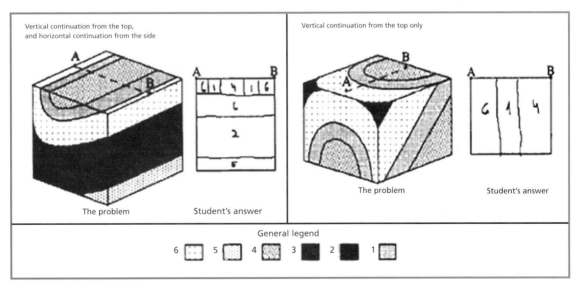

Examples of incorrect attempts by students to draw a vertical cross-section of a block of Earth's crust.

Although the evidence is limited, some research suggests that explicit instruction can improve students' spatial visualization skills. A review of several studies in engineering found that specially designed multimedia training courses enhanced these skills, especially for female students (Sorby, 2009). Some research indicates that teaching geosciences with visually rich materials can improve students' spatial visualization skills and in some cases reduce gaps in this area between male and female students (see, for example, Titus and Horsman, 2009). Evidence in chemistry is mixed; some studies have concluded that teaching analytic problem-solving strategies can lead to greater improvements in students' mental models than does emphasizing students' natural spatial ability (Hegarty, Stieff, and Dixon, 2013).

Animations and simulations

Animations, interactive computer simulations, virtual models, and other technology-based representations are widely used in the practice of science and engineering and are becoming increasingly popular in undergraduate education. By experimenting with a computer-based simulation of a projectile fired from a cannon, for example, students can see how the path of a projectile is altered (or not altered) when they change such variables as the type of object, initial speed, mass, and diameter—something that would not be feasible in a classroom setting. By rotating a three-dimensional model of a molecule, students can get a better sense of its composition than they would from a two-dimensional representation.

Animations and simulations have considerable potential for helping students learn. They enable students to conduct experiments that would otherwise be impractical or impossible. They can slow down or speed up the time involved in a particular process and allow students to work with entities and phenomena that are too tiny or huge to observe in the real world. In these ways, they not only can help students develop competence with representations, but also can make sophisticated concepts easier to understand.

It is not a foregone conclusion, however, that animations and their kin enhance student learning or do a better job than does using other types of representations. Simply showing an animation or simulation is not sufficient; this may confuse students without drawing attention to such issues as context, assumptions behind the model, and key features to look for. For example, some research suggests that animations should be implemented in a way that encourages students to predict what will happen before they work through a simulation and to reason why certain outcomes occurred after they do it (Hegarty,

Kriz, and Cate, 2003). In addition, animations, visualizations, and related tools do not necessarily reduce the demands on students' spatial ability; in fact, some research suggests that these tools may require greater spatial ability and visualization skills than static representations (Hegarty, 2011).

Implications for instruction

Improving students' skills in using visual and mathematical representations is an important part of moving them toward greater expertise in science and engineering. An understanding of the research on students' difficulties with representations and effective approaches for addressing them can inform efforts to design instruction. Some instructional issues to consider include the following:

- Instructors may need to provide students with more explicit introductions to the conventions that underlie the construction of various kinds of representations. Instructors might also highlight the relationships among alternative displays of similar information and explain how different types of representations are better suited to particular tasks.

- Providing extensive opportunities for students to practice interpreting and producing *multiple* types of representations can improve students' performance, according to research from physics and chemistry.

- When instructors construct representations, they should consider how people naturally interpret symbols like circles or use conventions like left-to-right processing.

Biologists at Michigan State University have adopted a model-based instructional approach in several departmental courses. The strategies used in these courses engage all of the three main aspects of learning emphasized by DBER studies: (1) building conceptual understanding, (2) solving problems, and (3) interpreting, constructing, and understanding representations. Although the example in the following case focuses primarily on ecology, modeling will work well for any scale in biology, including the cellular level, and for other science and engineering disciplines.

Modeling in the Broadest Sense

At Michigan State, plant biology faculty have transformed their introductory courses to emphasize scientific practices. (This project also included graduate students and post-docs at Michigan State University, as well as faculty members at other institutions.) A goal of the practice-based approach to instruction is to help students conceptualize and reason about complex biological systems. Students in these courses construct, apply, and evaluate scientific models, including visual representations like graphs, diagrams, and box-and-arrow systems models. "When they are learning a topic, they are learning modeling in the broadest sense, via the practices of science" says Diane Ebert-May,[a] who along with Tammy Long was one of two Michigan State University plant biology faculty involved in this effort.

The authors of a paper about this course transformation effort point out that practice-based instruction is particularly well suited to the study of ecology, which emphasizes an understanding of systems and the interdependence of the elements that comprise them (Long et al., 2014). Specifically, the authors also point out that models are an authentic

way of gaining insights into how students organize and connect knowledge.

A case study about the interaction of moose and gray wolves in Isle Royale National Park illustrates how students in an ecology course construct models as a way to understand the relationships among species in an ecosystem. In this park, moose are the primary diet for gray wolves, and the fitness of the wolves may be affected by congenital vertebral malformations. Students are given the following assignment:

Construct a box-and-arrow systems model that shows (a) the origin of genetic variations among wolves;

[a] Interview, April 17, 2013.

(b) the relationship between genetic variation and phenotypic variation among wolves; (c) the consequences of phenotypic variation on wolves' fitness. Include the following structures in your systems model but modify your language to make them specific to the case of the wolves' vertebrae. You may use structures more than once and add additional structures not on the list.

Allele, gene, DNA, protein, phenotype, nucleotides, fitness

A representative student response is displayed in the figure below.

As another example, students in Ebert-May's introductory biology course analyze graphs of current and projected patterns in atmospheric carbon during a unit on global climate change. Based on the data in these graphs, they determine what claims they can make about the projected consequences of global climate change. They are also asked what they can glean about the nature of science by analyzing graphs with seven different projections of future trends in carbon dioxide concentrations. "Our curriculum is based on three science practices: using data, modeling, and arguments," says Ebert-May. "Everything is data driven."

Faculty who teach the transformed courses note that "although many students struggle with using scientific models, particularly early in instruction, many report that over time, models help them to see 'the big picture' and how biological concepts are connected" (Long et al., 2014, p. 139). Models also provide a tangible way for students to assess and think critically about their own learning as they evaluate and revise their models to incorporate new knowledge.

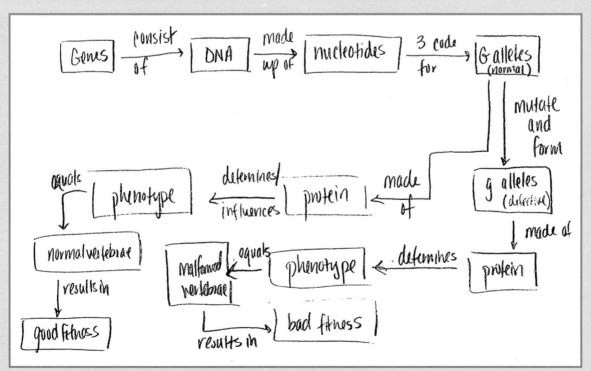

A student-constructed model of the interactions of moose and gray wolves in the Isle Royale ecological system.

Conclusion

The research summarized in this chapter indicates that effective instructors start from an understanding of how students think and learn, both in general and in science and engineering disciplines in particular. They emphasize students' prior knowledge and the role of students in constructing this knowledge instead of emphasizing the instructor's ability to transmit knowledge. Many researchers and science and engineering instructors are putting these findings into practice in their own classrooms, in ways that can be adopted or adapted by others. More ideas for how to do this are described in Chapter 4.

Resources and Further Reading

Discipline-Based Education Research: Understanding and Improving Learning in Undergraduate Science and Engineering (National Research Council, 2012)
>   Chapter 4: Identifying and Improving Students' Conceptual Understanding in Science and Engineering
>   Chapter 5: Problem Solving, Spatial Thinking, and the Use of Representations in Science and Engineering
>   Chapter 7: Some Emerging Areas of DBER

How People Learn: Brain, Mind, Experience, and School: Expanded Edition (National Research Council, 2000)

Designing Instruction

4

If the insights about learning in Chapter 3 have spurred you to think in new ways about improving your instruction, the question remains about which instructional strategies to try. This chapter describes a variety of practical strategies for instruction that are informed by evidence about how students learn best. The strategies discussed here are broader than those highlighted in Chapter 3 and are not discipline specific, although some instructors have given them a discipline-specific spin. The chapter first presents the kinds of student learning outcomes that these strategies are designed to produce. Next is a brief explanation of the characteristics of student-centered instruction, a pedagogical idea that undergirds the strategies in this chapter. The remainder of the chapter describes some of the most common research-based strategies for making lectures more interactive, promoting student collaboration and peer interactions, supplementing instruction with tutorials, and providing students with authentic experiences and instruction that engages them in the practices of science and engineering. Scattered throughout the chapter are examples of how skilled instructors have successfully implemented these strategies.

The strategies highlighted here are by no means the only research-based approaches for improving science and engineering education. Several more are described in Chapter 6 of the 2012 National Research Council (NRC) report on discipline-based education research (DBER), the source of much of the information in this chapter. In addition, information about tested and documented teaching methods can be obtained from professional organizations, resource centers, and other sources. The Pedagogy in Action Web portal of the Science Education Resource Center (SERC),[1] for example, offers descriptions, course activities, and other information and materials for more than 50 such teaching strategies.

---

[1] See http://serc.carleton.edu/sp/index.html.

When deciding on strategies to pursue, you might consider which ones will align well with the learning goals you established and the assessments you are using. You will also need to consider logistical issues such as class size, schedule, and classroom space, and your own teaching preferences and comfort level, among other factors. As the authors of *How People Learn* point out, "Asking which teaching technique is best is analogous to asking which tool is best—a hammer, a screwdriver, a knife, or pliers" (National Research Council, 2000, p. 22).

Goals of Research-Based Instruction

As mentioned in Chapter 2, decisions about how to teach should be based in large part on goals for what students should learn. These goals include general outcomes, derived from research on how students learn, that apply across science and engineering disciplines, as well as more specific goals for a particular course or program of study.

In engineering, the accreditation criteria for degree-granting programs developed by ABET, the accrediting agency, specify 11 general student learning outcomes. These outcomes address the specific knowledge and skills, as well as the more general habits of mind and professional conduct, that undergraduate students of engineering are expected to learn (ABET, 2009). (Chapter 7 of this book discusses the ABET criteria in more detail.) Many of these outcomes are best met through instructional methods that emphasize problem solving, communication, and teamwork, as well as other skills. Engineering instructors can use the program-level ABET criteria to guide their development of course-specific learning goals.

Across the science disciplines there is no consensus on a single set of learning goals for undergraduate education. Still, several general learning outcomes are largely consistent across the various fields of DBER. One useful list of general learning outcomes emerged from a series of workshops on promising practices held by the NRC (2011). Participants in these workshops identified these expectations for what undergraduate science, technology, engineering, and mathematics (STEM) students should eventually be able to do:

- Master a few major concepts well and in depth

- Retain what is learned over the long term

- Build a mental framework that serves as a foundation for future learning

- Develop visualization competence, including the ability to critique, interpret, construct, and connect with physical systems

- Develop skills (analytic and critical judgment) needed to use scientific information to make informed decisions

- Understand the nature of science

- Find satisfaction in engaging in real-world issues that require knowledge of science

The research-based instructional strategies presented in this chapter typically address several or most of these outcomes. You may need to combine more than one strategy to meet the specific learning goals you expect your students to achieve.

An Emphasis on Student-Centered Instruction

The chemistry curriculum developed by Vicente Talanquer and John Pollard, chemistry professors at the University of Arizona, encompasses several of the outcomes listed above from the NRC STEM workshop.

Shifting Instruction from What Chemists Know to How Chemists Think

An effort to redesign an undergraduate chemistry curriculum around findings about how students learn began as a conversation over lunch, says University of Arizona professor John Pollard.[a] Around 2006, Pollard was chatting with his Arizona

Students work in groups using a computer simulation to investigate the properties of gases in John Pollard's general chemistry class.

chemistry colleague Vicente Talanquer, and they discovered they shared similar frustrations with the lack of depth and focus on breadth in the traditional undergraduate chemistry curriculum. Talanquer[b] had become dissatisfied with the lack of intellectual demand in undergraduate courses and wanted to shift the focus "from presenting what chemists know to

[a] Interview, April 30, 2013.
[b] Interview, April 3, 2013.

illustrating how chemists think." Both professors saw a need to revamp a curriculum that was "fact-based and encyclopedic . . . focused too much on abstract concepts and algorithmic problem solving, and detached from the practices, ways of thinking, and applications of both chemistry research and chemistry education research" (Talanquer and Pollard, 2010, p. 43).

As a chemistry education researcher, Talanquer was already familiar with the literature on learning. He and Pollard began thinking about how to transform the curriculum and adapt the Process Oriented Guided Inquiry Learning (POGIL) approach, in which students work in small groups, to their own large introductory courses with enrollments of roughly 300 students. "We started, little by little, changing the emphasis of the curriculum; we created activities and pilot-tested them," Talanquer explains. They obtained grants to implement their ideas from the National Science Foundation (NSF) and the State of Arizona and assessed the effects on student learning of the changes they were making.

The curriculum they developed, called *Chemical Thinking* (2012), is intended to "promote deeper conceptual understanding of a minimum core of fundamental ideas instead of superficial coverage of multiple topics" and to connect ideas from one topic to another through a progression of learning experiences (Talanquer and Pollard, 2010, p. 43). Students "learn how to approach realistic problems from a chemical perspective, using the powerful and productive models, techniques, and ways of thinking developed in the field" (p. 44).

Although Talanquer and Pollard still lecture for short periods, they have moved from presenting a video or a simulation of a chemical process to having students create their own simulations and models. Students often work in pairs on what Talanquer and Pollard call "Let's Think" activities that require them to make observations, build models, make predictions and decisions, and construct explanations. Here is a Let's Think activity from a unit on predicting the physical properties of chemical compounds using their molecular structure (Talanquer and Pollard, 2012):

Let's Think—A Linear Molecule?

- Imagine for a second, that the water molecule was linear and not bent.

- How would this change the strength of the different contributions (i.e., dispersion, dipole-dipole, and H-bonding) to the IMFs [intermolecular forces] between water molecules?

- What would be the impact of this change on (a) the physical properties of water, (b) Earth's climate, and (c) life in our planet?

- Share and discuss your ideas with a classmate.

At the end of every learning module (the equivalent of about one week), students are given an interesting problem to solve, called "Let's Apply," which helps the instructor and the students themselves determine whether they have achieved the main performance outcome for that module. Based on a review of students' work, "we can get a sense of whether we need to emphasize something or go back and talk about other things," says Talanquer. Here is a Let's Apply task from the module on analyzing molecular structure:

Let's Apply—Water Repellent?

Some textiles are frequently treated with organo-fluorines to make them more hydrophobic. A layer of the fluorine compound reduces the ability of the fibers to absorb water.

- Build a reasonable explanation to justify why some organofluorine compounds may reduce water absorption by textiles.

- Share and discuss your ideas with a classmate. Do not forget to clearly justify your reasoning.

Talanquer and Pollard also administer formal exams, which they have redesigned to align better with their instructional approaches. "All of our exams are topical," says Talanquer. For example, the first unit of the course deals with how chemistry makes it possible to identify substances in one's surroundings. One of the exams designed for this unit focused on the composition of Titan, a moon of Saturn. Students were given data about Titan and asked to answer

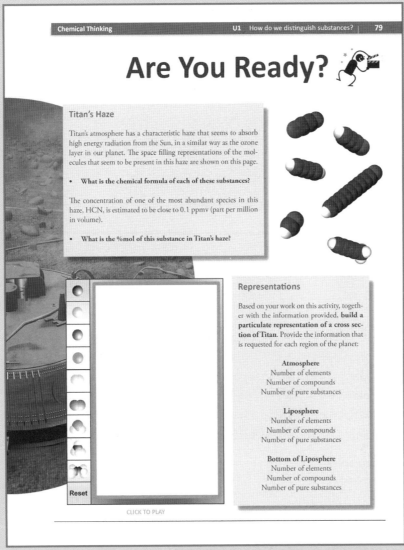

Are You Ready?

Titan's Haze

Titan's atmosphere has a characteristic haze that seems to absorb high energy radiation from the Sun, in a similar way as the ozone layer in our planet. The space filling representations of the molecules that seem to be present in this haze are shown on this page.

- **What is the chemical formula of each of these substances?**

The concentration of one of the most abundant species in this haze, HCN, is estimated to be close to 0.1 ppmv (part per million in volume).

- **What is the %mol of this substance in Titan's haze?**

Representations

Based on your work on this activity, together with the information provided, **build a particulate representation of a cross section of Titan**. Provide the information that is requested for each region of the planet:

Atmosphere
Number of elements
Number of compounds
Number of pure substances

Liposphere
Number of elements
Number of compounds
Number of pure substances

Bottom of Liposphere
Number of elements
Number of compounds
Number of pure substances

Reset

CLICK TO PLAY

Students complete topical exams in which they are asked to integrate their knowledge and apply it to the analysis of a relevant system.

questions about the types of substances found on this moon's surface and atmosphere.

Carly Schnoebelen,[c] who took Pollard's course as a freshman in 2009–2010 and became an undergraduate preceptor in the course the next year, found the active learning approach "absolutely more effective" than the lecture-based science courses she took. "A lot of times in lecture students memorize something for a test and immediately forget it," she says. "But if you're more active, you understand and remember it better."

Talanquer and Pollard are also evaluating the impact of their instructional approaches. On a traditional standardized exam that includes a heavy dose of algorithmic problem solving, their students perform the same as those in a traditionally taught class, but on an assessment of conceptual understanding, their students do significantly better (Talanquer, 2012). In addition, survey data show that considerably higher percentages of students taught with the redesigned curriculum find the course "challenging but rewarding," report that they were interested to learn about the material in the course, express interest in doing a chemistry research project, and agree that the teaching approach in the course motivated them to learn (Talanquer, 2012). Furthermore, says Talanquer, students who took an introductory course with the redesigned curriculum get better grades in advanced chemistry courses than those taught with a traditional curriculum. "That has become a powerful tool for changing people's minds," he adds.

[c] Interview, April 25, 2013.

Most of the strategies described in this chapter, like those used by Talanquer and Pollard, are student-centered. Student-centered approaches place less emphasis on the instructor transmitting factual information by lecturing and more emphasis on students building their own understanding with careful structuring and guidance from the instructor. As noted in the 2012 NRC report on DBER, these approaches include these characteristics drawn from evidence about how people learn:

- More time spent engaging students in active learning during class

- Frequent formative assessment of students' levels of conceptual understanding

- Attention to students' metacognitive strategies

In this type of instruction, students are expected to be actively and cognitively engaged in their coursework. Rather than being told what they should learn, students often do activities designed to help them discover key concepts or draw their own conclusions *before* the instructor explains a concept. In addition, students may be expected to acquire at least some of the basic knowledge for the course by doing assignments outside of class so they can come to class ready to apply and build on that knowledge.

Instructors still play several vital roles in student-centered classrooms. Instructors carefully design activities to support students in developing the desired knowledge and skills. They structure the activities to provide "scaffolding" during the learning process that builds on what students know and challenges them to gradually work beyond their current level. Instructors also assess students' prior understanding and frequently check how students' knowledge is progressing throughout the course. And while students are doing activities, the instructor observes, listens, asks questions, and guides students when they get off track. An understanding of research on learning can help with all of these roles.

Active learning is a critical element of virtually all of the research-based instructional strategies described in this chapter. Active learning engages students in answering and asking questions, thinking about and solving problems, and explaining and reflecting on what they are learning instead of just sitting and listening.

Some student-centered approaches differ radically from traditional lecture-based instruction. Observers of a classroom that uses formal cooperative learning, such as the problem-based learning approach or the Student-Centered Active Learning Environment with Upside-down Pedagogies (SCALE-UP) model, discussed later in this chapter and in Chapter 5, may wonder where the lecture went. Students work in small groups throughout most of the class period, tackle challenging and authentic problems, or do hands-on activities. The instructor circulates among the student groups, providing guidance and pausing the action only briefly to explain something to the whole class.

The "flipped classroom" approach, a term much in vogue, describes instructional designs in which students are responsible for learning most of the basic course content through out-of-class reading, research, or pre-recorded video lectures in order to free up class time for problem solving and other substantive activities. While a flipped classroom approach can be a dramatic departure from traditional instruction, this depends on how it is implemented. Flipped classroom models vary in the extent to which they use student-centered approaches or rely on lectures (albeit, prerecorded) to convey information.

In any case, you can implement active learning without devoting the entire class to cooperative work, or flipping the classroom, or eliminating your lectures. Less sweeping approaches can be effective, as explained in the next section.

Making Lectures More Interactive

DBER provides a strong base of evidence in multiple disciplines of the value of making lectures more interactive. Several research-based strategies intersperse lecture with shorter student-centered activities, such as interactive exercises or student discussions about probing questions intended to spur deeper thinking. Karl Smith (2000) has employed an approach in which he organizes a class by alternating between short, 10- to 12-minute lectures and even briefer, 3- to 4-minute opportunities for student discussion, "bookending" these activities with an introduction and summary. This is just one example. Other research-based methods, discussed below, use varying amounts of lecture and different types of interactive exercises.

Think-Pair-Share

Think-Pair-Share is an informal type of collaborative learning that can be implemented relatively easily in a lecture or a lab of any size in a fairly short time. This strategy engages every student in talking out loud about her or his ideas but requires less formal monitoring from the instructor than is recommended when students work in groups for longer periods.

The idea of Think-Pair-Share is an old one (Lyman, 1981), and its procedures have been refined over the years (Johnson, Johnson, and Smith, 1991). The instructor follows these basic steps (Allen and Tanner, 2002):

1. Pose a question during class, often one with many possible answers.

2. Give all students one or two minutes to THINK about their individual answer by having them jot down their ideas on a piece of paper.

3. Give all students a chance to discuss their answer and ideas with a neighbor in a PAIR or a small group. (This may take a few to several minutes depending on the complexity of the question.)

4. Invite pairs to SHARE what they discussed with the whole class.

5. Wrap up with a summary that emphasizes the main learning points.

The following examples illustrate how Think-Pair-Share questions can vary in topic, complexity, length of time required to answer, and presentation format:

Biology: Watch the video clip about the Human Genome Project and the designer baby. Work in pairs to answer the following questions: (1) What is the basis of making a designer baby? Think about the biology of DNA, genes, and traits. (2) What are the advantages and disadvantages of having a designer baby? (3) Do you agree or disagree with the idea of a designer baby? Why? (Chen and Ray, n.d.)

Geosciences: Look at this graph of satellite measurements of ozone concentration above Antarctica from 1979–1992. Put yourself in the mind of a scientist seeing this data for the first time. What complexities, patterns, or trends would be important to develop a theory for how this pattern has been generated? (Hancock, 2010)

Astronomy: Rigel is much more luminous than Sirius B. Rigel and Sirius B have the same temperature. Which star has the greatest surface area?: (a) Rigel, (b) Sirius B, (c) They have the same surface area, or (d) There is insufficient information to answer this question. (Forestell et al., 2008)

While students are discussing the question(s), the instructor can walk around the room and listen in on their conversations. This enables the instructor to assess what students do and do not yet understand, identify misconceptions, and note how students explain ideas to their peers. After the pairs' discussion, the instructor can acknowledge the good ideas heard and perhaps invite students who used insightful ways of explaining a concept or correcting a misconception to share their thoughts with the whole class.

The use of Think-Pair-Share and similar types of informal groupings has been associated with a variety of desirable outcomes, including improved achievement, critical thinking, and higher-level reasoning; better understanding of others' perspectives; and positive attitudes about their fellow students, instructors, and the subject matter at hand (Johnson, Johnson, and Smith, 2007).

Peer Instruction and ConcepTests

If you have ever given a traditional lecture, you have probably experienced that moment when you scan the rows of students—some listening attentively, some taking notes robotically, others yawning, whispering, or surreptitiously texting—and wonder, *How much of this are they really getting?* If you try to check students' comprehension by asking a question (hopefully something more pointed than the generic *Any questions?*), a motivated few will respond. As for the rest, you still do not know how well they understand.

One of the most influential, widely used, and time-tested strategies for making lectures more interactive builds on Think-Pair-Share but adds a more formal process for using carefully crafted questions to shed light on students' conceptual understanding. That strategy is Peer Instruction, developed by Harvard University physics professor Eric Mazur. As explained in Chapter 1, Mazur was motivated to change his teaching after recognizing that many of his students did not truly understand core concepts in physics.

In Peer Instruction, the instructor gives a short presentation focused on a particular topic and then asks all students in the class a multiple-choice question, or ConcepTest, designed to reveal common student misunderstandings about a central concept related to that topic. Students are given one minute to arrive at an individual answer and report their responses to the instructor; often students respond with clickers, but this can also be done with colored cards or other means. For the next few minutes, as the instructor circulates and listens, students discuss their answers and their reasoning with their peers in adjacent seats and try to convince each other why their answer is correct. At the end of the peer discussions, students are again polled for their answers, which often have changed based on the discussion. The instructor reviews the correct answer and addresses questions that arose during discussion, and then moves on to the next topic (Crouch and Mazur, 2001). To make time for the ConcepTests, students are expected to complete a reading assignment on the topic covered before class.

Since first introducing Peer Instruction, Mazur and his colleague Catherine Crouch have taken ideas from different sources to refine the approach. For example, before students come to class, they must do warm-up exercises in the form of Web-based, open-ended questions about their reading assignments. Tutorials (explained later in this chapter) and group problem-solving activities have been incorporated into a weekly discussion section that supplements the course. Evaluations of Peer Instruction show improvements in students' understanding of the course material as measured by their performance on the ConcepTests and on two standardized tests: the Force Concept Inventory and the Mechanics Baseline Tests (Crouch and Mazur, 2001).

For many instructors, one of the most appealing aspects of Peer Instruction is that it can be done with large courses in a lecture auditorium. "This is a great way for people to add an interactive component in inadequate spaces," says Mazur.[2] "Not many people may have the opportunity to redesign both the space and the course." The case study in Chapter 2 of David McConnell's geosciences course at North Carolina State University describes an effective way to implement ConcepTests with peer interaction in a large enrollment course; hundreds of ConcepTests in geosciences are available online (Science Education Resource Center, n.d.). Peer Instruction has been adapted in biology (Knight and Wood, 2005), chemistry, and other disciplines, and in a range of instructional settings and class sizes. Peer Instruction is also an attractive option because it can be incorporated into a standard lecture.

It is important, however, that any adaptations maintain the crucial element of peer interaction. Simply asking students to respond to clicker questions without this element loses the benefits of having students articulate a rationale for their answer, listen to their peers' reasoning, and try to reach consensus. "At times, it seems that students are able to explain concepts to one another more effectively than are their teachers," writes Mazur (1997, p. 13). This is likely because students who understand the concept "have only recently mastered the idea and are still aware of the difficulties involved in grasping that concept. Consequently, they know precisely what to emphasize in their explanations."

Designing good ConcepTest questions takes some thought. Crouch and Mazur (2001) recommend that the questions focus on important concepts, include incorrect answers based on common student misunderstandings, and be challenging enough that between 35 percent and 70 percent of the students answer correctly before the peer discussion (Mazur, 1997). Although multiple-choice questions are the easiest type to administer in a large class, ConcepTests can also take the form of open-ended questions or quantitative problems, or the students themselves can generate the answer choices that the entire class then votes on.

---

[2] Interview, April 13, 2013.

Here is an example of a ConcepTest question from Mazur (1997):

A SAMPLE ConcepTest QUESTION ON ARCHIMEDES' PRINCIPLE OF BUOYANCY

Imagine holding two identical bricks under water. Brick A is just beneath the surface of the water, while brick B is at a greater depth. The force needed to hold brick B in place is:

1. larger than

2. the same as

3. smaller than

the force required to hold brick A in place.

Correct answer: 2

Beth Simon,[3] a computer science and engineering instructor at the University of California, San Diego, organizes her 80-minute classes around a series of four to six multiple-choice clicker questions, administered using Mazur's model of individual answers, peer discussion, and a final vote. Students are expected to learn basic content before they come to class through reading assignments and prerecorded lectures, and they take a quiz on this homework at the beginning of each class. Designing clicker questions that target potential difficulties is a critical part of the instructor's role. "It's kind of like being a sports coach. If you hire a tennis coach for your kid, you don't want them to just assign the kids to play a game of tennis. Instead, they have them do little drills with particular things that they know are problematic. I think of my clicker questions as the exact same thing," says Simon.

"People say, where's the lecture? I do have some 'lectures,' but they generally come in response to questions," Simon explains. After completing a clicker question, for example, Simon might show a slide summarizing the most important things that students were expected to learn from that question. Or she might go into a deeper explanation of a topic that was not well explained in the textbook or do a demonstration of a process the students just studied.

---

[3] Interview, August 20, 2013.

Ongoing adjustments to lectures based on formative feedback

Some instructors adjust the content of their lectures based on the homework that students submit before class or on formative assessments they do in class. These strategies are informed by findings from research about the need for instruction to build on students' prior knowledge.

In Just-in-Time Teaching (JiTT), the most familiar of these methods, students do homework in the form of written responses to questions about reading assignments or solutions to problems, and then they submit their work on deadline via the Web, in time for the instructor to review it before the next class. The instructor can then modify the next lecture to clarify common misunderstandings or accommodate students' interests (Novak, 1999). A moderate amount of evidence suggests that JiTT is effective in teaching some physics concepts (Formica, Easley, and Spraker, 2010), is associated with positive attitudes about introductory geology (for example, Luo, 2008), and improves students' preparation for class and study habits in biology (Marrs and Novak, 2004). In its emphasis on learning certain material before class, JiTT might be seen as a precursor to the flipped classroom model.

In an approach called Just-in-Time-Teaching with Interactive Learning (JiTTIL), Stephen Krause and his engineering colleagues at Arizona State University and elsewhere have expanded on this basic idea by adding interactive classroom exercises and various forms of fast and frequent feedback (Krause, Kelly, and Baker, 2012b). In Krause's classes that use the JiTTIL approach, students spend much of the class time working in small groups at round tables on activities based on real-world situations. In one such activity, students select from a list of options the best materials to use to construct various components of a bicycle, based on their understanding of the properties desired in a particular component. To improve students' ability to transfer their learning to new contexts, certain activities include an "extension" question that challenges students to apply what they just learned to a new situation. In the bicycle example, the extension activity asks students to come up with substitute materials other than the ones listed for each bicycle component.

The Materials Concept Inventory, a standardized assessment in engineering developed by Krause and his Arizona State colleagues, provides information about students' conceptual knowledge at the beginning of a course. Day-to-day feedback comes from the "muddiest point" reflections described in Chapter 3 and from homework problems that emphasize the key concepts for the topic being studied. Immediate feedback comes from in-class ConcepTests, administered through the

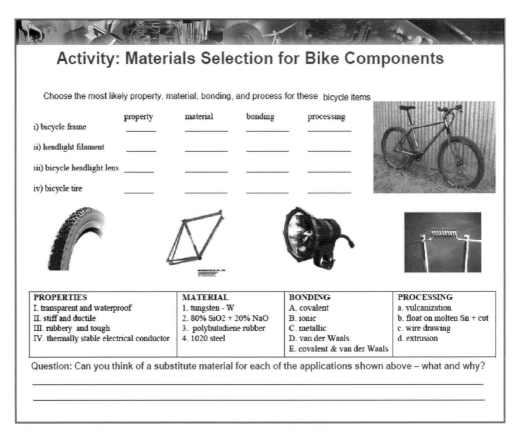

Activity: Materials Selection for Bike Components

Choose the most likely property, material, bonding, and process for these bicycle items

	property	material	bonding	processing
i) bicycle frame	_____	_____	_____	_____
ii) headlight filament	_____	_____	_____	_____
iii) bicycle headlight lens	_____	_____	_____	_____
iv) bicycle tire	_____	_____	_____	_____

PROPERTIES	MATERIAL	BONDING	PROCESSING
I. transparent and waterproof	1. tungsten - W	A. covalent	a. vulcanization
II. stiff and ductile	2. 80% SiO2 + 20% NaO	B. ionic	b. float on molten Sn + cut
III. rubbery and tough	3. polybutadiene rubber	C. metallic	c. wire drawing
IV. thermally stable electrical conductor	4. 1020 steel	D. van der Waals	d. extrusion
		E. covalent & van der Waals	

Question: Can you think of a substitute material for each of the applications shown above – what and why?

_____

_____

Students work in small groups to tackle real-world problems in an activity aimed at applying and extending newly acquired knowledge.

Web-based Concept Warehouse tool, and this information can be used to make on-the-spot adjustments in instruction.

These different types of formative assessments reflect the fact that students' prior knowledge changes as they progress through a course. "When you first walk into a class, it's your prior academic experience and life experience. But then after you've been in the class for a while, it's all the knowledge you've acquired in class," says Krause.[4] "Then there's the previous day's prior knowledge, which is critical, especially if there's a progression of three to five classes for a particular topic."

Evaluations of students taught with the JiTTIL pedagogy show greater gains in conceptual understanding than those in traditionally taught classes, as measured by the Materials Concept Inventory. The percentage of students who persist in the

[4] Interview, July 9, 2013.

course after the second week has also increased from 85 percent to 95 percent in the JiTTIL classes, and the withdrawal rate of female students has decreased from 40 percent to 10 percent (Krause, Kelly, and Baker, 2012b).

The most recent iteration of this pedagogy developed by Krause and other colleagues uses an even wider range of cyber-enabled tools to generate rapid and frequent feedback about student learning and includes more active learning exercises (Krause et al., 2013b).

Alternating lectures with interactive exercises

Although a few students may engage in meaningful conceptual reorganization during a lecture, the lecture mode of instruction is a fundamentally passive one. Interactive approaches are much more effective at promoting the mental processes involved in constructing new knowledge. Recognizing this, many skilled instructors have progressed from lecturing for the whole class period to alternating shorter lecture segments with various types of exercises that promote student interaction.

Clicker questions and other forms of ConcepTests are one way to do this, as are the Interactive Lecture Demonstrations described in the Sokoloff example in Chapter 3. Some instructors integrate group problem solving, "mini-labs," or other types of hands-on activities into their lectures. Often students work collaboratively on these activities, a form of instruction explored later in this chapter. According to a study of an approach to teaching introductory geology that alternated lectures with mini-lab activities, students who did a mini-lab with petrified wood and discussed their observations in online discussion groups showed statistically greater gains than did students in two control groups (Clary and Wandersee, 2007).

Mark Leckie,[5] a geosciences professor at the University of Massachusetts Amherst, describes his 75-minute oceanography classes as "part lecture, part student active learning." Every class includes a 15- to 20-minute collaborative activity, based on a set of exercises he developed with his colleague Richard Yuretich. (See Chapter 1 for examples of their exercises.) "In-class activities can be effectively used to 'set the hook,' to get students interested in what you have to teach, to challenge misconceptions, to initiate discussion of a new topic, to provide reinforcement of material presented in your lecture, to assess student understanding, or to practice critical thinking and problem-solving skills," writes Leckie (n.d.).

---

[5] Interview, March 22, 2013.

Student-to-Student Interaction

Drawing from research on the benefits of learning through social interactions, many forms of student-centered instruction—including some described above—incorporate activities in which students work together in groups. In well-designed activities of this type, students learn from interacting with each other; they build on one another's knowledge, ask questions and provide explanations, and come up with ideas that might not occur to an individual working alone. These activities can also help students develop the kinds of teamwork, decision-making, and interpersonal skills that are integral to the practice of science and engineering. These elements require students, both individually and collectively, to engage in the kind of thinking that leads to deep learning, to articulate their thinking, and to reflect on feedback from others in a way that causes them to reexamine and extend their thinking. Thus, while the social aspects of working in groups are important, the cognitive aspects of this process are also important.

Cooperative learning is a highly structured approach to learning through student-to-student interactions with a strong base of evidence of its effectiveness (see, for example, Smith, 2011). In a well-structured cooperative learning environment, students work together in small groups to accomplish a common goal. The activities foster interdependence by requiring the cooperation of all members of the group and hold both the individuals and the collective group accountable for successfully completing the work.

Collaborative learning is a more generic form of learning through peer interactions. Collaborative learning assumes that students learn best by constructing knowledge within a social context (see Chapter 3) and encourages students to coalesce into a "learning community." While collaborative learning, like cooperative learning, is intended to foster interdependence among students, it is less structured than cooperative learning and does not necessarily combine individual and collective accountability (Smith, 2011).

Research has shown that activities in which students collaborate with each other can be more effective than traditional instruction and can improve students' retention of content knowledge, according to several studies referenced in Chapter 6 of the 2012 NRC report on DBER and other literature. But results depend greatly on the care with which these activities are implemented. Collaborative approaches are not inherently effective and can be poorly implemented. The evidence is not conclusive about the conditions under which these strategies work.

Group activities often involve answering questions, solving problems, or conducting investigations. These activities can be as brief as 10 or 15 minutes or can last an entire class period or even longer. They can be integrated into a lecture format or can serve as the predominant form of instruction. While many instructors assert that they cannot do collaborative activities because their classes are too large, the experiences of expert practitioners prove otherwise. In large classes, the groups typically consist of students seated next to each other. In smaller classes, instructors use a variety of options to group students. Some assign students to groups to achieve a mix of personalities, abilities, or other characteristics, while other instructors let students form their own groups. Some instructors switch the group composition periodically to ensure that students get to know different people, while others keep the same groups to encourage bonding.

Grading group activities is tricky. Individual grades are critical to ensure that each student learns; in addition, Smith suggests that basing a small portion of a student's grade on group performance can be beneficial if done carefully (Smith, 1998).

Some common approaches to such student-to-student interaction as cooperative learning and collaborative learning are described below.

The jigsaw technique

In the "cooperative jigsaw" approach first described by Aronson and colleagues (1978) and refined later by other practitioners, each student member of a cooperative learning group "is responsible for learning a portion of the material and conscientiously teaching it to the rest of the group" (Smith, 2000, p. 32). The instructor chooses the material, structures the groups, provides guidance about student roles, monitors their functioning, and helps students summarize, synthesize, and integrate the material. Faculty who have used this technique find that it can foster students' interdependence and help them learn conceptual material. "Although it takes preparation and time to set up the jigsaw, students usually learn more material and remember it longer," Smith concludes (p. 32).

Barbara Tewksbury, a Hamilton College professor, often uses the jigsaw technique in her geosciences classes. Over the years, this technique has been the most popular cooperative learning strategy among participants in the On the Cutting Edge workshops in course design offered by Tewksbury and colleagues. As the example below demonstrates, the jigsaw technique emphasizes both individual accountability and achievement of group goals.

Putting Together the Pieces of a Geosciences Puzzle

In the early 1990s, Hamilton College professor Barbara Tewksbury[a] was considering ways to place more responsibility on students for learning the content in her geosciences courses. She came up with a plan to have individual teams learn a portion of the material about a particular topic and then reconfigure into new groups and share what they had learned—an approach she later realized had already been developed by others and dubbed the jigsaw technique. "I had no idea it had been formally invented and named in 1978 by Aronson," she says. "But it was one of these situations where I had a pedagogical problem to solve and thought, ah, this would be a good way to solve it. And it turned out I wasn't the only one who had done that," she says, adding that this "Lone Ranger" mentality was typical of geosciences faculty at that time, before geosciences education research had coalesced as an area of scholarship. (Today, she adds, instructors have no need to reinvent the wheel with all of the resources available.)

In Tewksbury's course on geology and human events in North Africa and the Middle East, one of the topics students study is the impact of climate changes on the development of Egyptian civilization around 3000 B.C. She uses the jigsaw technique as a way for students to analyze geological data on sediment accumulation in the basins of the Sahara in order to determine prehistoric changes in rainfall.

<hr>

[a] Except where noted, the information in this case study comes from an interview with Barbara Tewksbury, March 28, 2013.

To prepare for the in-class jigsaw, students do homework assignments that help them understand the extremely arid climate of the modern Sahara. These assignments include looking at Google images of the Sahara. Students also read historical accounts of traverses across the Sahara, a report from a British army expedition trapped in the desert, and descriptions of the modern salt mines operating in Mali.

The White Desert near Farafra Oasis, Egypt.

When the students arrive in class, they are divided into four teams of roughly four people per team. Every team receives a set of published data on the sediments in a particular paleolake; each of the four lakes is located in a different part of the Sahara and has a distinctive stratigraphic record. Their task as a team is to analyze the sediment record and figure out when the lake first appeared, when it dried up, and how the rainfall changed over thousands of years. "By the time the team is done analyzing, everybody has to be prepared to tell somebody else what they learned about their particular data. They have to be able to paint a picture—here's what I think is going on, and here's the evidence," Tewksbury explains.

At that point, she creates new groups composed of a member from each of the former teams. Each member of the new group shares the findings from the previous team's analysis of one particular lake. "They each teach each other what their data suggest," says Tewksbury. The new groups then do a two-part assignment: first, to determine what they can say about the timing and amount of rainfall changes in the Sahara as a whole based on sediment data from four lakes; and second, to analyze additional data about worldwide climate change and predict what will happen in the Sahara with future global climate change. "Of course, their intuition is that if it warms up, it's going to get drier, but the geologic record shows just the opposite: when it gets hotter, it rains more in the Sahara. So it ties back into the modern world," she says. In later class meetings, the students study other aspects of the impact of climate and geological events in order to understand why Egyptian civilization developed when it did.

"It's called a jigsaw because everybody has a piece of the puzzle," Tewksbury explains. "Each team has one stratigraphic column, so that means that four people in that team have the same jigsaw puzzle piece." When the groups are reconfigured, all four puzzle pieces are represented by each new member contributing one piece. As the students teach the members of their new group about what they learned, "that's equivalent to putting the piece down on the table." The final group assignment—to look across all four pieces and arrive at conclusions about Sahara rainfall trends and their implications

for global climate change—"puts the whole picture together." To instill individual accountability, each student must do a major analysis of the timing of the rise of Egyptian civilization that incorporates the earlier paleolakes analysis and other data.

This approach of having students reach their own conclusions based on data provides them with a much better learning experience than if she were to lecture on the topic, says Tewksbury. "They're perfectly capable of drawing the conclusions themselves."

It took Tewksbury time and professional development to arrive at an understanding of effective strategies for learning. Early in her career, she taught as she had been taught—by lecturing. "I had never heard of the word pedagogy," she says. Her "transformative" moment came in the late 1980s, she says, when she became involved as a content expert in a workshop on active learning and other strategies for middle and high school teachers. "I think I probably learned more about pedagogy and had my eyes opened a lot wider by what I learned from the Earth science teachers than they did from me. . . . That got me thinking for the very first time about what I was trying to accomplish in my classes," she says.

This example of a jigsaw in a geosciences class includes several elements associated with improvements in student motivation and learning:

- Students actively construct conceptual knowledge by analyzing data, seeing how it fits into a larger framework, and reaching conclusions.

- Students take control of their learning by doing advance reading, studying a variety of information, and explaining what they learned to their peers.

- The interactive element provides students with an incentive to do the work so they will not let down their peers or themselves.

- Students use the tools and practices of geology, much as a professional scientist would, by analyzing maps and data.

- The activity has relevance to the real-world problem of global climate change.

Natalie Yeo,[6] who was a student at the Community College of Rhode Island in 2013, participated in jigsaws and other cooperative learning approaches in a geology class with professor Karen Kortz. She describes the jigsaw groups as "kind of a mini–think tank because you're all trying to bolster the same idea." The variety of small group work in Kortz's classes keeps students constantly engaged, she says. "Sometimes I leave a lab and say, 'What a think marathon—my brain hurts, in a good way.'"

Group work on problems, experiments, and projects

In other types of cooperative or collaborative learning, students work in groups to solve problems, conduct investigations or experiments, or carry out projects. Some of these strategies involve more extensive changes in classroom organization and instructional practices than a short activity incorporated into a lecture would.

Process Oriented Guided Inquiry Learning (POGIL) began in college chemistry departments but has since been adopted by instructors in a variety of disciplines in numerous postsecondary institutions and high schools. Students in a POGIL classroom learn through a guided inquiry process in which they are presented with data or information, followed by leading questions designed to guide them in formulating their own conclusions (Process Oriented Guided Inquiry Learning, 2014a). Students work in small groups as the instructor observes and facilitates, stepping in as needed to address questions and provide guidance.

---

[6] Interview, April 10, 2013.

The following high school POGIL activity shows how the guided inquiry process works (Process Oriented Guided Inquiry Learning, 2014b):

LEARNING ABOUT ENZYMES THROUGH GUIDED INQUIRY

In a biology classroom that uses the POGIL "guided inquiry" approach, students explore this question: *What are the factors that regulate the rate at which enzymes catalyze reactions?* Students read a paragraph explaining how enzymes affect their daily lives and why the preceding question matters. In the specific activity, students look at the optimal conditions for two different enzymes: lipase, which breaks down lipids in the small intestine, and pepsin, which breaks down proteins in the stomach. They are presented with an initial model consisting of (a) a simple diagram showing that lipase breaks down triglycerides into glycerol and fatty acids and that pepsin breaks down large polypeptides into smaller polypeptides and amino acids, and (b) a graph of the effect of pH on enzyme activity. Students study the model and compare data in order to answer a series of questions of increasing complexity, including questions that require them to explain an answer in detail, justify their reasoning, and add a line to the graph. The final question in the series requires them to use their knowledge of protein structure to *explain in detail the effect of exposing an enzyme to a pH outside of its optimal range. Include the effect on both enzyme structure and function.*

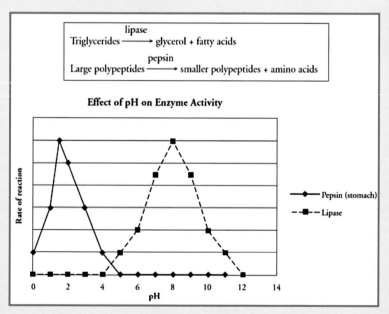

Model and graph provided to students in a POGIL guided inquiry on enzymes. SOURCE: Flinn Scientific, Inc., 2014.

This activity continues with a second model consisting of three graphs showing the effects of various factors on the function of the enzyme amylase in the body. Students work through another series of questions about that model. The activity also includes "extension questions," which require deeper thinking and might be used for homework or as an extra activity for groups that move quickly.

Within the basic POGIL framework, instructors use a variety of strategies to manage the groups and help students learn. Instructors might suspend the group work at various points to allow groups to report their answers to the whole class, and activities generally conclude with a whole-class discussion. At times, instructors may need to give a mini-lecture to the whole class or to an individual group to clarify an area of confusion or reinforce a vital point. Instructors may also set aside time for students to reflect on their learning and process skills. The strategies used will depend on what transpires during each class. "The principle is to have students do as much thinking and working as possible. No day is a typical day," says Rick Moog, a Franklin & Marshall College chemistry professor and executive director of The POGIL Project. Formative assessment is a central part of the POGIL process, as explained in Chapter 5.

Although POGIL has been used most extensively in smaller classes, it can also be adapted for large classes—for example, by framing a recitation section around POGIL activities or having students use clickers to give feedback to provide responses to questions based on POGIL activities (Amaral et al., 2005). Numerous resources in a range of disciplines—curriculum, instructional guidance, professional development workshops, and more—are available for instructors who want to use the POGIL pedagogy (see www.pogil.org).

Studies of the effectiveness of POGIL at a range of institutions and for a variety of courses provide evidence that this approach can improve achievement and reduce attrition as compared with courses taught through traditional methods (for lists of specific studies, see https://pogil.org/about/effectiveness). Other research has found improvements in test scores for general chemistry students when POGIL is combined with Peer-Led Team Learning, the approach described in Chapter 1 in which trained undergraduates lead supplemental problem-solving sessions (Lewis and Lewis, 2005).

Cooperative problem solving, an instructional approach that draws from research on cooperative learning, was originally developed for physics as a way to encourage students to develop expertise in problem solving while discouraging their tendency to use novice strategies (Heller and Heller, 2010). Working in small groups, students use a specially designed strategy to solve context-rich problems. These are problems rooted in real situations that would be difficult to solve by applying a few equations and plugging in numbers, seeking the recognizable patterns found in many traditional textbook problems, or looking for physics vocabulary cues. Instead, these problems are best solved by analyzing the situation, perhaps with the help of a visual representation, and logically constructing a path to a solution. These problems often require students to consider what they know and do not know and what assumptions they need to make.

Here is an example of a context-rich problem in one-dimensional kinematics:

> You have a summer job as the technical assistant to the director of an adventure movie. The script calls for a large package to be dropped onto the bed of a fast moving pick-up truck from a helicopter that is hovering above the road. The helicopter is 235 feet above the road, and the bed of the truck is 3 feet above the road. The truck is traveling down the road at 40 miles/hour. You must determine when to tell the helicopter to drop the package so it lands in the truck. (Heller and Heller, 2010, p. 242)

A typical 50-minute class organized around cooperative problem solving might look something like this: The instructor begins by articulating the concepts to be learned during that class session. For the next 35 minutes, students work in groups to solve the problem as the instructor observes and listens, diagnosing students' difficulties and occasionally interacting with groups that need help. At the end of the appointed time, one member from each group is randomly selected to put part of their solution on the board, with license to ask other members of the group for help. Students in other groups examine the solutions on the board to see how they parallel or differ from their own group's result. The instructor then leads a class discussion of the possible solutions but does not give students a paper with the complete correct solution until the end of class (Heller and Heller, 2010, pp. 1–2).

Cooperative problem solving can be used as the major focus of a course, as in the example above, or to make smaller recitation or discussion sections more interactive.

Findings from a study in chemistry also indicated that cooperative problem solving improved students' problem-solving abilities by about 10 percent, and that this improvement was retained when students returned to individual problem-solving activities (Cooper et al., 2008).

In *problem-based learning* (PBL), students learn disciplinary knowledge by working through problems that mirror real-world situations, most commonly in groups but occasionally individually. At the core of PBL is the notion of the "ill-structured" question, which reflects the complex, messy, and tentative nature of many of the problems facing science and society that have no simple, formulaic "right" solutions. Groups are presented with contextual situations and asked to define the problem, decide what skills and resources are necessary to investigate the problem, and then pose possible solutions (Duch, Groh, and Allen, 2001). To solve this type of ill-structured problem, students must engage in inquiry, information-gathering, and reflection. PBL activities can take up most of the teaching and learning time in a classroom or can be combined with a lecture.

Although the most striking thing about the **SCALE-UP** (Student-Centered Active Learning Environment with Upside-down Pedagogies) **model** is its redesign of the physical classroom space (described in Chapter 5), it is also a powerful example of how student collaboration can serve as the primary mode of instruction. In a SCALE-UP classroom, the lecture and lab components of a course are combined. Students learn some of the basic content through readings and homework before and after class. This arrangement makes it possible even for students in very large enrollment courses to spend most of their class time working in small groups on rich activities.

> "Strategies used will depend on what transpires during each class. The principle is to have students do as much thinking and working as possible. No day is a typical day."
>
> —*Rick Moog,*
> *Franklin & Marshall College*

The main learning occurs through interactions with peers under the guidance of the instructor and through classroom discussions among the students and with the instructor. Students do hands-on activities, problems, simulations, and experiments that challenge them to think deeply. Brief intervals of lecture are mostly limited to providing motivation and linking the collaborative activities to the bigger course content.

As one type of SCALE-UP activity, students do 10- to 15-minute experiments in groups using a "predict-observe-explain" model. For example, groups are given the task of rolling a racquetball through a curved path between a pair of concentric quarter-circle arcs drawn on a piece of paper. Some students tip the paper or spin or blow on the ball. The instructor asks them why they need to do this (making references to Newton's second law), with the goal of getting them to understand they are applying a force to the ball to change the direction of its motion. Once they understand, they are asked to specify the direction of the force. Through Socratic dialogue, the instructor eventually gets students to see that the force is always directed toward the center of the concentric arcs. Students recognize this as a centripetal force and then do a task in which they approximate the magnitude of the force from the mass of the ball and estimate its speed (Beichner et al., 2007).

Other SCALE-UP activities require students to think through a problem without making measurements. An example: *How far does a bowling ball travel down the lane before it stops skidding and is only rolling?* This difficult problem requires a great deal of estimation, but it provides students with insights about frictional force. When they have developed an answer, they can check it against a simulation of this scenario.

According to Robin Wright,[7] who teaches a SCALE-UP biology course at the University of Minnesota, an overarching theme of this approach to teaching is "to have students *doing* biology, not learning about biology, and to have that 'doing' happen in the classroom where we can watch and help and coach them."

Studies of the SCALE-UP model have found that participating students have better scores on problem-solving exams and ConcepTests, slightly better attitudes about science, and less attrition than students in traditional courses (Beichner et al., 2007; Gaffney et al., 2008). Failure rates among women and students from underrepresented groups have also been substantially reduced.

Mackenzie Tilley,[8] an engineering major at North Carolina State who took Robert Beichner's SCALE-UP physics course, benefited from this type of instruction in several ways. "What's great about the group work is that if you have a question, you don't have to wait for the professor to finish talking," she says. "You just turn to your partner and say, hey, how did you figure this out? Most of the time your partner will understand what you don't understand, or you'll understand when your partner or group members don't." In addition, she says, "the activities all worked in a way that clearly showed you the differences between certain principles. . . . You could distinguish what was going on and why it was going on that way."

SCALE-UP is just one example of an approach that combines the lecture and lab sessions of a course into a single, longer block of time to facilitate group investigations and projects. Some of these approaches include laboratory experiences aligned with scientific practices in which, for example, students record observations, develop and test explanations, refine existing models, and build and refine their own models of a scientific process by experimenting.

Another such approach is Modeling Instruction, developed by Eric Brewe and colleagues in the physics department at Florida International University.

---

[7] Interview, April 12, 2013.
[8] Interview, March 27, 2013.

Using Models as Physicists Do

Florida International University (FIU), a large, public research university with a majority Hispanic enrollment, graduates more Hispanic holders of bachelor's degrees than any other institution in the United States. In an effort to increase the participation of Hispanic students in physics courses

Eric Brewe engages in model building with his class at FIU.

and improve learning for all students, Eric Brewe and other faculty members in the physics education research group at FIU have designed and implemented a version of Modeling Instruction, an approach first explored by David Hestenes (1987) at Arizona State for whom Brewe was a graduate assistant. The Modeling Instruction approach used

by Brewe and his colleagues combines active student engagement, cooperative grouping, activities to foster conceptual understanding, and experience with the authentic practices of the discipline—features that can support the learning of students underrepresented in science, according to participating faculty (Brewe, Kramer, and O'Brien, 2009).

In the physics classes taught with the modeling method, students construct and validate models that allow them to explain, describe, and predict outcomes, much as scientists do. "If we think science is about building models, then we have to focus attention on getting students into authentic practices," says Eric Brewe,[a] who was instrumental in designing the modeling curriculum. The "cookbook" method of doing lab experiments fails to help students see the connection between their experiment and the theory behind it, he asserts. Instead of thinking about whether their approach to solving a problem is a useful model, students fixate on whether they arrived at the right answer. In Modeling Instruction, explains Brewe, "students think about what goes into a model. . . . We're careful to get students to understand how to use representations to make predictions or draw

---

[a] Except where noted, the information in this case study comes from an interview with Eric Brewe, April 16, 2013.

conclusions. A graph is only as good as the information you can draw out of it."

During his classes, which meet three times a week for two hours at a time, Modeling Instruction students work in small groups in a studio-format classroom with whiteboards and tables instead of desks. The longer class period has made it possible to integrate the laboratory and lecture components of the course, which mirrors the practices of scientists. "No reasonable scientist says, 'It's our day to do lab'—they do investigations when it's appropriate," says Brewe. The activities and lab experiments are designed to encourage model building. The groups share their ideas on portable whiteboards and come together for discussions, with the instructor moderating.

Stephanie Castañeda, a student who took two semesters of Brewe's course in 2012–2013, recalls a kinematics experiment. The students set up their equations and then tested whether their calculations were correct by rolling a ball down a ramp and placing a cup where they predicted the ball would hit the floor. "We basically learned that the model we had learned in class applied to real life," she says.

Other aspects of the course also attempt to replicate authentic practices. Students are assessed on their use of scientific apparati. Unlike the traditional approach of assigning many homework problems that are variations on the same thing, the homework in the courses taught with the modeling approach includes fewer problems that require deeper understanding. "We give homework every day, but just one problem that has to be done thoroughly and explained in words," Brewe notes.

Studies of Modeling Instruction indicate that students taught through this method outperform those taught in lecture-format classes, with benefits for Hispanic and white students and for male and female students (Brewe et al., 2010). Student

attitudes about physics, as measured by a standardized survey instrument, have also improved (Brewe et al., 2013). In addition, students in Modeling Instruction sections report 10 times the number of ties among themselves than students in lecture sections. Brewe, Kramer, and O'Brien (2009) see this as evidence that students in Modeling Instruction form richer and more deeply connected learning communities, which further contribute to learning gains.

Supplementing Instruction with Tutorials

Tutorials can serve as a ready-made tool for instructors who want to supplement their lectures with carefully sequenced, research-based learning exercises that students can do in small groups or independently. The widely influential *Tutorials in Introductory Physics* (McDermott and Shaffer, 2002) highlights tutorials created by Lillian McDermott,[9] Peter Shaffer, and the physics education group at the University of Washington that are a prototype for research-based tutorials designed to promote the kind of active intellectual engagement necessary to develop a functional understanding of physics concepts. Tutorials are often used in a recitation or discussion section in which students work in small groups, but they can also be incorporated into a lecture or assigned as homework.

The genesis of the physics tutorials, says McDermott, was her realization that even graduate students in physics had difficulties in understanding key physics concepts. "They were much more sophisticated, so they could get by with memorizing formulas; they could get by with knowing how to do things without necessarily understanding them. If you asked questions about understanding, they turned out to have the same problems as the other students." This led McDermott to begin documenting common student difficulties and researching the impact of instructional strategies to confront them.

Typically, tutorials target critical concepts and are designed to have students "elicit, confront, and resolve" common difficulties in learning, says McDermott. The questions on the tutorial worksheets are structured to help lead students through the steps of reasoning necessary to develop and apply basic concepts.

One of the Washington tutorials, for example, uses a simple optical system consisting of a light source, a mask with a small triangular hole, and a screen to help students understand and apply two basic principles from geometrical optics: light travels in straight lines, and light rays from every point on an object travel outward in all directions. The tutorial first asks students, working in small groups, to predict the images that will appear on the screen from different types of light-bulbs when the size and shape of the aperture changes. After the students have made predictions and explained their reasoning to one another, they observe what actually happens and try to resolve any discrepancies with their predictions. They are then asked to predict and explain up-down and left-right inversions of images produced by asymmetric sources. The point is to help students understand that the size and shape of the source, the size and shape of the aperture, and the distances

---

[9] Interview, April 18, 2013.

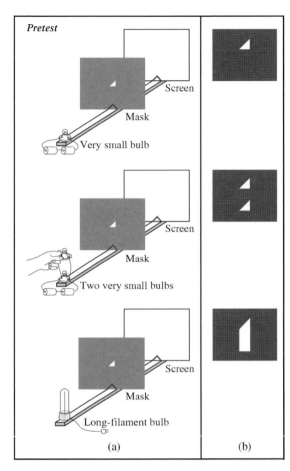

(a) Students were asked to sketch what they would see on the screen. (b) Correct answers.

involved can all have an effect on the image (Heron and McDermott, 1998).

The initial question is framed so that many students will make an incorrect prediction, says Paula Heron,[10] a professor in the physics department. When they actually try the experiment, such as turning on the lightbulb or changing the shape of the aperture, the results are not what they expected. "That's an opportunity to take advantage of that surprise, or confusion, or dismay, whatever the emotion is," says Heron. "It's a moment when you're likely to get strong intellectual engagement. By letting them see how their thinking led to one prediction and how a different way of thinking leads to a correct prediction, you can get them to not only see what the correct thing is, but give them an opportunity to reflect on the patterns of thought or beliefs they had, or the way that they were approaching the problem, that were incorrect or unproductive."

Numerous studies have demonstrated that the University of Washington tutorials significantly improve students' conceptual understanding and their more general scientific reasoning (see a review by Docktor and Mestre, 2011). These tutorials do require fairly extensive facilitation by teaching assistants.

Researchers and faculty have developed similar tutorials in astronomy, biology, geosciences, and other disciplines (see Chapter 2 for more information about the geosciences tutorials designed by Karen Kortz and Jessica Smay).

Science and Engineering Practices and Authentic Experiences

Think back to why you went into science or engineering. You likely became fascinated by something you saw or did that opened your mind to bigger ideas, such as your first view through a microscope of the amoebas that lived in a water puddle

---

[10] Interview, April 12, 2013.

or your realization that so much of the world around you could be explained by the principles of physics. But you probably also found satisfaction in *practicing* science or engineering—for example, by collecting and analyzing data, using the "tools of the trade," or designing a device or technology that can make our lives or our world better.

For students to be competent in science and engineering, they need more than knowledge of the content of a discipline. They also need to understand the practices, tools, and ways of thinking in that discipline—and how these can be applied to solve real problems. Although most students in science or engineering courses will not pursue careers in these fields, all of them can benefit from understanding the process of science and how it can be used to evaluate and make decisions about issues facing society.

Research at the K–12 level has shown that with well-designed curricula and instruction, students can become more competent in the practice of science at the same time they learn content at a deeper level (National Research Council, 2007). Some instructional strategies at the undergraduate level combine these goals. Using the practices of a profession and working on authentic problems also makes learning more relevant in a way that many students find motivating. These approaches may have students work on authentic problems or activities, analyze published data, use tools commonly used in the practice of a discipline, and participate in research experiences, as illustrated by the following examples.

In the SCALE-UP Foundations of Biology course for majors at the University of Minnesota, the lab and lecture components are integrated into thrice-weekly sessions of almost two hours each. As part of the course, students do a 5-week and a 10-week team project that explores an authentic problem of social value that they identify themselves, says Wright, one of the instructors. Past projects have dealt with the impact of climate change on coral reefs; the biological effects of an oil spill, Alzheimer's disease, or cancer; and even the design of camouflage clothing. Students apply their knowledge of genetics and evolution to propose solutions, says Wright.

As the culminating experience of the class, students present and discuss their proposals in a class poster session, just as biologists would. "We try in every way to represent the authentic work of the discipline," says Wright.

A unique undergraduate engineering program in the Iron Range mining region of northern Minnesota uses authentic engineering design projects to develop students' understanding of core competencies in engineering and professional engineering practices.

DESIGNING LEARNING

Prospective Engineers Learn Technical and Professional Competencies Through Authentic Projects

Through the Iron Range Engineering program, students learn both the technical knowledge and the professional practices of engineering by carrying out engineering design projects (Minnesota State University, Mankato, 2013). The program is a partnership between Itasca Community College in Grand Rapids, Minnesota, and Minnesota State University (MNSU), Mankato. Most of the participants are community college graduates who are completing the upper-division portion of an engineering bachelor's degree.

The majority of students' design projects are sponsored by the mining, milling, and manufacturing industries in Minnesota's Iron Range, says Rebecca Bates,[a] an engineering professor at MNSU, Mankato, although some students do entrepreneurial projects or work with faculty on a research project. One student project, for example, examined the problem of heat loss and transfer in a paper mill. This loss affects the quality of the paper produced because the paper must go through phases of dampness and dryness. The student team analyzed changes in the temperatures and airflow in the plant and made recommendations for improving insulation, air movement, and other factors.

Rather than attending lecture-based classes, students learn by conducting their design projects, participating in seminars and conversations with faculty and external experts, receiving feedback on their projects, and engaging in self-study and peer learning. Some of the required credits are related to engineering knowledge about areas such as digital logic and thermodynamics. Others are related to professional skills, such as teamwork, ethics, individual com-

munication, and time-management skills—"all of the things we connect with professionalism," says Bates.

In the proposal stage, students must develop both a work plan for their project and a learning plan that outlines their learning objectives for professional skills and technical knowledge. The plan also describes the methods students will pursue to meet those learning objectives and the means that will be used to assess and reflect on their learning.

Students present evidence that they have learned the requisite knowledge and skills to the faculty, who review the evidence and assess students' competency through oral and written exams.

Students' written reflections on what and how they are learning are an important part of the evidence used to assess their work. "When they start, they hate doing this because it's more work," says Bates. "They have produced a finished assignment and gotten the right answer, and then they say, 'You want me to write about how I got it?'" But, she adds, these reflections often lead to improvements in their projects, their learning processes, and their retention of content.

---

[a] Except where noted, the information in this case study comes from an interview with Rebecca Bates, July 8, 2013.

Students in Christopher Swan's[11] civil and environmental engineering and geotechnical engineering courses at Tufts University learn about engineering practices through projects with a community service angle. Working in small groups, students have tackled projects with environmental implications: for example, evaluating what happens when soils in a waste site are heated to high temperatures, as occurs in sites remediated with incineration. During the course of six to eight weeks, the students develop a research process and conduct a study of such questions as whether the resulting soil can be used as clean soil and how it differs from uncontaminated soil from the same site. The work of one student group was published as a symposium paper, says Swan. Students "get turned on by a research project—it may spark a deeper interest in engineering," he says.

Swan also works with students participating in service learning engineering projects in developing nations through Engineers Without Borders. In one ongoing project, students work with a village in Uganda to determine the most feasible way to continuously pump drinking water from a local source.

Conclusion

The approaches described in this chapter are intended to give science and engineering faculty a flavor of how research on how people learn can inform instructional practices in undergraduate education. Many other strategies backed by evidence of effectiveness, and many sources of information and support, await instructors who wish to explore these ideas in their courses. If you take the next step, you will be joining a community of practitioners engaged in learning, experimenting, and sharing results.

Resources and Further Reading

Discipline-Based Education Research: Understanding and Improving Learning in Undergraduate Science and Engineering (National Research Council, 2012)
Chapter 6: Instructional Strategies

Pedagogy in Action Web portal of the Science Education Resource Center (SERC)
http://serc.carleton.edu/sp/index.html

Process Oriented Guided Inquiry Learning (POGIL)
www.pogil.org

---

[11] Interview, August 27, 2013.

5 Assessing and Adapting

When Jessica Smay[1] took a position teaching geosciences and astronomy at San Jose City College in California in 2006, she was already persuaded of the value of interactive instruction. In her previous teaching job at South Suburban College, a community college in Illinois, she had attended a Center for Astronomy Education workshop and had started implementing ConcepTests. She had also begun to develop lecture tutorials in geosciences with her colleague Karen Kortz and was using them in her classes. With her move to a new community college with a highly diverse student body, Smay wanted to fine-tune some of her teaching strategies.

One approach Smay used to determine how well her students were learning was simply to *listen* to students' reasoning as they discussed a clicker question with a partner or worked in small groups on a tutorial. Smay would "walk around the classroom and see how the students were talking about or answering the questions—their thought processes," she says. If a student seemed confused, "I would say, 'How did you get this answer?' and they would talk me through it." Based on these discussions, Smay realized that in some cases she was expecting her students to "make too big of a leap" in their progression toward more accurate understanding, so she would revise a learning activity to provide students with more scaffolding. Some of the student misconceptions that emerged during these discussions also helped her to design better ConcepTests.

In a student-centered undergraduate classroom, many of the learning activities themselves are a form of assessment that provide instructors with richer information about students' understanding than they could obtain from traditional assessments and lecture-based instruction. While this is just one of several sources of assessment data in student-centered classes, it can be a valuable one, according

---

[1] Interview, May 21, 2013.

to Edward Price,[2] a physics professor at California State University San Marcos. "Very early in my experience as an instructor, I would often wonder what students were thinking, what they were getting from what we were doing in class. Other than just the 'nodding head' index of how many of them were asleep, you don't really know in a large lecture class." When Price began using ConcepTests, he found that the answers students gave to these questions and the discussions they had about them provided him with the immediate feedback he craved.

As you gain experience with research-based instruction, you will likely find that the same traditional tests—whether end-of-chapter textbook quizzes or the questions typically found on midterms or finals—do not adequately measure the kinds of conceptual understanding you want your students to develop. Student-centered approaches to teaching and learning call for different methods of assessment.

Student-centered instruction may also necessitate new ways of using technology. While technologies, ranging from clickers to interactive simulations of scientific processes, open up additional possibilities for instruction, their effectiveness hinges on how well they are implemented and whether they are aligned with sound pedagogy.

This chapter addresses three issues that often arise in the early stages of designing an effective, research-based approach to teaching undergraduate science and engineering.[3] The first is the appropriate use of assessment, which is an essential part of research-based instruction. The second is the effective use of technology, which has become commonplace in science and engineering classrooms. A third issue, the redesign of classroom spaces to support active learning, is by no means a prerequisite; many instructors have implemented research-based strategies quite well in whatever learning spaces are available, from large traditional lecture halls to smaller rooms with fixed desks. This issue is included here to show what can be done when changing the learning space is an option.

In a student-centered undergraduate classroom, many of the learning activities themselves are a form of assessment that provide instructors with richer information about students' understanding than they could obtain from traditional assessments and lecture-based instruction.

---

[2] Interview, August 23, 2013.

[3] Much of the information in this chapter is drawn from the 2012 National Research Council report on discipline-based education research; see, in particular, Chapter 4 of that report for more information about assessment of conceptual understanding; and Chapter 6 for more about technology and redesign of learning spaces.

Assessment and Course Evaluation

In a research-based science or engineering classroom, assessment serves several critical purposes for both instructors and students that go beyond the need to determine course grades. The most immediate purpose for instructors, and one that will help you with implementing the ideas in this book, is to obtain frequent feedback about what students know, how well they are learning, and where they are having difficulties. You can then use this feedback to modify your teaching to enhance student learning. The literature on assessment often refers to this as *formative* assessment. Formative assessments also serve an important purpose for students by providing them with information they can use to gauge their own learning and adjust how they study.

Summative assessments, which evaluate students' performance against a standard or benchmark at the end of a unit, in midterm, or at the end of a semester, continue to have a place in research-based instruction. They can tell you how students have progressed in their learning and can be used to determine students' grades. In addition, summative assessments can help you evaluate the effectiveness of your course design and determine which aspects to adjust in future iterations of the course.

Roles of assessment in a research-based course

Effective formative assessments conducted during the course of classroom instruction can make students' thinking "visible" to the instructor and the students themselves, notes the National Research Council (NRC) report *Knowing What Students Know: The Science and Design of Educational Assessment* (National Research Council, 2001, p. 4). They can reveal students' preconceptions and help both instructors and students monitor students' progress from a naïve to a more expert-like understanding. In a research-based classroom, formative assessments are not quizzes that students can ace by memorizing material the night before; rather, they should provide students with opportunities to revise and improve their thinking and help teachers identify problems with learning (National Research Council, 2001).

Rick Moog, a chemistry professor at Franklin & Marshall College, came to understand the various roles of assessment in the 1990s, when he began developing the group learning activities that would later evolve into Process Oriented Guided Inquiry Learning (POGIL).

But How Did You Arrive at That Answer?

ASSESSMENT IN AN ACTIVITY-BASED CLASSROOM

Rick Moog in his POGIL chemistry classroom.

Rick Moog,[a] the executive director of The POGIL Project (see Chapter 4 for a description), had already begun experimenting with ways to make his lectures more interactive when he attended a workshop on student-centered learning and assessment. After the workshop, he was determined to move away from lecturing in his general chemistry class and have students learn by doing group activities. And this, he realized, would require a different approach to assessment. "Historically, at least in my experience, instruction in science and math has really emphasized being able to generate correct answers to certain kinds of questions," he says. He attributes this to the nature of exams and the traditional approach to instruction—"which is to tell students what you want them to tell you back." But in a classroom that stresses process skills, critical thinking, problem solv-

ing, group work, and self-assessment, he realized he needed an assessment approach that was compatible with these goals. Moog explains:

> Most people, if you provide them simultaneously with formative feedback and evaluative feedback, pretty much ignore the formative feedback and focus only on summative feedback. For example, if a student hands in a lab report and you write all these comments on it about things they need to improve and how they could improve them, and then you write B+ at the top, many students only look at the B+. They either are or are not satisfied, but regardless, they put it in their book bag, and the next lab report you get from them has all the same issues. . . . If you want your students to actually get better at something, you need to find ways to provide them with constructive formative assessment that is independent of summative assessment.

[a] Except where noted, the information in this case study comes from an interview with Richard Moog, May 1, 2013.

Moog says this insight changed his approach to assessment. In POGIL classrooms, he explains, *how* a student arrives at an answer is at least as important as generating the correct answer. In his tests, he includes some traditional questions, such as asking students to calculate the pH of a particular solution. But he also includes questions that ask students to mark whether a particular statement is true or false and explain their reasoning. Students receive no points for a correct true or false answer; instead, credit is based solely on their explanation of their reasoning. In these explanations, students are expected to discuss what information they used to arrive at the answer and how they analyzed the statement. It's not uncommon, he says, for students to write out their reasoning and then go back and cross out or erase their original true or false answer and replace it with the opposite one.

In addition, Moog notes, the activities that students do in his POGIL classes are themselves a type of formative assessment. He starts each 80-minute class with a 5-minute quiz to check how well students understand the material they studied in the last class, after which he reviews any points that are unclear. Students then work in small groups on a learning activity while the instructor facilitates. To explore the concept of atomic number, for example, students analyze diagrams of atoms that identify the element and show the number and location of the protons, neutrons, and electrons in each atom. Students then answer a series of questions that guide them toward recognizing that all of the atoms with the same number of protons are identified as the same element—and that this number corresponds with the number on the periodic table for that element (Moog et al., 2006). Time is set aside at the end of each activity for students to reflect on and summarize what they have learned. Throughout this process of group work, debate, discussion, and reflection, both the students and the instructor receive feedback that helps them gauge students' level of understanding.

As the Moog example shows, such research-based activities as group project work and students' writings and reflections function as formative assessment as well as learning exercises. And as the Smay example at the beginning of the chapter illustrates, instructors can get rapid formative feedback simply by listening to student discussions during group work, such as the Peer Instruction component of a clicker question or a Think-Pair-Share activity done without clickers. With this type of formative feedback, instructors can adjust their teaching on the spot to clarify misunderstandings or address student questions. A study of geosciences classes that used ConcepTests and Peer Instruction to provide immediate feedback found a substantial improvement in students' scores on the Geoscience Concept Inventory (McConnell et al., 2006). A similar approach that used Peer Instruction with clicker questions in four introductory computer science courses reduced the student failure rate by 67 percent (Porter, Bailey-Lee, and Simon, 2013).

Something as low-tech as a whiteboard can be a useful formative assessment tool, says Eric Brewe,[4] a physics instructor at Florida International University (FIU). By walking around and looking at students' collaborative work on whiteboards, the instructor can quickly see how the groups are doing. "Without even talking to them, you can see what they're thinking. And sometimes you look at a whiteboard and see you need to step in and guide them in a different direction," he explains.

The importance of alignment

Various studies and guides to instructional design emphasize the importance of considering assessment in conjunction with content (or curriculum) and instruction (or pedagogy) (see, for example, Streveler, Smith, and Pilotte, 2012; Wiggins and McTighe, 2005). Aligning these three essential components of content, assessment, and instruction can serve as the backbone for designing or redesigning a course. The first step in the alignment process, write Streveler, Smith, and Pilotte, is to develop learning goals for what students should know and be able to do, which they see as "the activity that links content with assessment" (2012, p. 15). The next step, they propose, is to determine what constitutes acceptable evidence that students have met the learning goals—the assessment element—in the form of both summative and formative assessments. The final step is to decide on instructional strategies that will support the kind of learning embodied in the learning goals.

---

[4] Interview, April 16, 2013.

The NRC report *Knowing What Students Know* recommends that assessment be grounded in a scientifically credible model of how students learn—in particular, how they represent knowledge and develop expertise in a domain, such as a particular science discipline or engineering (National Research Council, 2001). This model can guide the choice of assessment tasks that will prompt students to say, do, or create something that demonstrates important knowledge and skills.

Instructors often include questions on their assessments that elicit the kinds of conceptual understanding and thinking skills they want students to develop in their classes.

"If you believe it's important for students to learn concepts in an introductory course, then you better also test them on that," says David Sokoloff,[5] a physics professor and discipline-based education research (DBER) scholar at the University of Oregon. "You don't often test them on concepts by giving them problems straight out of the textbook. You have to include conceptual questions on the test you use to grade them." Students get so accustomed to solving problems by memorizing algorithms that if a professor puts a question on the exam that deviates only slightly from the homework problems, "students will write that you were unfair because the problems on the exam were different," he notes. Sokoloff uses a combination of open-ended questions and multiple-choice "conceptual evaluations" with several incorrect "distractor" responses based on research about common student misunderstandings.

In his physics classes at FIU, Eric Brewe[6] also espouses the principle that "assessment should reflect what you're teaching." In addition to including questions about content that prospective physics majors would be expected to learn, he assesses how students use and interpret models or representational tools. And because he teaches an integrated laboratory and lecture course, he also asks exam questions that require students to use some type of lab apparatus.

---

[5] Interview, July 10, 2013.
[6] Interview, April 16, 2013.

Methods of assessment in research-based courses

A wide range of assessment methods are compatible with research-based approaches to teaching and learning. You don't need to design your own assessments; many research-validated instruments or items are readily available through resource centers, universities, professional organizations, and other sources. In deciding which assessment methods to use, you should consider how well the assessment aligns with your learning goals (as discussed above), which specific aspects of learning and teaching you are trying to measure, and how you intend to use the results. Assessment methods will vary depending on purpose.

Because different types of assessment have various strengths and weaknesses, researchers suggest using multiple forms of assessment, rather than relying on a single form, to obtain the richest information about students' learning (National Research Council, 2001). For example, if you are using a validated multiple-choice instrument to measure conceptual knowledge, you might supplement that with an assessment that requires students to write about and reflect on their learning to probe other aspects of their understanding and to encourage metacognition.

Steven Pollock and his colleagues in the physics education research group at the University of Colorado Boulder have employed different assessment methods at different stages of transforming several upper-division physics courses (Pollock et al., 2011). In the course design stage, they use student observations and surveys, analyses of student work, and interviews with previous instructors of the courses to investigate common student difficulties and determine what to teach. For formative classroom assessments, they use clicker questions and tutorials to pinpoint and address student difficulties. At the end of the course, they use a standard validated post-test and faculty interviews to assess student learning and evaluate the impact of the changes.

The sections that follow describe some of the most common assessment methods used in research-based courses.

Assessments of conceptual understanding

Improving students' conceptual understanding is a primary goal of research-based practice. Several research-validated tools have been developed to assess students' initial level of understanding and to measure their learning after instruction. Two common types are concept inventories and ConcepTests.

Concept inventories assess students' understanding of the core concepts of a discipline and are often administered as pre- and post-tests. Results of these inventories can also be used to compare learning gains across different sections or courses. Typically these inventories use a multiple-choice format, but they differ from traditional multiple-choice tests in that the questions and answers—including the distractor responses—have been developed through research on common student misunderstandings and erroneous ideas.

The widely used Force Concept Inventory (FCI) in physics is an early example of this type of assessment (Hestenes, Wells, and Swackhamer, 1992). The FCI consists of multiple-choice questions about the concept of force, which is central to understanding Newtonian mechanics, and many of the incorrect responses (distractors) are based on commonsense beliefs about these topics. Concept inventories have also been developed for other science disciplines and for engineering. These inventories can be used in large or small classes and with a range of students, which makes them useful for various types of comparative research.

The inventories vary in terms of their sophistication and validation methods, and the best ones have been validated in many instructional contexts. Like all multiple-choice tests, concept inventories address a relatively coarse level of knowledge and provide no guarantee that a student who answers such a question understands the concept, as noted in Chapter 4 of the 2012 NRC report on DBER. Thus, users should be attentive to the specific purposes for which a particular inventory has been designed, and to use the right assessment tool for the job.

ConcepTests, discussed in Chapters 2 and 4, are short formative assessments of a single concept.

Student writing as formative assessment

Many science and engineering instructors use short writing assignments to assess students' understanding and to develop their metacognitive skills. The reading reflections and the "muddiest points" reflections described in Chapter 3 are two examples. Other possibilities include writing "prompts" that require students to articulate their thinking in depth about a thought-provoking question or apply what they have learned to a real-world situation; and writing "one-minute papers" in which students identify the most important thing they learned and a point that remains unclear to them. These and other types of writing assignments can be done in a few minutes and can reveal different information about student learning than a multiple-choice question would.

Ed Prather[7] of the Center for Astronomy Education at the University of Arizona is a proponent of short, in-class writing assignments as a way to intellectually engage students and gather highly discriminating information that instructors can use to revise their teaching. In some cases, he says, instructors who thought their teaching was going well based on student responses to clicker questions are "in shock about how difficult it seems to be for their students to articulate a complete and coherent answer" to a writing prompt on the topic of the clicker question. Here are a few examples of prompts for five-minute writing assignments that Prather uses in his classes and offers in his professional development workshops on interactive learning (Prather, 2010):

- Explain how light from the Sun and light from Earth's surface interact with the atmosphere to produce the Greenhouse Effect.

- What three science discoveries made during the past 150 years have made the greatest impact on mankind's prosperity and quality of life? Explain the reasoning for your choices.

- What about the enterprise of science makes it different than business?

Erin Dolan,[8] a biology professor at the University of Georgia, often requires students to write about case studies of realistic situations in her biochemistry classes. "If you ask [students] to write something and they have to think about what they've written, they often recognize when they don't understand something," she explains, and they will ask for help to resolve their misunderstanding. For example, Dolan provides students with data from a case study of a patient with a biochemically based disorder and asks the students to explain in writing why the patient is experiencing particular symptoms, what might be causing them, and how they used the data to reach their conclusion. Her exams include similar types of open-ended questions based on case studies.

The time required to grade writing assignments and essay questions can be a deterrent to using them in large classes. Some instructors have relied on calibrated peer grading as a way to overcome this obstacle, particularly for low-stakes assessments in introductory courses; grading each other's written responses can also be a learning experience for students (see, for example, Freeman and Parks, 2010).

Assessments of group work

Because students often work in groups in research-based classes, some instructors have incorporated a group dimension into their assessments. These approaches require students to direct their collaborative skills toward an end result that "counts"—just as professionals collaborate on work products—and enables instructors to assess collaborative skills as well as individual knowledge. As students work together on assessment questions or problems, they must defend their reasoning and listen to others, so the assessment itself becomes a group learning activity.

Group assessment can be challenging. Smith (1998) and many others recommend including assessments of *individual* as well as group performance, even in a cooperative learning environment. In addition, grading assessments on a curve, in which students are graded relative to the performance of others and grades are assigned to fit into a predetermined distribution, does not align well with the spirit of cooperative learning.

Instructors have developed various approaches for combining group and individual forms of assessment in the same course. A popular one is the "two-stage" exam, which students first do individually and then redo collaboratively.

---

[8] Interview, July 2, 2013.

Two-stage exams are relatively easy to implement, can benefit learning, and are consistent with collaborative approaches to learning (Yuretich et al., 2001).

Mark Leckie and Richard Yuretich were early innovators of the two-stage exam approach in their geosciences courses at the University of Massachusetts Amherst (see Box 5.1).

BOX 5.1 TWO-STAGE EXAMS—ASSESSMENTS THAT *PRODUCE* LEARNING

How does an instructor balance the need for individually graded performance with the philosophy of cooperative learning? Geosciences professors Mark Leckie and Richard Yuretich[a] at UMass Amherst have come up with a method that Leckie describes as "very, very successful" and Yuretich calls the "number one" most effective piece of their course. Since the late 1990s, the instructors, who teach an oceanography course built on findings from research, have administered two-stage exams (Yuretich et al., 2001). These exams, which consist of about 25 multiple-choice questions, are given after each unit, or five times during the semester, in addition to a comprehensive final exam. (See Chapter 1 for a description of Yuretich's approach to pedagogy.)

The procedure goes like this: The students take the exam twice during a 75-minute class. The first time they take it individually. Then they turn in their answer sheets but keep the exam itself. The students are issued new answer sheets, and they retake the same exam "open book, open notes, and talking with their neighbors," says Leckie. "The whole room erupts in conversation. It's really kind of satisfying to watch them engage with each other. If you think about it, it becomes an active learning environment where they're discussing and debating and trying to convince each other of what the right answer is." While the few students who might be reluctant to "give away" their answers to others are not required to talk during this phase, most students

---

[a] Except where noted, the information in this case study comes from interviews with Mark Leckie, March 22, 2013, and Richard Yuretich, April 4, 2013.

Other assessment methods

Many other assessment techniques are compatible with research-based approaches to teaching and learning. The examples that follow illustrate just some of the possibilities.

In her biology classes at Michigan State University, Diane Ebert-May[9] bases her exam questions on daily learning objectives. The exams are aligned with the types of activities students do in class, such as analyzing real data, developing

welcome the opportunity. "I'll never forget the first time we did it; people were exiting the room and thanking you for an exam," says Leckie.

Seventy-five percent of a student's grade is based on the individual part of the exam, and 25 percent on the group part. To encourage collaboration and open discussion during the group phase of the exam, a score on the group part is not counted if it lowers a student's grade (Yuretich et al., 2001). The scoring is designed to be a "win-win," Leckie explains. Typically, the group score bumps up a student's grade a bit. "People learn that they can't not study for a test and take it the second time and get 100 percent," says Leckie.

By engaging students in active learning and critical thinking *during* the exam, the cooperative format has "increased the value of the exams as a learning experience," according to a study by Yuretich and his colleagues (2001, p. 115). This study included comments from students to illustrate how students prepare for the exam and negotiate their answers during the group part (p. 116):

- "In one case, studying involved simulating the group process of the exam in the home: 'I study with . . . five other people . . . we get in a big group and discuss it because we're going to be doing that in class anyway, and I benefit from that.'"

- "Students stated that they will change their answer on the group part of the exam 'usually because of peer pressure, but sometimes someone will give an explanation that sounds correct since they back it up with a scientific explanation.'"

- "One student's group '[went] over each question, and it's never just the answer is A, it's always: well, no, I disagree, why is it A?'"

When Leckie and Yuretich give presentations around the country, they realize how the idea of a cooperative exam has caught on elsewhere. "I've always been interested to hear a junior faculty member describing for me this really fascinating two-stage exam she's tried," says Leckie. "It's fun to hear it come back to you."

---

[9] Interview, April 17, 2013.

models, and structuring arguments based on evidence. One question intended to assess students' understanding of the dynamics of the carbon cycle—the sequence of events by which carbon is exchanged among Earth's biosphere, geosphere, hydrosphere, and atmosphere—presents students with the following scenario (Ebert-May, Batzli, and Lim, 2003):

> Grandma Johnson had very sentimental feelings toward Johnson Canyon, Utah, where she and her late husband had honeymooned long ago. Because of these feelings, when she died she requested to be buried under a creosote bush in the canyon. Describe below the path of a carbon atom from Grandma Johnson's remains, to inside the leg muscle of a coyote. Be as detailed as you can be about the various molecular forms that the carbon atom might be in as it travels from Grandma Johnson to the coyote. **NOTE:** The coyote does not dig up and consume any part of Grandma Johnson's remains.

To answer the question correctly, students must "trace carbon from organic sources in Grandma Johnson, through cellular respiration by decomposers and into the atmosphere as carbon dioxide, into plants via photosynthesis and biosynthesis, to herbivores via digestion and biosynthesis that eat the plants, and finally to the coyote, which consumes an herbivore" (D'Avanzo et al., n.d.). The question is also useful for identifying students' misconceptions about carbon cycling in an ecosphere.

Robin Wright[10] and her University of Minnesota colleagues who teach active learning biology courses based on the Student-Centered Active Learning Environment with Upside-down Pedagogies (SCALE-UP) model (see Chapter 4) "try in every way to represent the authentic work of the discipline" in their classes, and this extends to assessment. The "culminating experience" for each class, says Wright, is a poster session in which students present and discuss their team projects, which they have worked on for several weeks. In this type of authentic assessment, students demonstrate their mastery of essential knowledge and skills by performing a task of the sort that scientists do in their professional life. Students in Wright's active learning courses also do take-home exams that consist of just a few essay questions. Students can raise their grade on these exams by doing a reflection piece in which they analyze their strengths and weaknesses, consider the sources of information they used to answer questions, and develop a strategy for improvement.

In chemistry, researchers have developed a Metacognitive Activities Inventory (MCAI) to assess students' use of metacognitive strategies in problem

---

[10] Interview, April 12, 2013.

solving (Sandi-Urena et al., 2011). Data from this type of assessment can be used to determine interventions that are attuned to students' metacognitive level.

In addition to assessing academic learning and cognitive processes, some instructors also assess the affective domain—students' attitudes, beliefs, and expectations—which can influence their motivation to study science or engineering and their performance in these disciplines. An awareness of these characteristics can help instructors adjust their teaching to improve student learning, reduce attrition, and keep students in the science, technology, engineering, and mathematics (STEM) pipeline (McConnell and van der Hoeven Kraft, 2011). Several validated instruments are available to measure aspects of the affective domain.

Kaatje Kraft,[11] formerly a geology instructor at Arizona's Mesa Community College who currently teaches at Whatcom Community College in Washington, is one of more than a dozen instructors across the country who are participating in the Geoscience Affective Research NETwork (GARNET), a National Science Foundation (NSF)-funded effort to study the attitudes and motivation of students in introductory geology classes as a way to improve their learning. Kraft shares individualized pre- and post-responses from the GARNET assessments with her students and encourages them to use these data to reflect on how their motivation, self-regulation, and related characteristics affect their learning.

You should not feel limited by these examples. Many science and engineering instructors have adapted ideas from the general literature on assessment, such as the numerous techniques for classroom formative assessment suggested by Angelo and Cross (1993) and the general principles articulated in *Knowing What Students Know* (National Research Council, 2001). Additional assessment ideas are available in the 2012 NRC report on DBER and from professional networks and curriculum websites, such as On the Cutting Edge. The most important considerations are to choose assessments that are aligned with learning objectives and that engage authentic scientific or engineering thinking.

Evaluating the impact of instructional changes

The main reason for adopting research-based instructional practices is to improve students' learning and academic success. To determine whether you are meeting this goal, you need to assess the impact of any changes you are making, just as you would in a research study in your discipline. As discussed in Chapter 2,

---

[11] Interview, June 13, 2013.

> "You need to know what the results of your current practices are in terms of student learning, and you need to be able to compare them with what your reformed practices are. That was crucial to us. Otherwise it's all anecdote."
>
> —*John Belcher,*
> *Massachusetts Institute of Technology*

evaluating your teaching does not require you to do formal DBER studies, but it does mean analyzing some type of assessment data over time.

This type of evaluation of your courses can serve several purposes. It can indicate how well the reforms you have undertaken are working and reveal areas for future adjustments. It can help convince your department head and colleagues that your approaches are more effective than traditional instruction. It can provide evidence you can share with your students to explain why you are asking them to do certain things and how they are benefiting. And perhaps most importantly, it can convince *you* that the effort you've invested in reforming your teaching is worthwhile.

When John Belcher[12] began the Technology-Enabled Active Learning (TEAL) project in his physics classes at the Massachusetts Institute of Technology (MIT), he had already seen earlier teaching innovations come and go—in some cases because they lacked sufficient evidence to demonstrate their effectiveness to colleagues and to students who complained about the changes. Belcher recognized that having good assessment data could help increase the staying power of an innovation like TEAL, which uses media-rich technology to help students visualize and hypothesize about conceptual models of electromagnetic phenomena (Dori and Belcher, 2005). Students in TEAL classes conduct desktop experiments and engage in other types of active learning in a specially designed studio space.

As part of the TEAL project, which began in 2000, Belcher and his colleague Yehudit Judy Dori, who was then on sabbatical from Technion–Israel Institute of Technology, developed pre- and post-tests to measure students' conceptual understanding and determine the effectiveness of the visualizations and experiments. The TEAL students showed significantly higher gains in conceptual understanding of the subject matter than their peers in a control group (Dori and Belcher, 2005).

---

[12] Interview, July 9, 2013.

These assessment data were instrumental to TEAL's survival, says Belcher. When TEAL first made the transition in 2003 from a small-scale pilot to a large-scale project affecting nearly 600 introductory students per semester, the shift caused some organizational upheaval, and additional faculty had to be trained. "We got a lot of pushback from students," says Belcher. "If I hadn't had a lot of quantitative numbers in terms of assessment, I think we would have died that first year. Someone would say, 'They don't like it,' and I would say, 'I know they don't like it, but they're learning twice as much.' And I had reasonable proof that this was the case; it wasn't just my anecdotal feeling. I think that carried us through the first couple of years."

Belcher advises other practitioners who are undertaking major revisions in teaching to emphasize assessment in the early years. "You need to know what the results of your current practices are in terms of student learning, and you need to be able to compare them with what your reformed practices are. That was crucial to us. Otherwise it's all anecdote—it would be my anecdote against other people's anecdote[s]."

Many of the assessments described earlier in this chapter can be used to evaluate the impact of instruction as well as to assess individual students' learning. For example, an instructor might compare the post-tests of a group of students taught through a research-based approach with a control group of traditionally taught students.

Finally, as the 2012 NRC report on DBER emphasizes, DBER is a young and growing field. Some instructors who begin by assessing the impact of instructional reforms in their own classrooms may find this a stimulating area of scholarship and may choose to develop their expertise by not only using DBER, but also conducting DBER. Those who are so inclined will find many opportunities for contributions from new scholars.

Using Technology Effectively

Technologies for teaching and learning have particular relevance to science and engineering education. Becoming adept at using the technological tools of a discipline is part of the practice of science and engineering. In addition, technologies for learning, when used well, can advance research-based instruction through their capacity to engage students, facilitate interaction, and enable students to use hands-on approaches to explore scientific phenomena. Many technological tools have been expressly developed or adapted to suit the needs of research-based instruction. These range from the relatively simple, like clickers, to the more sophisticated, like interactive computer-based simulations.

The 2012 NRC report on DBER concludes that technologies for learning hold promise for improving undergraduate science and engineering but with this important proviso:

> Research on the use of various learning technologies suggests that technology can enhance students' learning, retention of knowledge, and attitudes about science learning. However, the presence of learning technologies alone does not improve outcomes. Instead, those outcomes appear to depend on how the technology is used. (p. 137)

Findings from research and advice from experienced practitioners about effective and ineffective uses of technologies can guide instructors' decisions about when and how to use these tools.

Learning goals drive technology choices

Before deciding whether and how to use technology in a course and which technologies to use, you need a clear set of learning goals and good assessments. You can then consider how technology can assist in meeting these goals and measuring students' progress. This point became clear to Edward Price, a physics professor at California State University San Marcos (CSUSM) as he experimented with a variety of technologies for teaching and learning physics.

"Don't Erase That Whiteboard" and Other Lessons from Teaching with Technology

Clickers, whiteboards, videos, simulations, tablet PCs, and photo-sharing websites—Edward Price[a] has tried these technologies and others in his physics classes at CSUSM. In the process, he has come to understand how various technologies affect classroom interactions and which tools work best with his teaching approach and student learning objectives.

"You have to have your own pedagogical goals and other goals for engaging the students, and that should drive your use of technology; it shouldn't be the other way around," says Price. "If you have some cool, neat toy it has to serve some purpose."

With this basic principle in mind, Price has changed how he uses technology over time. Price and several colleagues have developed a research-based, active learning curriculum called Learning Physics for larger enrollment classes taught in lecture halls (Price et al., 2013a). The curriculum incorporates videos of experiments and hands-on activities that students can perform in groups on small, lecture-hall desks. The pedagogy is designed to enable students to develop a deep understanding of such concepts as the conservation of energy and Newton's laws, as well as an understanding of important aspects of scientific thinking and the nature of science.

An earlier version of this curriculum used videos of experiments shot on the CSUSM campus but did not include a hands-on component. In many ways, the videos were successful, says Price. They took less time than hands-on experiments and they had some powerful features, such as allowing instructors to put two processes side by side to facilitate direct comparisons or to use a time-lapse feature for processes that took a long time. "But at the end of the day, doing experiments is an important practice in science. We wanted students to have an opportunity to do that for themselves," he says.

In later versions of the curriculum, students watch videos of experiments for about half of the class period and do hands-on experiments for the other half. Videos are used for experiments that are not practical to do in a large class, such as those that require expensive or complicated equipment or take up too much time or desk space. Hands-on experiments are used to teach concepts that students can study with inexpensive materials in a reasonable time and to give them practice in interpreting observations.

Students conduct the experiments, which take from 5 to 15 minutes, in groups of three or four. For example, as part of a unit on magnetism, students float various materials on a styrofoam disk in a bowl of water and see if a magnet reacts to them and whether the interactions are different for a rubbed and an unrubbed magnet. To aid students in setting up the experiments properly without wasting time, the instructors provide short videos or photos of what the setup should look like.

Clickers also play a role in Price's classes. After students have watched a video or a simulation, they discuss the outcome with a neighbor, and then they vote on their conclusions with clickers. When students conduct an experiment, they answer clicker questions as a way to establish a consensus about their results. "That kind of mirrors how things work in science, where you establish a consensus," says Price. "Students appreciate that because

_____
[a] Except where noted, the information in this case study comes from an interview with Edward Price, August 23, 2013.

they have some uncertainty about whether the outcome observed is the one we intended them to see. The whole-class vote and discussion gives them a lot more confidence in doing the experiments."

Students in Price's courses often use whiteboards to brainstorm, solve problems, and present results to the rest of the class (Price et al., 2011). The low-tech whiteboard has several features that make it a suitable collaborative work-space. "It's big, it's very approachable, it's easy to start with—I joke that the whiteboard always boots up," says Price. The work that students display on whiteboards is a valuable record of their thinking, but this record is lost when the whiteboard is erased. Price and his colleagues hit upon a technological solution to this problem, which they tried out in an introductory physics course for biology majors. Using wireless-enabled digital cameras, they created an archive of students' work on the photo-sharing web-site Flickr.com. With Flickr, images can be organized into hierarchical collections that match the course structure. Flickr also supports tags and comments, which enable students, instructors, or learning assis-tants to discuss or ask questions about an image (Price et al., 2011).

"The availability of the photo archive changed the class culture in an unintended but productive way," write the researchers (Price et al., 2011, p. 427). "Before Flickr was used, whiteboards were seldom corrected during the class discussions. Errors were pointed out, but there was typically no rea-son to mark them, especially since the whiteboards would be erased when the class moved on to a new topic." After the whiteboards were archived

on Flickr, however, students began correcting their whiteboards in class so that the photo would pre-serve an accurate solution. Whether this behavior stemmed from a desire to have a useful and clear photo archive or from an effort to avoid embarrass-ment, the act of photographing the whiteboards "initiated a final round of instructor feedback and student revision that presumably helps students con-solidate their understandings." This process of stu-dents correcting their solutions is another example of how technology can restructure a classroom.

In some of their courses, Price and his colleagues have used tablet computers and Ubiquitous Presenter software as an alternative to whiteboards (Price et al., 2011). With these technologies, students can write on the tablet screen as they would on a whiteboard and then send their work to the instructor, who can pre-view, project, and annotate submissions from any of the groups in the class. The instructor can also create and write on lecture slides. The student submissions, instructor slides, and annotations are automatically archived and can be reviewed on a website. Students have made extensive use of this Web archive, and in an end-of-semester survey, 75 percent of students reported that access to other students' work was use-

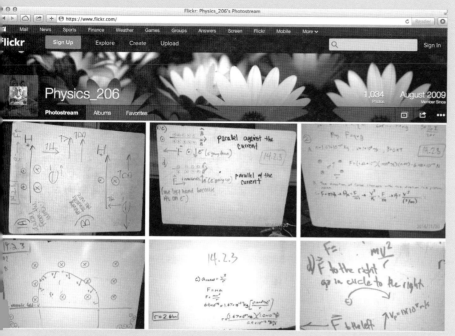

Example of Flickr whiteboard photo archive.

explanations of the scientific phenomena they have studied in class. Students write a response to a prompt in the CPR system. Then they use instructor-prepared questions to evaluate sample responses and receive feedback on their evaluations, which allows them to "calibrate" their evaluation skills. Students then score their peers' work. "As the instructor, my role shifts to developing these materials but with less of an emphasis on grading them," he explains. "The students' role changes dramatically. They're put in the position of having to become expert enough to evaluate other people's work. It's a really different kind of expectation." Price and his colleagues have independently analyzed the validity of the CPR tool as used with the Learning Physics curriculum and found that students' scores for their peers' essays correlate very closely with the instructors' own expert evaluations of the same work (Price et al., 2013b).

According to an evaluation by Price and colleagues (2013a), students taught with the Learning Physics curriculum learned significant physics content and developed more expert-like views about science and learning science. Their performance on a conceptual content assessment was similar to that of comparison students taught with an inquiry-based curriculum developed for smaller enrollment classes that met for more hours per week. Moreover, Learning Physics students outperformed the comparison group on an end-of-semester written explanation.

ful or very useful (Price et al., 2011). The instructors note, however, that these benefits must be weighed against the expense and technological complexity of the approach and the small size of the tablet screen compared with a whiteboard.

Learning is a social process, says Price, and introducing new technology or changing the technology can impact that social process. The experience with the photo archive of students' whiteboard work illustrates this. He suggests that instructors think beyond what a particular technology enables them to do and also consider "How is it going to restructure the roles of the different people in the classroom? How is it going to change the social interactions?"

In Price's classroom, one technology that has transformed the students' and instructor's roles is Calibrated Peer Review (CPR), a Web-based tool developed at the University of California, Los Angeles, that enables students to learn and apply a structured process for evaluating their own and their peers' written work. In a class of 100 students, it is difficult for the instructor to read and grade writing assignments with any frequency. But with CPR, Price can assign homework in which students must write

If you want to gradually integrate learning technologies into your courses, you might take some of these tips from Price's experience:

- Basic technologies like clickers—or even a whiteboard—have a place in a research-based, high-tech classroom.

- Just because a technology is new or visually impressive does not mean it will serve the purpose of increasing student interaction.

- Some technologies may prove to be more successful than others in achieving your teaching and learning goals. If a certain technology turns out to be less effective than you hoped, you can abandon it, revise its application, or try something else.

- Technologies can change how students interact with each other and with the content of your course.

- After you gain experience with various technologies, you may see possibilities for adapting new technologies to meet specific learning needs in your course.

- You need to weigh the costs of a technology against its benefits for student learning. Technologies that are expensive, time-consuming, or complicated to use may not be worth the cost or effort.

Clickers

Using clicker questions is often the first step that instructors take toward a more interactive style of teaching. But "a clicker is a technology, not a pedagogy," as pointed out by Alex Rudolph,[13] a physics and astronomy professor at California State Polytechnic University, Pomona, and an experienced clicker user.

Clickers in and of themselves do not transform learning. Their efficacy depends on how they are used. Many instructors who maintain that they are implementing research-based strategies because they have integrated some clicker questions into their lectures are omitting important elements, such as peer discussion or sufficiently challenging questions.

When used properly, clickers have certain advantages. They make it possible for instructors to obtain rapid feedback for themselves and their students. They allow instructors to collect an answer to a question from every student and hold

---

[13] Interview, August 20, 2013.

each student accountable for participating. They can tell instructors when students are disengaged or confused and why this has happened, and can help instructors immediately fix the situation. Good clicker questions can generate more discussion and questions from a much wider range of students than occur in a traditional lecture. When clickers are implemented correctly, students are more engaged and learn much more of the content covered. Students will overwhelmingly support their use and say they help their learning (Wieman et al., 2008).

"The most compelling evidence on clicker use shows that learning gains are associated only with applications that challenge students conceptually and incorporate socially mediated learning techniques" concludes the 2012 NRC report on DBER (p. 124). Examples include posing formative assessment questions at higher cognitive levels and having students discuss their responses in groups before the correct answer is revealed.

A guide on effective clicker use developed by the Science Education Initiative at the University of Colorado Boulder and the University of British Columbia contains numerous suggestions, including the advice paraphrased below (Wieman et al., 2008, p. 2).

- Have a clear idea of the goals to be achieved with clickers, and design questions to improve student engagement and interactions with each other and the instructor.

- Focus questions on particularly important concepts. Use questions that have multiple plausible answers and will reveal student confusion and generate spirited discussion.

- Take care that clicker questions are not too easy. Students learn more from challenging questions and often learn the most from questions they get wrong.

- Give students time to think about the clicker question on their own and then discuss with their peers.

- Listen in on the student discussions about clicker questions in order to understand how students think, and address student misconceptions on the spot.

Jacob Smith,[14] a student at Cal Poly Pomona, was exposed to clickers for the first time in Rudolph's physics class. The clicker questions and ensuing discussions "had the whole class engaged," he says. "I learned different ways [that]

---

[14] Interview, August 23, 2013.

people's thought processes worked—how they would develop their idea and why they believed it was correct." Formulating an explanation to convince another student who disagreed with him "helped me engage my mind to better grasp each concept," he adds.

Research by Michelle Smith and colleagues (2009) has found that the peer discussion process enhances students' understanding even when none of the students in a group initially knows the correct answer. A representative comment from a student in the study by Smith and colleagues clarifies how this works: "Often when talking through the questions, the group can figure out the questions without originally knowing the answer, and the answer almost always sticks better that way because we talked through it instead of just hearing the answer." In addition, the authors note, students develop communication and metacognitive skills when they have to explain their reasoning to a peer.

> You need to weigh the costs of a technology against its benefits for student learning. Technologies that are expensive, time-consuming, or complicated to use may not be worth the cost or effort.

Conversations around clicker questions can cause students to confront their misconceptions and realize they have to adjust their thinking, says Derek Bruff,[15] director of the Center for Teaching at Vanderbilt University. "That idea of collective cognitive dissonance is exciting," he adds. A common faculty error is to use clicker questions that are too easy, he points out; all that does is "ensure at some minimal level the students were awake." Another common failing occurs when a large percentage of students answer incorrectly and the instructor quickly gives the correct answer and moves on; a better approach is to give students time to discuss and rethink their answers, and then to follow up with additional clarifications if necessary.

Simulations, animations, and interactive demonstrations

Other popular learning technologies used in science and engineering courses include simulations, animations, and interactive demonstrations. These tools can help students visualize, represent, and understand scientific phenomena or engineering design problems. While more research is needed on their educational efficacy and the conditions under which they are effective, expert practitioners around the country have studied and used these tools and found them to be valuable teaching and learning aids.

---

[15] Interview, April 29, 2013.

One research-validated example of this type of tool is the suite of Interactive Lecture Demonstrations developed by David Sokoloff and Ron Thornton (discussed in Chapter 3). Another example is the collection of PhET (Physics Education Technology) simulations developed at the University of Colorado Boulder (see Box 5.2).

In chemistry, Michael Abraham and John Gelder (n.d.) at the University of Oklahoma have developed interactive Web-based simulations of molecular structures and processes, along with materials for using these simulations as part of an inquiry-based instructional approach. For example, students can use a Web-based simulation of Boyle's law to observe the activity of molecules in a gas sample and collect data and answer questions about the relationship between gas pressure and volume. Abraham, Varghese, and Tang (2010) have also studied the influence of animated and static visualizations on conceptual understanding and found that two- and three-dimensional animations of molecular structures and processes appear to improve student learning of stereochemistry, which concerns the spatial arrangement of atoms within molecules.

Numerous other simulations, animations, demonstrations, and videos are available for use in research-based science and engineering classrooms. Here are some issues to consider when using these types of tools:

- Interactive simulations are flexible enough to be used in a variety of class settings, but they are most effective when they are used in ways that encourage students to predict and discuss possible outcomes and propose "what if" scenarios, or that allow students to explore the simulation for themselves.

- Simulations that are *interactive* are particularly well suited to research-based instruction because they enable students to develop and test their conceptual understanding by changing different variables.

- Well-designed simulations have some advantages over real-life experiments because they can be designed to help students see a phenomenon in the way that experts do. They can also require less class time, fewer materials, and less space to carry out.

- Simulations and interactive demonstrations can be ineffective for learning if an instructor's demonstration omits opportunities for student predictions, discussion, and suggestions, or if an instructor discourages student exploration by being too prescriptive about what to do.

A student scrutinizes an image on a computer screen that simulates fluid running through a pipe. What will happen to the velocity of the fluid if a section of the pipe is constricted from 2 meters to 1 meter? Using the mouse, the student narrows a section of the pipe and sees that the velocity of the flow increases through the narrower passage. She calculates the change in pressure between the 2-meter and the 1-meter diameter and writes down the answer. Now, what will happen if the density of the fluid is changed from that of water to that of honey?[a]

This is one of dozens of PhET simulations developed at Colorado. These interactive simulations enable students to make connections between real-life physical phenomena and the underlying scientific concepts. The PhET simulations are based on research findings about how students learn in science disciplines and have been extensively tested and evaluated for educational effectiveness, usability, and student engagement (University of Colorado Boulder, 2013).

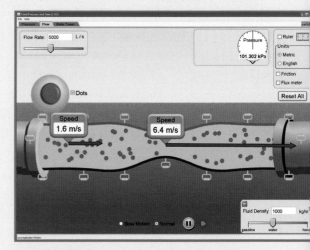

PhET simulation.

The first group of simulations was developed for physics, but simulations have since been added in other science disciplines and for the elementary through undergraduate levels. As of early 2014, 128 simulations were available for free on the Web.

"An important goal for these simulations is to help students connect the science to the world around them. We try to embed it in the context of something familiar," says. Kathy Perkins,[b] a Colorado physics professor who directs the PhET project. "Students can get engaged in scientist-like explorations to discover and build up the main concepts behind a particular topic."

The PhET simulations include appealing graphics, and students can manipulate certain variables with the easy-to-use controls. The simulations encourage students to explore quantitative changes through measurement instruments such as rulers, stop-watches, voltmeters, and thermometers. "As the students work with the simulation, they can be asking their own questions, and the simulation will help them answer those questions by what it shows," Perkins explains.

Another simulation allows users to build circuits involving lifelike resistors, lightbulbs, wires, batteries, and switches.[c] They can measure voltages and currents with realistic meters and see lightbulbs lighting up. Unlike real-life experiments, the PhET simulations show visual representations of the models that experts use to understand phenomena that are invisible to the naked eye—in this case, the flow of electrons around the circuit and how their velocity changes in response to changes in the circuit (Wieman and Perkins, 2005). One of the common student misconceptions about circuits is that "students think that current is used up in the circuit—that it starts out large and gets used up, and there's zero current at the end," Perkins notes. "But showing the electrons flowing around helps to mitigate that

---

[a] See http://phet.colorado.edu/en/simulation/fluid-pressure-and-flow.

[b] Interview, June 18, 2013.

[c] See http://phet.colorado.edu/en/simulation/circuit-construction-kit-dc.

difficulty because they can see that the current isn't changing; they see the electrons are not slowing down, they are not losing them."

This ability to replicate expert-like perception is one of the advantages that a carefully designed computer simulation has over a real-life experiment, write Wieman and Perkins (2005). In a simulation, certain important features of a scientific phenomenon can be enhanced while peripheral features that would distract students in a real experiment can be hidden; and time scales and other features can be adjusted to point students to the desired perception. In addition, using an existing simulation often takes less preparation time than assembling the materials for a traditional experiment.

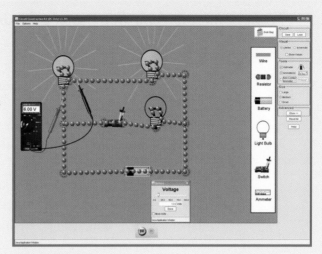

Circuit simulation.

The simulations can be integrated into class instruction in various ways, says Perkins. She often recommends that instructors start by allowing students to explore the simulation on their own for a few minutes, which helps students gain some familiarity with how it works and generate their own questions. Then the instructor can move into a guided activity with the simulation—"not telling students what to touch and do exactly, but asking open-ended questions where the simulation is providing the 'sandbox' in which to explore these questions," Perkins says.

Integrating the simulations with interactive teaching techniques is preferable to simply using them as a visual demonstration during a lecture, in Perkins's view. When the simulations are used in a lecture, Perkins suggests that instructors first have students predict the outcome and discuss their predictions before showing them the simulation. This might be done through a clicker question, such as asking students to predict, vote on, and discuss what will happen to the brightness of one of the lightbulbs in a circuit if a certain switch is closed. After the instructor demonstrates the simulation, students can then propose changes in certain variables—for example, "'What if you add another battery? What if you flip that battery around? What if those are in parallel instead of in series?' I call that whole class inquiry," says Perkins, "when you're operating the simulation up front but the questions are coming from the students." Alternatively, instructors in a large lecture class could use the simulations as tutorials that students do on their own laptops or in groups.

In smaller classrooms, simulations can form the basis of collaborative student activities, says Perkins. For example, for the PhET simulation on projectile motion, the instructor might challenge the students to explore all the ways in which they can make the projectile go further. Simulations can also be used for pre-lab learning or in the labs themselves "At [the University of Colorado] we have circuit labs with the simulations and real-world equipment in the same lab, where students will be going back and forth."

Simulations can also be used ineffectively, Perkins cautions. "One of the things we see that really short circuits the learning from the simulations is when you give students really explicit directions about what to set up"—in other words, when they are used "in a cookbook style."

Other computer- and Web-based technologies

Computers and Web-based technologies are essential to the practice of science and engineering, and their applications to undergraduate education in these disciplines are innumerable. The following examples highlight a few of the ways in which computer technologies are being used to enhance teaching and learning, facilitate student-teacher and peer-to-peer interaction, and encourage students to take greater responsibility for their own learning.

Workshop Physics, a research-validated approach developed at Dickinson College by Priscilla Laws and her colleagues, teaches calculus-based introductory physics without formal lectures (Dickinson College, 2004). Instead, students learn collaboratively by conducting activities and observations entirely in the laboratory, using the latest computer technology. The process encourages students "to make predictions, discuss their predictions with each other, test their predictions by doing real activities, and then draw conclusions," says Laws.[16] In addition to directly observing real phenomena, students in Workshop Physics use computers to collect, graphically display, analyze, and model real data with greater speed and efficiency than they otherwise could. Recently, Laws and a group of colleagues have created and are evaluating Web-based, interactive video vignettes that demonstrate physics topics like Newton's third law.[17]

In many undergraduate geosciences courses, students are using Google Earth to support hands-on projects, create maps and models, measure features, organize geospatial data, and accomplish many other purposes (Science Education Research Center, 2013).

Some science and engineering instructors and students are using blogs, social media, and other common Web resources to promote student interaction and learning. John Pollard at the University of Arizona has created a YouTube "Chemical Thinking" channel on which he posts videos he made to explain general chemistry concepts.[18] Facebook groups are also an important part of Pollard's class, says student Courtney Collingwood,[19] who took the course in 2013. "People will post, and Pollard or Talanquer will answer. There's a lot of opportunity for help if people are willing to ask," she says.

Students in Eric Brewe's introductory modeling physics course at FIU decided to put together a course "textbook" in the form of a class wiki as a study

---

[16] Interview, July 30, 2013.
[17] See http://ivv.rit.edu.
[18] See http://www.youtube.com/user/CHEMXXl.
[19] Interview, April 24, 2013.

resource.[20] Students took turns doing the wiki page for each class session, and other students could make comments, additions, and suggestions.

Learning Spaces

Many instructors vacillate about adopting student-centered instruction because they are not sure it can be done in an auditorium with fixed seats or other standard classrooms designed for large enrollment courses. But this is more a problem of mindset than of physical constraints, as illustrated by the case study of Scott Freeman's biology class in Chapter 1 and other examples in the preceding chapters. Many DBER studies directly address the viability of using student-centered approaches in large classes, and the evidence emerging from these studies has been quite positive. In addition, clickers, computer-based simulations, and other technologies have been particularly useful in facilitating interaction in large courses, as the previous discussion makes clear.

That said, some instructors, departments, and institutions have designed or redesigned learning spaces that are particularly suitable for interaction, group work, project-based learning, and other research-based approaches. These redesigns are typically accompanied by dramatic changes in instruction, including reductions in the amount of lecturing and the integration of lecture and laboratory courses. These models for redesigning learning spaces are particularly worth considering when an institution is planning a remodeling or new construction program.

Early examples of redesigning learning spaces in conjunction with reforms in pedagogy include the Workshop Physics approach described above and Studio Physics, an integrated lecture/laboratory model developed at Rensselaer Polytechnic Institute in 1993. The best known example is the SCALE-UP approach, which as of 2013 was being implemented at 250 sites in the United States, including North Carolina State University, MIT, the University of Minnesota, Old Dominion University, and many other institutions. While the motive for redesigning the learning space in many of these sites was to promote more active learning in courses of 100 or more students, the approach has also been used in smaller settings of 50 students or fewer. The SCALE-UP model is described in Chapter 4; what follows in Box 5.3 is a discussion of how institutions adopting this approach have transformed the classroom environment.

---

[20] Interview, April 16, 2013.

At NC State, a pioneer of the SCALE-UP model, the redesigned classroom space is an obvious departure from the standard lecture hall. The room holds roughly 100 students. The students sit at 11 round tables arranged banquet-style, each large enough to accommodate 9 students working in teams of 3. Everything about the room's design—from the three networked laptops, whiteboards, and lab equipment on every table to the strategically placed larger whiteboards and computer screens that afford every student a view—is intended to maximize collaboration and hands-on work among students and interaction between students and faculty.

Robert Beichner,[a] an NC State physics professor who was frustrated with the stadium seating, wooden chairs, and wobbly paddle-shaped desks in his institution's lecture halls, approached his department head about designing an optimum space for the types of research-based strategies he wanted to use. He was told that if he could find matching funds, the department would provide the furniture. He obtained grant money from NSF and the U.S. Department of Education's former Fund for the Improvement of Postsecondary Education (FIPSE) program and found a space on campus that could be remodeled.

The transformed learning space sent an obvious signal to students that teaching and learning in SCALE-UP classes would be different. "[Students] know how a lecture hall is supposed to be used—you essentially sit and write down notes," says Beichner. "When you walk into a space that's different, your expectations are violated."

Beichner recognizes that institutional issues, including funding constraints, competition for space allocation, and scheduling, make this type of renovation

[a] Interview, March 26, 2013.

Phase II classroom seating 55 before renovation.

Phase II SCALE-UP classroom seating 54 after renovation.

Phase III classroom seating 99 students.

Robert Beichner believes his role in a SCALE-UP classroom is to listen to students and guide their thinking.

difficult to undertake. If an institution is willing to commit to this approach, he recommends that the faculty involved be specific about what they want and closely monitor the remodeling process. Often the people who do the work are not accustomed to faculty being particular about such details as the size of the tables or the placement of projection screens and ceiling lights, but these types of design features affect learning, Beichner says.

At the University of Minnesota, another institution that has adopted or adapted the SCALE-UP approach, the biology department's plan to transform a course using an active learning approach coincided with the Office of Classroom Management's plan to remodel a learning space. The biology department offered to combine one of its classrooms with an adjacent room controlled by Classroom Management in order to create a larger classroom patterned after NC State's SCALE-UP design, says Minnesota biology professor Robin Wright.[b] The result was the creation of the university's first remodeled active learning classroom. The success of this first classroom helped to convince her university to incorporate 17 additional active learning classrooms in a new campus building.

In Minnesota's active learning classrooms, "the space invites" student peer-to-peer discussion and innovative instructional approaches, says Wright. The feedback on the redesigned rooms has been positive among faculty members who have taught there, she reports. "Generally, faculty said they never want to teach any other way."

SCALE-UP classrooms are also equipped with computer-based simulations and many other technological supports for project-based learning. And what does Beichner consider the most important technology in the room? "The round tables."

---

[b] Interview, April 12, 2013.

While these types of redesigned classroom spaces can facilitate active learning, they are expensive and may not always be feasible. If the opportunity for remodeling or construction arises, then a department or institution should give thought to research on learning in their design. But if the opportunity is not there, a redesigned classroom is by no means necessary to realize the benefits of research-based instruction. As Colorado professor Steve Pollack[21] notes, instructors can adopt "transformed pedagogy in old-fashioned classrooms."

Conclusion

This chapter has offered ideas for appropriately assessing learning and teaching, using technology effectively, and redesigning classroom spaces when that option is available. These and other aspects of research-based instruction are likely to present challenges, but these challenges need not derail you. They can be tackled head-on, as discussed in Chapter 6.

Resources and Further Reading

Discipline-Based Education Research: Understanding and Improving Learning in Undergraduate Science and Engineering (National Research Council, 2012)
Chapter 6: Instructional Strategies

Interactive physics simulations
http://phet.colorado.edu

Interactive video vignettes in physics
http://ivv.rit.edu

Knowing What Students Know: The Science and Design of Educational Assessment (National Research Council, 2001)

Student-Centered Active Learning Environment with Upside-down Pedagogies (SCALE-UP)
http://scaleup.ncsu.edu

YouTube "Chemical Thinking" channel
http://www.youtube.com/user/CHEMXXl

---

[21] Interview, April 25, 2013.

Overcoming Challenges

In pursuing your scientific or engineering research you have undoubtedly encountered obstacles: an experiment or design that did not work as anticipated at first, a grant that fell through, a peer review that identified a problem in your methodology. But surmounting these obstacles can sometimes lead to greater understanding, a stronger design, and better results.

The same is true with instructional design. Many leaders in research-based instruction readily admit that some of their early attempts were not as successful as they had hoped, and many faced challenges that rattled their resolve. As in scientific research or engineering design, the best response to the inevitable stumble or obstacle is not to give up but to reflect on what you can do better, make adjustments, and persist.

"Be patient," advises Alex Rudolph,[1] a physics and astronomy professor at California State Polytechnic University, Pomona. "Don't expect everything to work the first time out. Realize that these things take time to learn and do well. . . . Be willing to try something and get better at it, because if you do it a few times you almost always get better."

Just as many of your students need time, guidance, and encouragement to be successful with new ways of learning, you will need time, practice, and support to become more comfortable and competent with new ways of teaching, and even longer to become adept. Ed Prather,[2] an astronomy professor at the University of Arizona, tells participants in his faculty development workshops that "while the first time out of the gate it might not be perfect, they're making slow and steady progress toward a goal that is part of their profession." Even instructors who have been using research-based approaches for several years continue to tweak their

---

[1] Interview, August 20, 2013.
[2] Interview, April 29, 2013.

courses to incorporate promising strategies, fine-tune their curriculum or teaching techniques, and address new challenges.

The advice in Chapter 2 to start small and revise your teaching gradually can help you gain confidence that the changes you are making are "effective, doable, and rewarding," notes Cynthia Brame,[3] assistant director of Vanderbilt University's Center for Teaching. "[E]ven a partial change in this direction can lead to significantly increased learning gains," conclude Knight and Wood (2005), and can help people adapt to challenges little by little.

This chapter offers a view from the trenches about common challenges to implementing research-based strategies and advice about how to address them. The suggestions come from experienced practitioners who have encountered and surmounted bumps in their own roads and from scholars who have studied faculty innovation.

Not all of the challenges discussed in this chapter can be fully resolved at the instructor level. Some require actions from department heads, institutional leaders, and others with broader influence. This chapter focuses on steps that can be taken at the individual level to advance research-based teaching and learning, while Chapter 7 describes what departments, institutions, and other entities can do to support these efforts.

Common Challenges to Broader Implementation

Studies of faculty adoption of instructional innovations and surveys of instructional practices in science and engineering have identified several factors that instructors often perceive as obstacles to using more research-based practices (for example, Henderson and Dancy, 2011; Jacobson, Davis, and Licklider, 1998; Knight and Wood, 2005):

- Time involved in learning about new strategies and redesigning courses

- Concerns about ensuring that students are taught important content

- Concerns about students' reactions to an unfamiliar teaching method and the impact on student course evaluations

- Concerns that a different strategy will not work as well, especially if it impacts tenure

---

[3] Interview, April 29, 2013.

- Departmental norms about teaching methods and other expectations

- Class size and classroom facilities

- Course scheduling issues

Although some of these factors are more myth than reality, several can present genuine challenges. Henderson, Dancy, and Niewiadomska-Bugaj (2012) suggest that about one-third of the faculty who try at least one research-based strategy abandon their reform efforts, often when they are confronted with implementation challenges, such as student complaints, concerns about losing important content, or weaker than expected student outcomes. In addition, faculty members frequently modify a research-based strategy to suit their needs—a reasonable reaction, but one that can compromise effectiveness *if* the modifications omit elements that are critical to the strategy's success.

The good news is that real challenges can be overcome, particularly if departmental and institutional leaders can be brought on board to address challenges that cannot be dealt with by individuals alone. Of the faculty in multiple science disciplines at the University of British Columbia (UBC) who adopted research-based instructional strategies with the support of the Carl Wieman Science Education Initiative, only a tiny fraction—1 out of 70 individuals—quit using them, according to a study by Wieman, Deslauriers, and Gilley (2013). In addition, more than 90 percent of the faculty adopters in the UBC physics and geosciences departments, both of which had grants of five or more years to transform their undergraduate courses, started using research-based strategies in other courses when they had the opportunity, with minimal or no support from the Initiative. Sections taught using research-based instruction had better student attendance, higher student engagement, and greater learning gains than sections taught in traditional ways (Wieman, Deslauriers, and Gilley, 2013). The study authors speculate that the direct support provided to adopting faculty members by a trained science education specialist in their discipline was instrumental in helping them persist through the initial stages of implementation, and that a supportive departmental environment was also a critical factor.

While departmental and institutional support is desirable and helpful, the lack of this support is not an excuse for retaining the status quo. Individual instructors can still adopt and advocate for research-based strategies even without the active involvement of their department or institution. Some well-known pioneers of research-based practices report that when they started out many years

ago, their department provided little to no encouragement for their efforts or took a neutral stance—or "tolerated" them as long as they brought in grant money, as one senior professor of physics at a state university noted.

In fact, many of the programs, models, and strategies highlighted in this book began with one or a few instructors who were committed to improving their practice. While "lasting change is not created by lone visionaries" (Chasteen et al., 2012, p. 75), individuals can plant a seed that blooms, propagates, and flourishes with the right sustenance from colleagues and institutional leaders.

"The thing that transforms a department is not the department but the faculty in the department," says Eric Brewe,[4] a physics professor at Florida International University. "If I'm a department chair and I want to change the way my faculty teach, [I] have to support it—commit resources to it. But the research on institutional change says that once you get to 20 percent of an organization, you can start to see some momentum. In a department of, say, 30 faculty members, that's 6 people. That's not too much to ask for." This speaks to the need for instructors in the vanguard of reform to reach out to their colleagues in their own institution.

_____
[4] Interview, April 16, 2013.

The sections that follow examine the most common challenges that can be addressed by individuals—those relating to time, content, and student reactions—and offer ideas for overcoming them. In addition, the chapter suggests ways in which instructors can expand their knowledge and skills in research-based practices so they are better prepared to face implementation challenges and to secure funding and other resources to support more ambitious reforms. A final section suggests ways in which individual instructors can help to create a departmental or an institutional culture that fosters research-based innovations in teaching and learning. Broader challenges that require actions from departments or institutions, such as those related to tenure, departmental expectations, class size, and scheduling, are addressed in Chapter 7.

Taking Time for Reform

Finding time to learn about research-based approaches and to redesign courses is one of the greatest challenges to implementation. Science and engineering faculty members work an average of 55 to 60 hours per week (Fairweather, 2005). Although they may be interested in research findings about effective teaching and learning, most cannot afford to spend an unspecified amount of work time figuring out how to apply these findings to their own practices (Fairweather, 2008).

Faculty at research universities may be hesitant to take time away from their own research, especially if they're seeking tenure, and from related tasks such as supervising graduate students and writing papers and proposals. As discussed more in Chapter 7, teaching is often viewed as a lesser priority, and one that is not promoted by the institutional reward structure. Instructors with heavy teaching loads may fear that redesigning their courses could mean they must spend even more time developing materials, preparing for class, meeting with students, and grading assignments and exams. At all types of institutions, faculty have other responsibilities that put additional demands on their time.

It does take some time to become skilled at using new strategies and even more time to redesign a course. But there are ways you can reduce the time involved, allocate your time differently, or share the effort involved in transforming instruction. Here are some suggestions from experienced practitioners and studies of course transformation:

- *Use materials developed by others that have been shown to be effective.* As noted in Chapter 2, research-validated curricula, assessments, and other instructional resources are available from a variety of sources. While you may want to adapt or add to these materials, starting with existing materials can save considerable time and effort.

- *Do what you can with the time and resources available, and then expand.* This complements the advice in Chapter 2 to start small. "Think about one new thing you can do during the class period, or one class session you can teach that's structured a little bit differently," suggests Derek Bruff,[5] a senior lecturer and director of Vanderbilt's Center for Teaching. Bruff gives the example of an engineering professor who worked with the Center for Teaching over a few semesters and "added one layer after another to his teaching over time . . . making small changes along the way. After a few semesters, his teaching implements more [research-based] practices than it did before."

- *Consider using your preparation time differently.* To prepare for a student-centered class, instructors may spend less time creating well-organized and engaging lectures but more time selecting and adapting good questions and activities tied to their learning goals. "It clearly takes effort to change your practices and engage in discussion and reflection," says chemistry professor Vicente Talanquer[6] of the University of Arizona. "If you are motivated, you're using the time you take to prepare for classes in a different way." In addition, while it does take extra time and effort to transform an existing course, designing a new course around research-based approaches may not require significantly more effort than preparing a semester's worth of lectures.

- *Obtain support, where available, from education specialists, postdoctoral fellows, or similar positions.* The Carl Wieman Science Education Initiative at UBC and a sister initiative at the University of Colorado Boulder provide science education specialists to help faculty with course transformation. At the University of Wisconsin–Madison, graduate student interns in the Delta Program in Research, Teaching, and Learning serve as "capacity building for faculty," says Don Gillian-Daniel,[7] the program's associate director, by helping faculty create research-based instructional materials. "For some faculty, it's simply having new materials," explains Gillian-Daniel. "For other faculty, it's

---

[5] Interview, April 29, 2013.
[6] Interview, April 3, 2013.
[7] Interview, April 26, 2013.

an opportunity to start a progressive revision of a course." People trained in providing this type of instructional support not only can save faculty time, but also can be a source of new ideas and expertise.

- *Share the effort with one or more interested colleagues.* Several instructors interviewed for this book worked with one or more colleagues to redesign a course, and in some cases they decided to co-teach or team teach that course. Part of the UBC/Colorado Science Education Initiative involved doing away with the "glaring example of inefficiency [of] the large multi-section, multi-instructor courses where all the instructors prepare independent lectures and exams" (Wieman, Perkins, and Gilbert, 2010).

- *Use graduate assistants or undergraduate learning assistants to help with some of the logistical demands of research-based instruction.* These types of assistants can assist with a range of the day-to-day tasks in student-centered courses: preparing materials, providing guidance to students as they work in groups, reviewing students' reflective writing assignments, or managing a course wiki, to list just a few possibilities.

- *Consider your priorities for using the time you have.* Often the real issue is not so much a lack of time to revise your teaching, but priorities for allocating time. Once they had gotten a taste of the possibilities, some instructors interviewed for this book made a point to set aside time to expand their initial efforts at research-based reform. Some have used sabbatical time or summers for this purpose. Priorities for using one's time are also shaped by departmental and institutional incentives, so encouragement from these levels can help instructors feel they have the latitude to shift a portion of their time toward improving teaching and learning.

Some of these options may require approval or support at the institutional level, and some may be easier to do for instructors who are not seeking tenure. Thus, departmental and institutional support can be extremely helpful in reserving time for implementing research-based practices. When administrative leaders recognize the value of investing time in making significant course changes, faculty feel supported and the change process can proceed more quickly.

Focusing on Important Content

Some instructors fear that if they shift to more student-centered instructional approaches, their students will miss exposure to important content, including content they need to know to be prepared for upper-level courses. Nearly one-half (49 percent) of the physics faculty surveyed by Dancy and Henderson (2012) cited concerns about "content coverage" as a factor that prevented them from using more research-based strategies. Other instructors may worry that the content taught through student-centered activities will be less rigorous than that covered in a traditional lecture.

Scholars and practitioners with experience in research-based course redesign point out that students are not well served by a curriculum in which they are exposed to many topics but gain mastery of none. What really matters is how much content students actually learn, not how much content an instructor presents in a lecture. "[R]ather than worry about cramming more material into an already bloated curriculum, it would be best to focus on teaching a few of the major concepts/principles well in order to help students see 'the big picture,'" writes Jose Mestre (2008, p. 3). In a paper about insights on implementing small-group learning from successful practitioners, Cooper and colleagues (2000) noted that about two-thirds of the faculty members they interviewed said they covered fewer topics in class when they used group work "but that students learned and retained more of the 'big ideas' that they chose to address relative to using lecture formats" (p. 64).

> What really matters is how much content students actually learn, not how much content an instructor presents in a lecture.

In a related vein, not all of the material addressed in a typical lecture course is vital for students to learn. In the process of writing learning objectives for an engineering course, Jacobson, Davis, and Licklider "discovered that about 10 percent of course material covered was not connected to a learning objective. We were also able to focus the course on a few key objectives that could be assessed and evaluated throughout the course" (1998, p. 2).

Moreover, using research-based, instructional strategies does not necessarily result in significant reductions in the content taught, as some instructors fear. As documented in a study by Deslauriers, Schelew, and Wieman (2011), an instructor using research-based methods in a section of a physics course covered the same amount of material in the same amount of time as an instructor using a strictly lecture-based approach, but students taught with research-based approaches showed dramatically higher gains in learning.

There are steps you can consider to make sure that students learn the most important content in your discipline and are adequately prepared for subsequent courses.

- *Make students responsible for learning some content outside of class.* What matters most is what students learn in an entire course, rather than what they learn through "in-class" and "out-of-class" activities. Some content can be covered by homework, reading, or study guides. This is what Knight and Wood (2005) did when they revamped an upper-division biology course to reduce lecture time and include more student interaction. Students were asked to take responsibility for learning some of the material by doing assigned readings (with quizzes to make sure they learned the reading material) and working in groups outside of class to complete homework problems and post their answers on the course website. Students in the interactive course had significantly higher learning gains and better conceptual understanding than a group that previously took the same course taught with a lecture-based method.

- *Identify and focus on the most important content.* If you begin the process of instructional change by setting learning goals, as recommended in Chapter 2, this will help determine the most essential topics and enduring ideas to be addressed in a course. Topics that are nice but not necessary to know can be omitted. When Mark Leckie[8] and Richard Yuretich redesigned their oceanography course to make it more interactive, "it forced us to really identify the absolutely important things" that they wanted students to learn, says Leckie. This was a "refreshing" exercise that made it possible for them to devote class time to interactive learning, he adds.

- *Focus on fewer topics in greater depth.* Faculty are often concerned that this approach will be less rigorous than traditional lecture, but actually it is more so, says Vicente Talanquer, because the activities focus on developing students' conceptual understanding. Students learn by going into depth on core concepts rather than by working their way through a list of many topics.

- *Consult with colleagues to identify the topics students need to know to be prepared for subsequent courses.* Instructors who teach introductory courses may hesitate to use a more student-centered approach because they fear their students will seem ill-prepared for upper-level courses in a discipline if they have not studied certain topics. But these expectations about topics may

---

[8] Interview, March 22, 2013.

be based on longstanding tradition or the assumptions of individual faculty about what is important rather than on a real analysis of learning goals. If you engage your departmental colleagues in a discussion about which content is important—or, better yet, in a full-blown effort to identify broad learning goals across multiple courses—the result might be a shorter list than you imagined.

Helping Students Embrace New Ways of Learning and Teaching

What you are asking students to do in a research-based classroom is not necessarily easy. At first, some students may be puzzled, uncomfortable, or even resistant when they realize they are expected to learn in unfamiliar ways or to prepare differently and participate more actively in class. They can't get by with just taking notes and cramming for exams. You may hear comments like these:

You're the expert—I'm paying a lot for you to teach me.

Wouldn't it be faster if you just told us?

Why should I have to work with someone else who knows less than I do?

Why do I have to do these grade-school-type activities? I've done well in my other classes by doing the homework, taking notes, and studying.

This is biology, not English—why do I need to write something for each class?

I'm shy; I don't feel comfortable talking in a group.

Why are you doing this to us?!

Many students have grown comfortable with being told facts to memorize, and some pushback from students is understandable (Cummings, 2008). Sometimes the greatest resistance to change comes from the highest achievers or upper-division students, who have succeeded to date through traditional approaches (Silverthorn, 2006).

At institutions where student course evaluations play a role in assessing and retaining instructors, instructors may fear that trying new approaches will lower their good evaluation results. A sense of perspective is necessary, however; often it is a minority of students who balk at new ways of teaching and learning. Faculty who spearheaded the research-based transformation of numerous courses at Colorado found that ratings on student course evaluations before and after the course transformations "remained essentially the same for the same instructors independent of the pedagogy used," with two exceptions that appeared to be related to "poor planning and/or technology bugs rather than resistance to the pedagogy" (Wieman, Perkins, and Gilbert, 2010, p. 14). Some studies (for example, Hativa, 1995; Silverthorn, 2006) have documented improvements in student course evaluations after the adoption of research-based teaching practices. At North Carolina State University, students who took a first-semester physics

class taught using the Student-Centered Active Learning Environment with Upside-down Pedagogies (SCALE-UP) model (see Chapter 4) universally selected the SCALE-UP version, rather than the lecture version, for their second-semester physics course. In focus groups, students who had taken the lecture version for their first semester and SCALE-UP in their second semester reported that they were learning at a deeper conceptual level in the SCALE-UP class, a point that is corroborated by evidence of gains in learning (Beichner, 2008).

Seidel and Tanner (2013) reviewed research literature on student resistance to active learning and concluded resistance is often less a reaction to the pedagogy than to negative instructor behaviors in the classroom, such as sarcasm, absenteeism or tardiness, and unresponsiveness or apathy to students. Seidel and Tanner also posit that a faculty member's own barriers to embracing innovative instruction may find a parallel in students' attitudes. Priscilla Laws,[9] a Dickinson College professor who was an early user of a workshop approach to teaching physics, cautions that any amount of resistance from students "can give disgruntled faculty an excuse to drop what they didn't want to do in the first place."

Still, student resistance can be a real issue even when the instructor has a positive attitude about new approaches to teaching. In upper-level biology courses that were redesigned by Knight and Wood (2005), many students at first disliked and distrusted the interactive approach and the group activities. After additional

---

[9] Interview, July 30, 2013.

exposure, however, most students became comfortable with the unfamiliar format and ultimately reported that it helped their learning.

Seasoned practitioners and researchers suggest several strategies that instructors can use to create positive student attitudes about research-based strategies:

- *Make clear from the first day why these teaching strategies are effective, and be explicit about how they benefit students, and what is expected of students.* "It's really critical that you explain to students why you're doing what you're doing and acknowledge how it may differ from their expectations," says Edward Price,[10] a physics professor at California State University San Marcos. "They must see you are convinced that they will learn more . . . and must see that you have a specific rationale." Robin Wright,[11] a biology professor at the University of Minnesota, emphasizes the importance of making students feel as if they have teamed with the instructor to foster their own learning. The first day of a course, Wright leads her students in a discussion of the roles and responsibilities of students and instructors and how they differ from what students are accustomed to. She explicitly acknowledges that they may be uncomfortable at first. Suggestions for setting a positive tone for a student-centered classroom on the first day of class can be accessed through the Starting Points module on the Science Education Resource Center (SERC) website (http://serc.carleton.edu/introgeo/firstday/index.html).

- *Show students evidence of how research-based strategies will help them learn and prepare for their future life.* Some instructors share evidence with their students of increased learning among students in research-based classes. Karl Wirth,[12] a geosciences professor at Macalester College, shows students lists of the skills that employers want and how those correlate with the activities they will do in his class. Stephen Krause,[13] an engineering professor at Arizona State University, displays a graphic that compares the work environments of "yesterday's engineer" and "tomorrow's engineer" and correlates the former with teacher-centered instruction and the latter with student-centered learning.

- *Use a variety of interesting learning activities.* "[D]ifferent teaching approaches and activities are likely to resonate in different ways with different students," write Seidel and Tanner (2013, p. 592). They suggest that varying the

---

[10] Interview, August 23, 2013.
[11] Interview, April 12, 2013.
[12] Interview, July 8, 2013.
[13] Interview, July 9, 2013.

teaching approaches used throughout a course may "provide points of access to positive classroom experiences for diverse populations."

- *Encourage word-of-mouth among upper-level students who have already taken the course.* Many instructors interviewed for this book talked about the power of the student grapevine in convincing other students to enroll in courses that use research-based approaches. After a few years of teaching a SCALE-UP biology course, Wright noticed that students who had previously taken the course were succeeding in upper-division courses, including courses taught in a more traditional way. Eventually, she says, the upper-division students tell the lower-division students, "You're going to work your butt off, you're going to be really frustrated sometimes, but it's really worth it because it will prepare you well for what you're going to do next." Undergraduate learning assistants and graduate teaching assistants who have helped to facilitate student-centered classes can also spread the word about the benefits of this approach.

- *Listen to students' concerns and make changes to address legitimate ones.* The first few semesters of teaching more interactively may be somewhat rough. Virtually all of the instructors interviewed for this book continued to refine their approaches after their initial effort to introduce a research-based strategy. While some pushback from students may stem from their lack of familiarity with new teaching strategies, other student criticisms may be legitimate responses to aspects of a class that could be improved. Price reports that "the reaction from students has been generally positive, and as we have listened to them and refined what we're doing, it's become more positive."

- *Make sure that grading and other policies are fair.* In classes that involve extensive collaborative work, some students may resent having a portion of their grade depend on the contributions of others, especially if their team includes a weak or lazy student. As discussed in Chapter 5, it is important to assign students an individual grade even in a collaborative learning environment, and to ensure that a grade for group performance does not unduly penalize a student (Smith, 1998). Seidel and Tanner (2013) suggest that instructors provide students with clear and explicit criteria, or rubrics, for how their work will be evaluated before they start a task.

Professor Dee Silverthorn at the University of Texas (UT) uses a combination of strategies to help students adapt to the interactive strategies used in her physiology class.

Acclimating Students to an Interactive Biology Class

On the first day of Dee Silverthorn's[a] upper-division physiology course at the University of Texas (UT), she informs her students this will be a different kind of class. "You spend a lot of your career at UT going to class, taking notes, going home and rewriting notes, and then memorizing them," Silverthorn tells her 200-plus students, most of whom are majoring in biology or health care fields like nursing, pre-med, or physical therapy. "And then you get a test that's short-answer, multiple-choice, and there's going to be enough content on the test that you're going to be able to recall what you've memorized. This class is not like that. On the test you're going to get a piece of paper—one page with three lines of text at the top—and the rest of the page is blank. For the rest of your life no one is going to be telling you what need to know. . . . You've got to have the information stored and organized [in your brain] and be able to retrieve it flexibly."

"And the students don't believe me," says Silverthorn, who has been teaching since 1986. In the weeks that follow, students come to realize that their professor meant what she said. She spends minimal time lecturing, and many of her slides consist of figures and graphs. Students are expected to learn basic facts, such as definitions or functions of major bodily systems, outside of class by doing reading assignments. She makes sure they do the assignments by requiring them to take online, open-book quizzes on the readings that must be completed before class starts and that factor into their grade. A portion of their grade is also determined by their attendance in class.

---

[a] Except where noted, the information in this case study comes from an interview with Dee Silverthorn, June 25, 2013.

In class, students answer clicker questions that target common misconceptions and then find another student with a different answer and do a Think-Pair-Share exercise, as Silverthorn wanders through the large lecture hall with a cordless microphone. "It's really loud and noisy and a lot of fun," she says. Then the students vote again on the correct answer.

Students also work on more demanding problems in class. After studying normal and abnormal electrocardiograms (ECGs), for example, students are given one of six different abnormal ECGs to analyze. Working in teams, they try to determine the heart rate and rhythm, label all the waves, compare their abnormal ECG with a normal ECG, and decide what physiological problem caused the abnormality. "The more you can make it practical, the more you teach them to think critically in context," says Silverthorn. She once received an email from a student who attended a Johns Hopkins University summer program and was excited that he knew more than the Hopkins medical students in the program, she reports.

The exams generally consist of an essay question, including some that require students to make concept maps. For example, students might be given a question about a clinical scenario: somebody gets lost in the desert and becomes dehydrated. Students must map the physiological responses that the person's body goes through as it tries to adapt to a decrease in blood volume and water volume and an increase in osmolarity. "I tell them the tests are a teaching tool as well as an evaluation tool," says Silverthorn. She informs her students that "I'm pushing you out of your comfort zone, but if you're not challenged, you don't know where you need to improve."

Most students accept the reality of the course structure and begin to adapt, writes Silverthorn (2006). At this point, she says, the instructor needs to be ready to help by encouraging students and giving them alternative ways of approaching the

course, such as new study strategies. Once students' attempts to adapt meet with some success, most regain their confidence. "Often these students have to redefine what 'success' means. Before this class, success was making an A on an exam. Now success is measured against progress ('I'm doing better than I was') and is related to mastery of the material," writes Silverthorn (2006).

Despite her efforts to prepare students from the beginning about how the class operates and why she teaches as she does, some students have difficulty adapting. After the first test, when some students are disappointed in their grades, she talks to the class again about the rationale and evidence for interactive teaching and learning. "You have to keep telling them over and over what you're doing and why and that it's okay." High achievers in particular, including pre-med majors, may become frustrated when they suddenly are not doing as well as they expect in a class that requires them to learn in a different way. Many students have not learned to study for understanding, she points out.

Silverthorn's advice to other instructors who are implementing research-based strategies is to challenge students but be fair about it. Instructors need to examine why students develop misconceptions and how they can address them. While many students later say that this physiology course was one of the hardest undergraduate classes they took, they also give it good evaluations. "Students can appreciate being pushed as long as they know it won't hurt their grade," she says.

It took Silverthorn several semesters of observation and experimentation to develop her teaching strategy. Even now, she continues to tweak aspects of the course. "Teaching is an interactive process," she says, "and I believe that when we stop trying to improve our teaching, it is time to retire."

Developing the Expertise to Meet Challenges

The ability to handle challenges generally improves as instructors gain more experience and knowledge of practices based on discipline-based education research (DBER) and related research. In addition, many instructors have collaborated with more experienced colleagues and participated in faculty development—not solely to get started, but also to get better. These modes of self-improvement are not just for novices at research-based teaching and learning; they can also benefit instructors who are well under way with implementation and want to learn new strategies or master approaches they have already tried.

"Effective teaching needs to be seen as a scholarly pursuit that takes place in collaboration with departmental colleagues, faculty in other departments in the sciences and engineering, and more broadly across disciplines," notes a National Research Council (NRC) report on improving undergraduate science, technology, engineering, and mathematics (STEM) teaching (2003, p. 31). "Faculty can learn much by working with colleagues both on and beyond the campus." For example, the report notes, colleagues can help improve the effectiveness of teaching by directly observing each other's instruction, analyzing course content and materials, discussing problems they encounter, and other means.

The learning communities discussed in Chapter 2 not only can support faculty's initial forays into research-based instruction, but also can offer advice on dealing with challenges that arise during implementation (Vergara et al., 2013).

Another way to find and give collegial support for research-based approaches is by observing the classrooms of other instructors who are implementing these strategies or by inviting colleagues to observe your own classes and offer feedback. Some instructors do two-way observations and critiques of each other in real time. Instructors have also videotaped their classes and arranged for trusted people to give them feedback on their own time.

Becoming a skilled user of research-based approaches often requires following up an initial workshop with more in-depth faculty development. Steve Pollock at Colorado went through such a progression. He received his first exposure to using ConcepTests with colored cards (a low-tech predecessor to clickers) from a colleague in the physics department in the 1990s. He began reading more of the physics education research literature. Next he took a course in theories of learning from Valerie Otero, a faculty member in the School of Education at his university. "This awakened me to the research base, and I submitted an application to the Carnegie teaching scholars program" run by the

Carnegie Academy for the Scholarship of Teaching and Learning. That experience consisted of two one-month learning opportunities during consecutive summers, with work in between on an individual implementation project. Later on, after receiving tenure, Pollock spent two months of his sabbatical visiting institutions that were leaders in physics education research (PER). "I really tried to observe as much as I could about what PER groups were doing. I came back and I started implementing it in my classroom and engaging in a more serious level of research," he says.

While it is not necessary to delve as deeply into the scholarship as Pollock has, it is helpful to continue taking advantage of faculty development opportunities after an initial exposure, particularly ones that are taught using the same methods of active learning, group work, and intellectually rich activities that you are seeking to use with your students (Felder and Brent, 2010). Chapter 7 describes additional short- to longer-term professional development options offered by individual institutions, professional societies, foundations, and other entities.

In the "situated apprenticeship" workshops offered by Prather, director of the Center for Astronomy Education, participants receive feedback as they practice implementing research-based strategies in a simulated classroom environment. In this way, faculty gain a better understanding of the kinds of challenges that they and their students will face in a more interactive classroom.

Instructors as Active Learners

PRACTICING RESEARCH-BASED STRATEGIES IN A WORKSHOP ENVIRONMENT

In the workshops offered by the Center for Astronomy Education, instructors struggle in real time with the implementation issues they're likely to have with using active learning strategies in their own classrooms. During the workshops, they are surrounded by other faculty whose role is to observe, question, critique, and "highlight when things are going awry," says Ed Prather,[a] who leads the workshop, directs the Center, and serves as an astronomy professor at the University of Arizona. The "situated apprenticeship" model developed for these 2-day, 16-hour "boot camp" workshops uses a mock class environment in which participants take turns playing the roles of instructor, students, and friendly critics. The goal is to promote real change in instructional practices and skills by evoking and examining participants' ideas about implementation of a particular instructional strategy.

In one version of the workshop, participants gain experience with developing and using Think-Pair-Share questions. In a plenary session, participants first critique questions provided by workshop leaders. Next they develop their own questions in collaborative groups. To guide the development process, participants are prompted to consider these questions:

- What discipline topics could an Astro 101 student realistically understand at a deep conceptual level?

- What would a student need to say to you to convince you that he or she had a deep understanding of the topic?

- What are students' common conceptual or reasoning difficulties about the topic?

- What are the essential discipline ideas that illustrate or define the topic?

- What question would serve as a vehicle to promote a rich discussion among your students about the topic that would address the difficulties students have?

Each group then takes a turn practicing implementation of its question while the rest of the participants assume the roles of students in a mock class, a colleague who critiques the implementation, or critiquers of the Think-Pair-Share question itself. This process enables participants to see firsthand the kinds of errors that instructors commonly make when they implement a strategy like Think-Pair-Share. For example, some instructors reveal the correct answer to the "students," as well as the percentage of students who chose that answer, before the students have had a chance to discuss and debate their answers with one another. "Providing students with this information before they talk to each other and before they are encouraged to defend the reasoning behind their vote has the potential to take the intellectual responsibility off the students and turn the pedagogical value of TPS [Think-Pair-Share] into a thought-less migration toward the most popular vote" (Prather and Brissenden, 2008). In this situation, the workshop leaders have found that a powerful way to instigate an immediate, lively discussion among students is to use a verbal prompt such as "turn to your neighbor and convince them you are right, and if you have the same answer, that

---

[a] Except where noted, the information in this case study comes from an interview with Edward Prather, April 26, 2013.

does not mean you are right, so be sure to explain your reasoning."

"One thing that is quite clear is that a professional development environment has to be as well-informed and intellectually rich as you would hope your classroom would be," says Prather. The mock classroom exercises and peer feedback are intended to foster change in implementation knowledge and skills by creating a situation in which participants encounter cognitive dissonance, much as students would in a research-based learning environment.

The current workshop design "came out of this moment when I was disenchanted with what I knew was happening in the workshop, in much the same way that a faculty member has to become really dissatisfied with what they see in their classroom," Prather explains. In the earlier iteration of the workshop, Prather used a more traditional approach of telling participants about the implementation issues they were likely to encounter—which was "essentially a glorified lecture environment about interactive teaching," he says.

Participants who have attended other workshops on Think-Pair-Share report that after attending the Center for Astronomy Education workshops, "they feel much more confident in their ability to successfully implement this instructional strategy in their own classes" and "are better able to fully articulate

the underlying pedagogical reasons for its use" (Prather and Brissenden, 2008).

In another version of the workshop, participants practice implementing tutorials. The participants are divided into teams of three and are told to do the tutorial but to "write all your answers as if you're only as good at astronomy as a good 101 student," Prather explains. Participants are also asked to write in the margins what they would ask a student who is stuck on that question. "If you can't write out an answer in Astro 101–speak about these topics or envision what [students] might be struggling with when they get to that question and what you would ask, then you're not ready to use it in the classroom," he adds.

In a follow-up activity, participants who did not do that particular tutorial play the role of students doing the tutorial for the first time and ask questions of the instructor based on what they think students would struggle with. The workshop leaders then analyze whether the questions the "students" asked are legitimate issues that students would have trouble with.

The length and intensity of the workshops are critical, says Prather. It takes a while for faculty to be "willing to let their guard down enough to be honest with each other; it can't happen in a one-hour workshop," says Prather.

Since its inception in 2004, the Center for Astronomy Education has provided comprehensive, multi-day professional development to more than 2,200 astronomy and space science instructors, post-docs, graduate students, and other professionals. The workshops are jointly funded by NASA's Jet Propulsion Laboratory and the National Science Foundation (NSF).

A Word About Funding and Other Resources

Implementing a research-based approach involves both actual and opportunity costs. While many instructors have developed research-based strategies and materials without any dedicated time or funding or other supports such as release time, it is obviously easier to do this with resources.

Once you have taken initial steps to implement research-based strategies, funding or in-kind resources can provide the impetus to go deeper into redesigning a course or to expand into additional courses. Many people highlighted in this book applied for and received grants or fellowships to subsidize some of the time and other costs involved in studying research-based strategies, designing or redesigning courses, developing materials, purchasing learning technologies, and pursuing other activities associated with instructional reform.

In some cases, grants, release time, or other types of resources may be available from one's own institution. In many cases, instructors have sought external support. NSF has been and continues to be a notable source of funding for reform of science education. Other sources include disciplinary societies, professional associations, foundations, or other government agencies. Chapter 7 gives some examples of the types of support that are available from institutional and external sources.

Taking Individual Steps to Influence Peers and Departments

The attitudes of one's peers and the culture of a department can facilitate or impede efforts to implement research-based strategies. Based on interviews with faculty about constraints on their use of STEM innovations, Henderson and Dancy (2011) conclude that it is easier for instructors to use research-based methods if other members of their department are also doing so, but it is much more difficult if traditional methods are the norm. While research evidence about increased student learning can be persuasive, colleagues often have a major influence on whether instructors use an instructional innovation: two-thirds of the faculty surveyed by Henderson and Dancy reported learning about an innovation through a colleague.

Based on her current work on innovative strategies in materials science engineering courses, Cindy Waters[14] asserts that instructors are more likely to see the value of changing their teaching if others in their faculty peer group also value that effort. Moreover, she notes, the faculty who continue a research-based inno-

---

[14] Interview, September 3, 2013.

vation once they have started are often those who "feel that someone who is their superior has acknowledged its value."

Although a department typically cannot be turned around by an individual instructor, there are things individuals can do to build support for research-based practices and to contribute to changes in their department's culture.

- *Start building an informal community around research-based practice.*
  Having a critical mass of faculty in a department that can demonstrate positive results may be enough to spur wider change and convince a department or an institution to provide funding, programs, or other supports to foster and sustain research-based approaches.

- *Share evidence about the effectiveness of instructional improvement efforts.*
  Collecting evidence of the impact of your efforts is an important part of research-based teaching and learning and can help to persuade some other instructors of its value. David Sokoloff,[15] a professor at the University of Oregon who leads workshops on physics education, acknowledges that while it is not always easy to convince other faculty to consider research-based approaches, the evidence is a natural starting point. "There's so much evidence out there that traditional strategies don't work. And so if you have people who have an open mind and are willing to listen to that, eventually you get them to do it. . . . If you see the research results and are kind of hit over the head with them, the best thing is for somebody to go back from a workshop and test it with their own students."

- *Recognize that evidence may not be enough.* As the 2012 NRC report on DBER makes clear, evidence alone has been insufficient to spur widespread changes in teaching and learning practices. During presentations about his physics SCALE-UP program at NC State, Robert Beichner[16] has encountered some faculty who are skeptical about findings from cognitive science research in general. "A faculty member may say, 'After you get done with games, when do you actually teach?'" When confronted with that attitude, Beichner suggests that users of research-based approaches "show them things your students can do that their students can't."

- *Invite colleagues to observe your class.* One way for your colleagues to see what students in a research-based environment can do is to observe, or even

---

[15] Interview, July 10, 2013.
[16] Interview, March 26, 2013.

volunteer in, a class. "Faculty members typically have misunderstandings about research-based innovations," says Waters.

- *Talk to your department chair and other academic leaders about major changes you plan to make.* Some instructors are afraid that if they try something new it could lead to a rocky semester or two, which could be particularly problematic for faculty who have not yet gotten tenure. Barbara Tewksbury,[17] a geosciences professor at Hamilton College, advises instructors in this situation to "address the issue up front" and explain to your department chair, and perhaps to a division head or academic dean, what you are planning to do and why. "The response you get will guide how much risk you want to take."

Conclusion

This chapter has focused on "bottom-up" approaches that you can pursue individually or with colleagues to address common challenges to implementing research-based practices. The suggestions in this chapter may assuage some of your concerns about finding time to improve instruction, covering important content, and managing student reactions, and may help you gain expertise to meet other challenges.

But, as the 2012 NRC report on DBER emphasizes, efforts to promote research-based practices are most effective when they are also reinforced by "top-down" actions to address the complex factors that affect instructors' work. Chapter 7 provides several examples of ways in which departments, institutions, and other entities can initiate broader reforms to improve the effectiveness of undergraduate teaching and learning in science and engineering.

Resources and Further Reading

Discipline-Based Education Research: Understanding and Improving Learning in Undergraduate Science and Engineering (National Research Council, 2012)
  Chapter 8: Translating Research into Teaching Practice: The Influence of Discipline-Based Education Research on Undergraduate Science and Engineering Instruction

---

[17] Interview, March 28, 2013.

7

Creating Broader Contexts That Support Research-Based Teaching and Learning

When Cathy Manduca[1] arrived at Carleton College in 2001 to direct the Science Education Resource Center (SERC), a national network for professional development, curriculum, research on learning, and community building, she found a strong faculty engaged in understanding teaching and learning. A decade earlier in her career, she had taught geology at Carleton on a temporary appointment, and so she already knew about the institution's history of supporting research-based instruction and faculty development. Carleton also has its own center for teaching and learning aimed at improving instruction across the entire curriculum. In short, at Carleton, Manduca found "a campus-based example of the same kinds of activities that we're engaged in on a national level" through SERC.

"[C]hanges in teaching require an environment that is supportive of change, as well as a culture that engages in learning about teaching" writes Manduca (2008). While external funding can breed these kinds of cultures, it is not sufficient. "Cultural change has to come not just from the top and not just from the bottom, but from all directions," she adds.

The National Research Council (NRC) report on discipline-based education research (DBER) confirms this point: "Faculty members' teaching decisions depend on the interplay of individual beliefs and values, which have been shaped by their previous education and training, and the norms and values of the contexts in which they work. These contexts include the department, the institution, and external forces beyond the institution" (National Research Council, 2012, p. 177).

If you are a current or aspiring instructor, you are probably already aware of how departmental or institutional factors can encourage and sustain—or hinder—your pursuit of research-based practices in undergraduate science and engineering courses. If you work in a context that lacks explicit support for these

---

[1] Interview, May 13, 2013.

practices, it may be tempting to forego the effort to change how you teach. But departmental or institutional norms are not static; support for research-based teaching and learning can be cultivated over time.

If you have a leadership role in a department, an institution, or some other influential stakeholder group, you have an exciting opportunity to support and encourage the wider use of research-based practices—and increase student learning in the process.

Top-down and bottom-up strategies can be mutually reinforcing. The success of instructors in implementing research-based practices depends to some extent on the policies of their departments and institutions. At the same time, the success of departments and institutions in effecting change depends in part on a sincere commitment from their faculty. Departmental and institutional support can help to create a culture that values and encourages research-based teaching and learning, which in turn provides an incentive for more instructors to get involved.

A variety of external organizations also provide pedagogical, professional, and financial support for reforming science and engineering education. These include disciplinary societies, education associations, resource networks, foundations, government agencies, and others.

This chapter describes several ways in which departments, institutions, and external organizations can promote research-based approaches to teaching and learning. The information is drawn from Chapter 7 of the 2012 NRC report on DBER, particularly the section titled "Putting Reform Efforts into Context"; from papers commissioned by the NRC and other research; and from interviews with practitioners who have implemented research-based reforms in their departments or institutions or on a regional or national scale.

If you are a science or an engineering instructor, department head, or institutional leader, you'll find ideas in this chapter for creating a culture at your campus that nurtures effective teaching and learning. You will also find possible sources of professional development, curricula, collegial networks, funding, and other support for reform.

Creating Departmental and Institutional Cultures That Support Change

"Faculty members are situated within contexts that exert considerable influence on how they think about their work, how they approach teaching, what they value, why they select particular teaching approaches, how they assess the relative value and impact of their teaching choices, and how they assess effort spent on teaching in relationship to effort on other activities," writes Ann Austin (2011, p. 2), a Michigan State University professor who has studied faculty development, instructional reform, and organizational change. Various elements of these contexts, such as institutional leadership, departmental peers, and reward systems, can interact in different ways to encourage—or discourage—research-based teaching practices (Austin, 2011; Fairweather, 2008). Thus, efforts to promote change should take into account the multiple departmental and institutional factors that influence instruction (National Research Council, 2012, p. 184).

Indeed, a lack of attention to the larger institutional context is one reason why research-based practices in undergraduate science and engineering education have not produced more widespread change, despite evidence of their effectiveness (Fairweather, 2008). Faculty at research institutions may resist adopting more effective teaching strategies, writes James Fairweather, "in part because they perceive that the teaching process is at odds with the research process, and that research is more interesting and more valued." Thus, efforts to promote change must acknowledge that reform takes place in a social context that "typically rewards research more than teaching and asks faculty members simultaneously to be productive in research, teaching, and service" (Fairweather, 2008, p. 26).

Faculty at public undergraduate institutions and community colleges may face a different set of contextual factors that affect their implementation of research-based instructional strategies. Examples include heavy teaching loads that may impinge on the time available to redesign courses, a lack of teaching assistants to help manage more interactive classrooms, or limited access to on-campus professional development and expertise in innovative instruction.

Any sustained attempt to foster research-based teaching and learning must focus on creating a supportive culture in key departments and the institution as a whole. Culture is not easy to define, but it is shaped by such characteristics as the values and beliefs about teaching of leaders and faculty members, the dominant teaching style, the emphasis placed on teaching versus other priorities, and the willingness of leaders and faculty members to engage in discussions and interactions around teaching and learning (Austin, 2011).

The departmental context

The context with the most direct impact on instructional practices is the department. "The department is the important unit of change at the university," says Kathy Perkins,[2] who has studied institutional change through the University of Colorado Boulder's Science Education Initiative (SEI). "They're the ones that are really connected and cohesive and are tied to how instruction happens in actual courses. So if you can facilitate the department as a whole in thinking about undergrad science education and improving understanding of student learning, that can be really effective."

Departments play a pivotal role because they "sit at the intersection of institutional and disciplinary influences" (Manduca, 2008, p. 9). While departments are a critical part of the institutional administrative structure, they are also responsible for maintaining and advancing the knowledge, practices, and culture of their discipline. In addition, instructors are more often swayed to change their teaching practices by colleagues in their own department and discipline than by general evidence about the effectiveness of research-based approaches (Wieman, Perkins, and Gilbert, 2010).

Decisions made at the departmental level may influence, either overtly or inadvertently, how instructors teach and whether they adopt research-based approaches. For example, departments typically determine what content is taught in their discipline, how courses are sequenced, and what requirements must be met by majors. They also decide how many courses and which courses an instructor teaches and how teaching assistants are used. Furthermore, departments may have some say in how instructors are evaluated and recommended for tenure and whether they have opportunities to attend professional development.

Efforts to change departmental culture are most effective when they involve the greater part of a department's faculty—which might number in the dozens at a large research university—and affect a majority of its undergraduate courses. This is what Colorado and UBC have sought to accomplish through their SEIs. This initiative has benefited from a high level of funding, beyond what is available to many struggling institutions, but it has also yielded processes, materials, and lessons about reform that can be helpful to other institutions, regardless of their financial situations.

---

[2] Interview, June 18, 2013.

Departmental Support for Instructional Change

THE SCIENCE EDUCATION INITIATIVE

Fourteen departments at Colorado and UBC have undertaken efforts to transform their undergraduate science courses using evidence from research through the SEI, begun in 2005 by Carl Wieman, a Nobel Prize recipient in physics and former professor at both institutions who is now at Stanford University. Rather than trying to change the teaching practices of isolated individuals, the SEI focuses on departments as critical units of change that decide what and how to teach and can influence large numbers of faculty. "If you can facilitate departments as a whole in thinking about undergrad science education and improving student learning, that can be really effective," says Kathy Perkins,[a] who succeeded Wieman as director of the SEI at Colorado.

As a first step, the SEI invited departments to submit competitive proposals for grants to improve all of their core undergraduate courses for majors and non-majors. Each department received up to $1 million at Colorado and $2 million at UBC— "sufficient funds to attract serious attention" and to create an incentive for departments and faculty at large research-oriented institutions to focus on teaching (Wieman, Perkins, and Gilbert, 2010, p. 2). "So the department as a whole had to decide if this is something that they wanted to engage in," says Perkins. "Instead of being top-down, 'you must do this,' the SEI was structured as, 'if you want to engage in this, we'll give you resources to do it.'" The grants, she explains, funded improvements in three areas aligned with research on effective teaching and learning: (1) identifying what students

should learn by setting learning goals, (2) assessing what students are learning through interviewing students and giving assessments tied to learning goals, and (3) identifying and implementing instructional approaches to improve learning. The proposals also had to address how the changes being envisioned in instruction, materials, and assessment would be disseminated and sustained. Departments were encouraged to make changes course by course rather than trying to redesign an entire curriculum at once.

Colorado's investment of $5 million funded seven departmental grantees at various levels (Chasteen et al., 2012; Wieman, Perkins, and Gilbert, 2010). UBC provided $10 million, which has gone to seven departments. All of the departments that received grants have used a large portion of their money to hire science teaching fellows—post-docs in the department who understand both the content and the pedagogy—typically with a Ph.D. in the discipline and training in science education and cognitive science. These fellows collaborate with individuals or small groups of faculty to transform courses and, in the process, transform the faculty members' approach to teaching.

This model of using fellows has worked well according to the SEI leaders, and some departments have made them permanent positions (Wieman, Perkins, and Gilbert, 2010, p. 5). Collaborations between the fellows and the faculty have been most successful when a department chair or leader first obtained a commitment to the process from the faculty member and established clear roles and expectations.

As a result of the SEI, more than 100 faculty members at Colorado have changed their teaching practices, and more than 10,000 students each year

---

[a] Interview, June 18, 2013.

are taught in courses that have been transformed to incorporate research-based practices, notes Perkins. The numbers from UBC are even larger, notes Wieman.[b] In a 2010 survey of faculty in the participating departments, 62 percent of respondents reported that they had developed learning goals and used them to guide their teaching practice, 56 percent reported using information on student thinking and/or attitudes, and 47 percent reported using pre- and post-measures of learning (Wieman, Perkins, and Gilbert, 2010). At UBC, 99 percent of the faculty who have changed to research-based teaching methods as a result of the SEI report that they are continuing to use those new methods (Wieman, Deslauriers, and Gilley, 2013).

The initiative has also helped to shift the culture in the physics department at Colorado, says physics professor Noah Finkelstein.[c] "The culture has been one of saying, 'I'm not simply teaching, I'm engaging in a professional and scholarly activity of education.'" The impact has been similar in many of the other SEI departments, notes Wieman.[d]

The efforts of the physics department at Colorado to introduce research-based strategies into what had been a traditionally taught, junior-level course in electricity and magnetism illustrate the synergy that can occur when committed instructors receive support from their department and institution. With assistance from a science teaching fellow, faculty members established explicit learning goals for the course, developed and refined course materials that addressed known student misconceptions, and adopted interactive instructional strategies such as ConcepTests and small-group tutorials. They also documented student outcomes and studied the course transformation process (Chasteen et al., 2012).

At both universities, several factors have been significant in sustaining the transformed courses and successfully transferring the reforms across multiple instructors (Chasteen et al., 2012; Wieman, personal communication[e]):

- A **supportive department,** as evidenced by financial and staff resources, the involvement of groups of faculty in setting learning goals, the support of the chair and associate chair, and the presence of faculty involved in DBER

- A **team-teaching approach** that pairs faculty who have experience in redesigning courses with instructors who do not have such a background

- The provision of **dedicated staff,** including science teaching fellows and undergraduate learning assistants

- The creation of a **one-credit "co-seminar"** in which students work on tutorials that reinforce what they are learning in the main course

- An **archive** of course materials[f]

The formal funding period for the SEI ended in 2013, but Perkins expects several of its activities to continue at Colorado through the Center on STEM Learning, established in December 2012 to coordinate more than 75 science, technology, engineering, and mathematics (STEM) improvement efforts across campus and disseminate information, research, and resources. At least some teaching fellow positions are likely to be maintained, says Perkins, but perhaps in a different form depending on the available funding.

[b] Email from Carl Wieman, March 20, 2014.
[c] Interview, April 23, 2013.
[d] Email from Carl Wieman, March 20, 2014.

[e] Email from Carl Wieman, March 20, 2014.
[f] See http://www.colorado.edu/sei/fac-resources/index.html; http://www.cwsei.ubc.ca/EOYevent.html.

Several lessons and observations about transforming courses and changing departmental culture have emerged from the SEI experience as a whole (Wieman, Perkins, and Gilbert, 2010):

- *Implementing new research-based teaching approaches has increased student learning.* In cases where comparable measures of student learning were administered in the course before the transformation and after, students performed better in the transformed course. In the Colorado course in electricity and magnetism, for example, students in the transformed course had higher average scores on an assessment in electrostatics than students in a traditionally taught semester of the course. This kind of data is not always available, however, because in many cases faculty changed their assessments to better match their learning goals or did not have detailed assessment data from before the transformation.

- *Focusing on the department as the unit of change is a sound approach.* The most successful and dramatic improvements in teaching have occurred when the whole department has made reform a departmental priority.

- *Providing incentives and rewards increases faculty buy-in.* Departments have provided various incentives, such as giving faculty involved in course transformation release time; offering extra support from a teaching assistant, research assistant, or post-doc; and providing faculty with course materials developed by science teaching fellows. Participating faculty also mentioned two implicit rewards that have increased their commitment to the initiative: greater student engagement and opportunities to think about and discuss teaching as a scholarly activity with their colleagues.

- *Providing research and data on the effectiveness of new instructional approaches is seldom enough to change teaching practices among skeptical faculty.* Faculty members tend to be more convinced by data from their own courses and observing and talking with their colleagues than by general findings from DBER.

- *Change takes time and effort.* Developing learning goals, for example, was more difficult than the SEI leaders expected. It required faculty to reorient their view of education from one that emphasizes the delivery of content to one that helps students acquire important competencies.

- *Barriers to change persist.* Resistance to using shared course materials among some instructors of large, multi-section courses is one such barrier. Another is the unproductive belief that "students these days" are deficient and that shifting to more student-centered forms of instruction is tantamount to lowering standards. Contrary to common thinking, resistance from students has *not* proved to be a barrier to course transformation at these institutions.

The SEI experience at Colorado and UBC reinforces the effectiveness of focusing on departments as units for change and engaging faculty in discussions about learning goals. It also suggests that making changes course by course is more feasible than trying to reform an entire curriculum. The efforts of individual faculty to redesign courses can proceed more quickly and effectively with a repository of shared course materials and the assistance of a fellow or similar individual who has knowledge of teaching and learning in a particular discipline. Collecting evidence about the impact of reforms on teaching practices, as well as on student achievement, is also quite valuable.

> "The department is the important unit of change at the university. They're the ones that are really connected and cohesive and are tied to how instruction happens in actual courses."
>
> —*Kathy Perkins,*
> *University of Colorado Boulder*

Research also indicates that department chairs and deans have a critical influence on instructional practices in positive or negative ways. For example, chairs can signal the relative priority placed on teaching excellence and can shape how faculty members view their responsibilities, demands, and work priorities. Early career faculty members, in particular, look to their chairs for signs about institutional priorities in order to make choices among competing expectations (Rice, Sorcinelli, and Austin, 2000). Departmental leaders who support reform can help bring around faculty who are unlikely to adopt research-based strategies on their own (Fairweather, 2008).

Ann Austin (2011) suggests several actions that department heads and deans can take to help create cultures that value and reward excellent teaching:

- Regularly discuss the relationship of student learning to institutional missions and the relationship of teaching excellence to student learning

- Initiate opportunities for collegial conversations about research-based teaching

- Allow instructors time for innovation

- Provide specific support for professional development on teaching and learning, coupled with incentives for faculty members to participate

The institutional context

The colleges and universities in which departments are situated also have an impact on issues that affect teaching and learning. These institutions set policies for tenure, promotion, and evaluation. Institutional priorities affect the time and effort instructors devote to teaching versus research or other activities. Institutional leaders can create a climate that supports and rewards excellence in teaching—or reinforces negative incentives. Institutions can provide resources for professional development on effective teaching, create incentives to reform teaching, and construct or remodel campus facilities to make them well suited to interactive teaching and learning (Manduca, 2008).

The joint efforts of faculty, university staff, and university leaders to introduce and expand problem-based learning (PBL) and other innovative practices at the University of Delaware shows how change can flourish in a hospitable institutional climate.

Meeting in the Middle

FACULTY ADVOCATES AND UNIVERSITY ADMINISTRATORS COME TOGETHER TO SUPPORT INSTRUCTIONAL INNOVATION AT DELAWARE

Science faculty at the University of Delaware were among the early adopters in the 1990s of problem-based learning (PBL), an instructional model in which students tackle complex, challenging problems and work collaboratively to resolve them. (See Chapters 2 and 4 for more about PBL.) Since then, the university has developed an institution-wide system of faculty development and other supports for research-based instruction.

Creating a community of faculty to improve teaching and learning

Deborah Allen,[a] who directs the university's Center for Teaching and Assessment of Learning, was one of the first faculty members at her institution to embrace PBL when she was a biology professor. She credits Barbara Duch, a consultant to an earlier iteration of the center that Allen now heads, with helping to build a community among the individual faculty, scattered across different science departments, who shared a concern about the effectiveness of traditional methods of instruction. Duch had a gift for "knowing what our comfort zone was, and then just pushing us gently a little bit outside of that," says Allen.

With support from the center, this group of faculty developed courses, wrote PBL curriculum, assessed the effectiveness of their teaching strategies, and conducted research on student learning in the sciences. They met weekly for informal conversations about teaching and learning and served as a support group for each other. "I could not have survived without that group of people I could go to," says Allen.

Another outgrowth of this multidisciplinary collaboration was the development of a "Science Semester" curriculum for education majors. The university agreed to combine the required cluster of courses in life sciences, earth science, and physics for these students into a 12-credit interdisciplinary course, which students took exclusively for an entire semester. The PBL curriculum consisted of units that explored interdisciplinary topics, anchored by problems that students would work on for as long as a month. One unit, which Allen helped to develop, was called Kids, Cancer, and Chemicals. During this segment of the course, students studied a possible "cancer cluster" in a New Jersey community that was home to a chemical manufacturer. As part of the unit, students researched the chemistry of groundwater, studied the movement of chemicals through different types of soil, and analyzed epidemiology data, among other activities.

Faculty collaboration continues to be a vital force in encouraging instructional reform in the sciences at the University of Delaware. In biology, for example, faculty who may be reluctant to embrace new research-based modes of teaching are invited to serve as group facilitators in classrooms that use collaborative learning. "That was very effective because the students in a sense acted as the advocates," says Allen.

As newer faculty members have come on board with additional strategies for improving instruction, the university has become less "monomaniacal" about PBL, Allen explains. A high percentage of faculty use some type of collaborative learning at least some of the time, but they feel as if they have more options than just PBL.

---

[a] Except where noted, the information in this case study comes from an interview with Deborah Allen, April 11, 2014.

Institutional support for instructional reform

The passion of this group of early reformers helped to persuade the university administration to support their efforts. Faculty who were interested in PBL submitted and won a National Science Foundation (NSF) grant. "I think that's what got our administration's attention," says Allen. "Getting federal funding can really help to give your effort legitimacy, and then your administration will pay attention."

At Delaware, says Allen, "the strongest things are [those] that percolate up from faculty interest. We're the creative force, the ones who want to see it happen, and the administration met us in the middle." As the number of faculty interested in research-based instruction grew, the administration began providing them with additional support—although the economic climate was better in those days, Allen notes.

Recognizing that students working in small groups will sometimes need more guidance than a single instructor can provide in a large course, Allen hit on the idea of using undergraduate seniors as group leaders in collaborative classrooms. The university agreed to fund a course to train these peer facilitators, and the program remains strong on campus.

Eventually, faculty who were implementing PBL advocated for classrooms that were better suited to student collaborative work. They gathered evidence of the effectiveness of their instructional strategies in order to convince the administration to invest in classroom redesign. The administration at the time recognized that "all you're asking is for us to change the furniture," Allen recalls. As part of a regular classroom renovation plan, the administration designed several rooms specifically geared to PBL. The university has since built additional rooms equipped with new technologies to facilitate group work. "The highest-tech ones have a huge computer monitor that sits on the wall for each group, and not only whiteboard space," says Allen. "They can use collaborative docs and project them on the screens. The instructor can select which screen we'll view."

The university also founded an Institute to Transform Undergraduate Education and provides it with line-item funding. The Institute offers faculty-led professional development on PBL to instructors from around the world, sponsors an online clearinghouse of peer-reviewed problems and resources, and provides other services. The administration "saw this as a signature program," Allen says. "There was a real synergy. We weren't just asking for handouts; we were building something in collaboration with them."

Both new and more senior faculty can find additional support for effective, research-based instruction through the center that Allen directs. This center sponsors workshops and follow-up consultations with faculty, distributes internal grants for instructional improvement, and conducts federally funded initiatives to strengthen best practices. "We're not just sending people to workshops," Allen explains. "We do the workshops here, and then we continue to support them. We do informal consultations all the time—the typical classroom observations, but from the perspective of having done this ourselves."

Working with faculty developers who have firsthand experience implementing research-based instruction can be reassuring for those who are struggling to make the transition. "We've faced these issues in the classroom, and so we have that reality that faculty really appreciate," Allen notes. "We've done it and we know what we're up against. That's good strategy."

As the University of Delaware's experience indicates, when a core group of faculty who are committed to change come together with open-minded and cooperative administrators, this can create a synergy that stimulates reform across a wider segment of the institution. While the impetus for reform bubbles up from the "bottom," the support necessary to maintain and expand it comes from the "top."

The sections that follow discuss specific areas that can be addressed by departments and institutions to encourage research-based teaching and learning:

- Curriculum and instruction

- Workloads and schedules

- Institutional priorities, tenure, and reward systems

- Institutional support for professional development

Curriculum and Instruction

Instructors' adoption of research-based practices may be influenced by departmental decisions about curriculum, such as course content and sequencing or faculty assignments to teach particular courses (Fairweather, 2008). For example, if the members of a department have not set overall learning goals or are more focused on covering content than on making sure students learn core concepts, this may create concerns about how well a course redesigned around research-based approaches will mesh with later courses in a sequence. If different sections of the same course are taught by different people, then this could discourage an instructor from attempting to incorporate new strategies into one section.

Some of these potential problems can be averted if the faculty members in a department can agree on a set of broad learning goals for a program of study and particular courses, as discussed in Chapter 2. This has the added benefit of coordinating learning goals that require more than one course to achieve. During these types of departmental discussions, faculty can also discuss difficult concepts within the curriculum and which courses would best address them.

Departments and institutions can encourage faculty to adopt research-based reforms through other means, such as those described in the following examples.

Create opportunities for faculty to discuss learning and teaching

These opportunities can range from regular meetings on research in learning and teaching to informal brown bag lunches. At Delaware, Allen[3] is implementing a new take on the old faculty lounge by setting aside a room for conversations about teaching and learning. "People can just drift in whenever they want in a place where you know there will be these conversations." Devoting a significant portion of a departmental retreat to teaching and educational issues, as has been done at UBC, can have a powerful impact.

Provide fellowships for faculty to work on instructional reform

At Michigan State, the Lilly Teaching Fellows program provides pre-tenure faculty, including STEM faculty, with a year-long fellowship to engage in scholarship on effective teaching practices. A large majority (85 percent or more) of faculty who participated in the program between 1991–2004 and 2004–2009 reported that their involvement had a positive impact in these six areas: (1) beliefs about teaching and learning, (2) practice of teaching and learning, (3) effectiveness of teaching and learning, (4) networking with administrators across the university, (5) networking with faculty and other academic staff, and (6) views about Michigan State (Moretto, 2011).

Vanderbilt University provides fellowships with a stipend to faculty, including STEM faculty, in the second through sixth years of their careers to help them improve their instruction using ideas from research. "We ask them to commit for a whole academic year to a sequence of activities—one-on-one consultations, course design, teaching visits, and dinners with senior faculty," says Derek Bruff, director of the university's Center for Teaching and a senior lecturer in mathematics. "The idea is to help them become more effective teachers in the short run in their own classrooms but to also give them exposure to a certain set of ideas and skills that will serve them well as they take on leadership positions at Vanderbilt down the road," he explains.

Provide grants for faculty to reform instruction

Institutional grants can range from substantial grants to departments, such as those made through the SEI described above, to small grants to individual faculty to

---

[3] Interview, April 11, 2013.

design or redesign courses or improve teaching. At Dickinson College, the dean's office provides funding for faculty to work together during the summer on curriculum reform or department change. This funding enabled the physics department to devote faculty time to designing curriculum for student-centered instruction, says professor Priscilla Laws, which in turn helped create more faculty buy-in for the curriculum changes.

Hire DBER scholars or other faculty with expertise in teaching and learning

Within a science or an engineering department, instructors who have expertise in DBER can help build a supportive culture. At the University of Georgia (UGA), says biology professor Erin Dolan,[4] "We have a really strong group of people who are very knowledgeable about the research base in biology education and can think about putting that research into practice in the classroom." As a result, she notes, most of the department's introductory courses use instructional strategies that actively engage students, and faculty are now working on transferring those strategies into upper-level courses. "We are hopefully moving the whole biology faculty toward a more evidence-based approach," she says. This effort at UGA has been bolstered further by the participation of biology faculty in the regional workshop of the National Academies Summer Institute hosted at the university (see Chapter 2 for more about the Institute). "We have enthusiastic administrative support, which is great," says Dolan.

Create graduate or postdoctoral fellowships to assist faculty with reform

A number of institutions have implemented fellowships for graduate students and/or post-doctoral candidates to improve their knowledge and skills in research-based instruction, as described in the professional development section below. These programs not only benefit the participating graduate students and post-docs from whose ranks many future STEM faculty will come, but they can also benefit current faculty by providing a source of assistance in designing and implementing research-based courses.

Such programs can be a "win, win, win," says Bruff of Vanderbilt. "The graduate student gets a really valuable professional development experience. . . . The faculty member gets some help in the form of a graduate student to implement some part of their course that they want to improve or enhance. And the undergraduates in the course benefit by having a better learning experience."

---

[4] Interview, July 2, 2013.

Train undergraduates to assist instructors with large courses

Many institutions across the country have mounted learning assistant or preceptor programs in which undergraduates with an interest in teaching are trained to assist faculty in introductory courses. These programs not only provide participating students with classroom experience and, in many cases, with seminars on research-based pedagogy, but they also provide faculty with individuals who can help their peers with active learning or can lead tutorial workshops.

At Colorado, faculty must apply to have learning assistants for a course, a process that "requires that they think about teaching in new ways," says Valerie Otero,[5] director of the learning assistants program. At the University of Arizona, Carly Schnoebelen,[6] who served as a preceptor for chemistry professor John Pollard, describes her duties in this way: "I go to all of the lectures. . . . [W]e do a lot of in-class activities and problem solving. I walk around, help other students, and answer questions." In addition, she says, preceptors staff an office where students can go to get help with homework or to study for exams.

Assist faculty with research-based reforms through centers for teaching

Many colleges and universities have created centers for teaching and learning or similar units. These centers perform a range of functions. While their services often include workshops and other types of professional development, many of these centers provide teaching evaluations, observations, mentoring, and consultations to help instructors improve their teaching; oversee new faculty induction programs; give out teaching awards; and conduct other activities. The impact and effectiveness of the programs offered through these centers varies, but they can be one component of a multi-pronged effort to create an institutional culture that supports effective teaching.

Workloads and Schedules

Decisions about workloads, access to teaching assistants, and related professional issues can affect the capacity and desire of instructors to implement new teaching approaches (Schuster and Finkelstein, 2006). From the department's perspective, the need to provide instructors for 10 sections of a large introductory course may

---

[5] Interview, November 18, 2013.
[6] Interview, April 25, 2013.

supersede considerations of whether those instructors are using the most pedagogically sound strategies.

Departments and institutions, often at the request of forward-thinking instructors, have taken various steps to facilitate research-based teaching and learning. Below are a few examples.

Allow instructors to team teach or co-teach a course

Sharing responsibilities for designing, preparing for, and teaching courses can be more efficient and can also facilitate the sharing of ideas. Robin Wright[7] team teaches a course at Minnesota in foundations of biology with a colleague. Both instructors attend each class session, and they take turns leading the class. "It might be my turn to be the lead instructor, but my colleague will be there in the room the whole time, interacting with students and making corrections for me or asking questions on behalf of the students. And I do the same thing for him," she explains. "It's just wonderful."

A teaching team that includes both an experienced and a new faculty member can benefit both instructors. The more experienced instructor can provide guidance on developing materials and managing classrooms efficiently, while new instructors can often share fresh ideas and up-to-date research on teaching practices.

Colorado uses the strategy of rotating faculty assignments to teach redesigned courses to expose more faculty to new research-based teaching strategies. In this way, says physics professor Noah Finkelstein,[8] faculty who have less experience with research-based instruction "learn by enculturation and participation."

Use innovative approaches to scheduling to facilitate classroom interaction

Several of the courses taught by instructors highlighted in this book use block scheduling in which classes meet for fewer days but for longer periods to allow more time for in-depth class projects. When John Belcher[9] and other physics instructors at the Massachusetts Institute of Technology adopted the Technology-Enhanced Active Learning approach, they switched from three hours of lecture and two hours of recitation sections per week to two two-hour periods and one one-hour period of lecture with clicker questions combined with active learning exercises and lab experiments. They were emulating practices introduced by Robert Beichner's Student-Centered Active Learning

---

[7] Interview, April 12, 2013.
[8] Interview, April 23, 2013.
[9] Interview, July 9, 2013.

Environment with Upside-down Pedagogies (SCALE-UP) program at North Carolina State University.

Another option is to set aside one course session per week for small-group activities led by a teaching assistant or a learning assistant. When David Gosser[10] and his chemistry colleagues at the City College of New York implemented Peer-Led Team Learning, they took away one of the four hours of lecture per week and devoted it to peer-led sessions in which students solved problems in small groups.

Use teaching assistants differently

Rather than assigning a few teaching assistants (TAs) to handle all the responsibilities for a particular introductory course, faculty in the physics department at the University of Washington "pool" their TAs so that some grade homework while others help students with tutorials in the classroom, says Paula Heron.[11]

Offer faculty release time from teaching to redesign courses

California State Polytechnic University, Pomona, not only paid faculty to attend a university-sponsored workshop on how to implement innovative approaches to teaching physics; the university also provided some with release time from teaching to implement new approaches, according to Alex Rudolph,[12] a professor of astronomy and physics. "This is a case where they're backing a very strong research-based change that discipline-based education research is informing," he says. "It's helping a lot." Paying for some of a faculty member's summer time to work on new teaching methods can also be effective.

Institutional Priorities, Tenure, and Reward Systems

Policies for evaluation, promotion, tenure, salaries, and other reward systems send strong signals to instructors about what they must do to get and keep a faculty appointment and what their department and institution value. Institutional priorities, such as the relative emphasis given to teaching and research or the need to secure outside grant money, also affect how much time and effort instructors invest

---

[10] Interview, July 3, 2013.
[11] Interview, April 12, 2013.
[12] Interview, August 20, 2013.

in making their teaching more effective (Fairweather, 2005; National Research Council, 2012). Instructors are more apt to focus on improving their teaching when institutional reward structures and priorities are aligned with this goal.

An important set of institutional priorities relates to how instructors are expected to allocate their attention among their teaching, research, grant seeking, and service missions. These expectations vary considerably depending on the type of institution, its history, its available resources, the type of position an instructor holds, and other factors. Several studies have shown, however, that higher education institutions in general value research more than teaching (Fairweather, 1996, 2008; Massey, Wilger, and Colbeck, 1994). Faculty in four-year institutions report increasing pressure to do research, according to an extensive quantitative study by Schuster and Finkelstein (2006). Fairweather (2005) found that as faculty time in class increases, salary level decreases and that across four-year institutions, scholarly productivity and publications are the strongest predictor of faculty pay.

> "I've met tenure-track faculty who were good teachers who weren't interested in being great teachers until after they achieved tenure. They felt they needed to focus more on their research than taking their teaching to the next level."
>
> —Derek Bruff,
> Vanderbilt University

"If you're at a traditional research-oriented institution, survival—or your opinion of what survival is—determines your behavior," says University of Washington professor Lillian McDermott,[13] co-developer of the research-based tutorials described in Chapter 4. If instructors believe that their future or their standing depends more on the quality and productivity of their research and their ability to bring in research grants than on the effectiveness of their teaching, they will be less inclined to spend time changing their instructional practices. It is understandable, then, that some instructors choose to just "suffice" in their teaching responsibilities (Austin, 2011).

At research institutions, policies often signal to instructors that research performance is valued more highly than teaching performance, notes Bruff. Although that may be appropriate given the mission of a research university, these policies "sometimes lead faculty and administrators to take a 'good enough' approach to teaching," he says. "If your teaching is problematic, then people will pay attention.

---

[13] Interview, April 18, 2013.

You might get extra help from your chair, you might be sent over to a teaching center for assistance, and, if the problems persist, you might not get tenure. But once you reach a 'good enough' bar, there can be few incentives to be better. I've met tenure-track faculty who were good teachers who weren't interested in being great teachers until after they achieved tenure," Bruff adds. "They felt they needed to focus more on their research than taking their teaching to the next level."

Similarly, the quality of teaching is often evaluated in a far less careful and rigorous way than the quality of research, notes Carl Wieman,[14] which is both an indication of an imbalance in institutional priorities and a contributing factor to its continuation.

The relative emphasis given to teaching versus research really hits home in decisions about tenure, promotion, or reappointment. At four-year colleges and universities, publishing research is the most important factor in faculty tenure and promotion decisions, according to an analysis by Braxton, Lucky, and Holland (2002). In this environment, it is not surprising that faculty members on a tenure track at a research university might put less effort into improving their instruction. Once tenure is received, they may feel more at ease in exploring new areas, including improvements in teaching.

This pressure to do research is far less of a factor at community colleges, where tenure is based to a large degree on teaching performance, with some consideration for service to the community and institution. The priority that community colleges place on faculty participation in professional development has a positive influence on teaching effectiveness, says Kaatje Kraft,[15] who until recently taught at Arizona's Mesa Community College. "Professional development is expected at a community college. That's important because that's where you get access to the research base on teaching practice."

Students' end-of-course evaluations are another institutional factor that can inhibit instructors from taking risks in their teaching, out of fear that integrating new approaches may not immediately be successful from the students' standpoint (Austin, 2011). Student evaluations are often used to gauge teaching performance, but they are far from complete in their appraisal of teacher effectiveness. In surveys and interviews conducted by Henderson and Dancy (2011), faculty overwhelmingly expressed the view that student evaluations were not a particularly effective way of measuring teaching quality. These authors conclude that an over-reliance on these evaluations can impede reform.

---

[14] Email from Carl Wieman, March 20, 2014.
[15] Interview, June 13, 2013.

Some departments or institutions at large universities have formal policies to give greater recognition to teaching excellence. At UGA, the criteria for promotion and tenure in the Department of Plant Biology require faculty to demonstrate excellence in teaching through peer evaluations (in addition to student evaluations), teaching awards, innovation in teaching methods, and other criteria (University of Georgia, 2007). In the peer-evaluation process, a longstanding part of the department's teaching evaluation criteria, assistant professors may undergo a mentoring or formative evaluation of their instruction in which senior faculty and a faculty mentor attend a representative subset of their classes for one course and make helpful comments and suggestions. Following that formative evaluation, which occurs early in the faculty member's career, all assistant and associate professors go through a more formal peer evaluation by a committee of three senior faculty. These committee members attend at least three lectures each and score various aspects of instructional skills and success. The criteria for the peer evaluation include the following factors: preparation, presentation, stimulation of students' interest, instructor's enthusiasm for the subject, mastery of the subject matter, an overall rating, and other special observations about aspects that add to or detract from teaching effectiveness. The faculty member being evaluated has an opportunity to discuss the findings with the committee and suggest possible changes before the committee submits its report, which becomes part of a promotion dossier, to the department head.

In addition, half of the Department of Plant Biology faculty at all ranks at UGA had participated in the National Academies Summer Institute in biology as of spring 2014, according to Michelle Momany, the department head.[16] Momany has found that involving new faculty in the Institute and having them sit in on an effectively taught class from the very start helps them "use scientific design for their first course, and [they] don't have to go back and spend time fixing it later." Generally, she says, new faculty members "welcome the opportunity to get familiar with the research on how best to help students and are happy to pick up tips along the way."

At UBC, the Department of Earth, Ocean, and Atmospheric Sciences conducts class observations of each faculty member every year, using two tools developed by the SEI. The first tool, a Teaching Practices Inventory, is a checklist of whether a lecture course includes characteristics that research has deemed to be effective. Examples include learning goals or outcomes; supporting materials for students; in-class activities, such as pauses to ask for questions, small-group

---

[16] Email from Michelle Momany, March 18, 2014.

discussions or problem solving, demonstrations or simulations, clicker questions, student reflection activities, and student presentations; opportunities for two-way feedback between the instructor and the students; diagnostic assessments; collaboration or sharing in teaching; and other characteristics. The second tool, the Classroom Observation Protocol for Undergraduate STEM (COPUS), allows trained observers to reliably characterize how faculty and students are spending their time in the classroom (University of British Columbia, n.d.). Similar tools are also available in other disciplines, such as the Revised Teaching Observation Protocol being used in geosciences.[17]

In general, however, most institutions have a way to go in making an explicit commitment to teaching excellence in their faculty evaluation and priorities and reward systems. Some DBER scholars have recommended that teaching evaluations be based on actual student learning gains, as gauged by pre- and post-assessments of learning, in addition to student course ratings (Knight and Wood, 2005).

Institutional Support for Professional Development

Many institutions have mounted their own professional development programs that emphasize research-based approaches to teaching (Gappa, Austin, and Trice, 2007). As one example, the 22 research universities that belong to the NSF-funded Center for the Integration of Research, Teaching, and Learning network, or CIRTL, are providing long-term professional development and mentoring to build a cadre of future STEM faculty who are committed to using research to improve teaching and learning. While CIRTL is implemented somewhat differently at each institution, each program is founded on three core ideas: (1) teaching-as-research, in which STEM graduate students and post-docs engage in the systematic use of research to develop and implement effective teaching practices; (2) learning communities that encourage groups of program participants and their mentors to share knowledge and ideas for practice and that prepare participants to learn to use learning communities in their own work; and (3) learning-through-diversity, which capitalizes on the diverse experiences, backgrounds, and skills of students and faculty to enhance learning. The following case study shows how these ideas are being applied in the CIRTL programs at Michigan State and the University of Wisconsin–Madison.

---

[17] See http://serc.carleton.edu/NAGTWorkshops/certop/index.htm.

Universities Target Future Faculty as Agents of Change

At their regular biweekly meeting, a select cadre of doctoral fellows in science, engineering, math, and related fields at Michigan State University (MSU) work in smaller groups with their mentors and program staff. Taped on the walls of the meeting room are copies of PowerPoint slides containing the main research questions for the "teaching-as-research" project that each fellow will develop and carry out during the course of an academic year. A biology fellow presents her research question—*Do active learning strategies improve student learning in a genetics course?*—and explains her initial ideas for addressing it. "What type of active learning strategy do you plan to use?" asks one fellow. "What assessments will you use to measure the results?" asks her mentor. Fellows will take into account this input to narrow and refine their research questions; in later meetings, they will receive feedback about their objectives, methodology, and other aspects of their project.

This hypothetical example is based on the experiences of real fellows in the Future Academic Scholars in Teaching (FAST) program at MSU. Begun in 2006 with funding from the university's Graduate School and NSF, FAST is a project of the CIRTL network, which provides professional development to STEM doctoral students to prepare them to implement and advance effective teaching practices. Each year, 10 to 14 FAST fellows are chosen from a group of applicants with an interest in teaching and a strong record in their disciplinary work toward their doctorate. During the course of an academic year, FAST fellows participate in mentored teaching experiences, workshops, and seminars on research about instruction, learning, and assessment. After completing the program, fellows may reapply for an additional year.

"Just because people are smart and they know research doesn't always mean they can teach it effectively to a diversity of other people," says Henry "Rique" Campa III,[a] director of FAST, associate dean in MSU's graduate school, and professor of wildlife ecology. "And that is the essence of what we're trying to change" (Michigan State University, 2011). When Campa was an MSU Lilly Teaching Fellow in the 1990s, he recognized that the things he was learning about pedagogy and assessment during the year-long fellowship would have been helpful to him as a graduate student. This spurred him to work with CIRTL and collaborate with STEM colleagues on developing the FAST program to target future faculty.

Consistent with CIRTL's Teaching-as-Research approach, the centerpiece of the FAST program is a scholarly project on an aspect of teaching and learning that each fellow designs with support from a faculty mentor and the university's CIRLT steering committee. The fellows then implement their projects in an undergraduate course and present their findings at a final symposium. Each fellow receives $2,000 to help conduct the project and to disseminate the results at conferences or through journal articles or other avenues.

Twice a month, the fellows participate in meetings with the steering committee members to discuss their projects or interact with guest speakers who have expertise relevant to their projects. On the off weeks, they meet in informal "journal clubs," led by a post-doc and FAST program graduate assistants, where they prepare for the larger meetings and review pertinent research.

---

[a] Interview, April 23, 2013.

Chris Richardson, a former FAST fellow who is now an assistant professor of physics at Elon University, is putting into practice several of the strategies he learned through the FAST program. "When you get your Ph.D. and go to grad school, everyone comes out with the ability to do some form of independent research. . . . What you don't have much experience doing, and what they don't teach you to do well, is actually teach," says Richardson.[b] "I knew that I needed more preparation than just teaching a couple of classes. That's what I got from FAST."

Richardson's first FAST project analyzed gender differences in responses to clicker questions in an introductory physics course and found that while the number of correct answers and response times were similar for men and women, the average number of responses for a given question was significantly higher for men and that men were slightly more likely than women were to change their response within the allotted time (Richardson and O'Shea, 2013). His second-year FAST project correlated students' clicker-question responses and grades with data from a survey of attitudes and beliefs; he found that for men as a group, their confidence in how well they learned the course material did not correlate with their grade, while women were under-confident about their learning as shown by their grades.

Like Richardson, many former fellows have published their research on teaching and gone on to faculty positions. "They can show scholarship across the mission—and that looks pretty good on a CV," says Campa.

For Allison Rober,[c] an assistant biology professor at Ball State University, her time as a FAST fellow not only shaped how she herself teaches, but also influenced her colleagues. "My department chair was

excited I had these types of skills," she says. In her classes, she uses a range of research-based strategies, such as collaborative learning, one-minute reflection papers, modeling, and Think-Pair-Share. "I feel fortunate that I don't even know how to teach without using student-centered pedagogy," she says. "I'm always trying to engage students in behaving like scientists, regardless of what profession they aspire to." Rober shares materials with other faculty at her institution who are interested in the scholarship of

teaching and learning. In addition, she collaborated with a colleague to align the laboratory and lecture parts of a biology course to cover the same topics at the same time. That change contributed significantly to improvements in student learning, she says.

At the University of Wisconsin–Madison, the graduate students and post-docs in the Delta Program in Research, Teaching, and Learning (Wisconsin's version of a CIRTL program) can take courses and participate in small-group facilitated programs, internships, and other activities (Gillian-Daniel, 2008). As part of their coursework and their internships, Delta participants team up with a

[b] Interview, May 2, 2013.
[c] Interview, April 29, 2013.

faculty member or other instructor to develop new instructional materials and to conduct research on teaching. These relationships benefit the mentoring faculty as well as the Delta participants, says Don Gillian-Daniel,[d] associate director of the Delta Program. "The students are capacity building for faculty. They bring in new ideas and training and provide the energy to help faculty move into doing something new with their course."

Some of the Delta participants' Teaching-as-Research projects are "phenomenal," says Gillian-Daniel. One Delta student, for example, turned a traditional "cookbook" laboratory session in an ecology course into an inquiry-based lab session in which the undergraduate students asked their own research questions and took field trips to local sites to investigate resource management. In another project, a computer science graduate student and a post-doc, working with a civil engineering professor, found that undergraduates were having difficulties with translating word problems into a conceptual framework and with solving the problems. The team designed an interactive Web tutorial that guided students through step-by-step solutions of problems and then required them to solve similar practice problems on their own (Gillian-Daniel, 2008).

A longitudinal study of participants in a doctoral and postdoctoral teaching development program at Wisconsin, including the Delta Program, found that 76 percent of the study respondents reported that they had applied the knowledge and skills gained from these programs to their subsequent undergraduate teaching. Respondents frequently reported delivering student-centered instruction and applying what they had learned about assessment, course preparation, and planning, including setting learning goals (Benbow, Byrd, and Connolly, 2011, cited in Pfund et al., 2012).

Broader evaluations of the impact of CIRTL-related professional development, which also relied largely on faculty's self-reported data, suggest that participants gain knowledge and skills about teaching and awareness of a wider range of approaches to analyzing teaching problems. They also develop a better understanding of the value of teaching as part of their careers and a greater ability to encourage student learning (Austin, Connolly, and Colbeck, 2008). Furthermore, participants often indicate that they feel better prepared for undergraduate teaching, have a greater sense of self-efficacy about teaching, and value opportunities to interact with others with similar interests in teaching (Austin, 2011).

---

[d] Interview, April 26, 2013.

Several ideas that may resonate with staff at other institutions can be drawn from the CIRTL projects at MSU and Wisconsin.

- Exposing prospective faculty to research-based approaches to teaching can be an effective strategy for improving undergraduate instruction over the long term. When participants in these programs become faculty, they tend to apply what they learned in their own classrooms, and their influence will last for years to come as they progress in their careers.

- Focusing on future faculty can have a spillover effect by inspiring faculty who are mentoring participants to revise their own courses.

- Professional development that involves mentoring experiences, communities of learning, and a year-long time frame appears to have a greater impact on practice than a short-term workshop.

- Participants in professional development should be encouraged to assess the impact of the changes they make in their own classrooms, not only to inform their own practice, but also to monitor the effectiveness of a professional development model.

- Having multiple professional development programs with similar goals at the same institution can create synergy around reform. At MSU, for example, the FAST program grew out of the university's Lilly Fellows and the CIRTL network.

It can be a challenge to get busy instructors with many competing demands to participate in professional development, whether it is sponsored by the institution itself or by outside groups like those mentioned later in this chapter. If professional development programs are going to serve as an effective lever for change, they need to attract more than the "usual crowd" of instructors who are already interested in effective teaching (Austin, 2011). Faculty development experts suggest several strategies that department chairs, deans, and other institutional leaders can take to encourage participation and broaden the reach of professional development efforts (Austin, 2011; Hilborn, 2012; Sorcinelli et al., 2006):

- Send a clear signal that the institution values participation in professional development focused on improving teaching.

- Recognize that instructors have different needs for and interests in professional development at different stages of their career and offer a range of options and formats that appeal to faculty in various circumstances.

- Present professional development as a prestigious and growth-oriented opportunity rather than a remedial situation.

- Ensure that professional development activities make effective use of participants' time and result in substantial and positive outcomes.

- Link rewards with faculty involvement in professional development.

- Provide funding to cover the costs of participation.

Professional development can have an impact beyond the instructor who directly participates. When Elizabeth Derryberry[18] was hired as a biology professor at Tulane University in 2011, she hoped to be able to use the instructional strategies she had honed as a postdoctoral fellow in the NSF-funded FIRST IV (Faculty Institutes for Reforming Science Teaching) program. As part of this program, Derryberry had attended two consecutive summer workshops where she

learned about effective research-based strategies and designed an inquiry-based undergraduate course in animal behavior. During the academic year between the workshops, she co-taught the course she had designed. With input from a FIRST IV mentor, she analyzed the effectiveness of her teaching through an assessment of students' conceptual learning and videotapes of her classes. The assessment showed gains in learning, which was "very useful both as feedback for teaching and in job applications," says Derryberry.

In her initial meeting with her department chair at Tulane, "one of the things I made evident is that teaching is really important to me," says Derryberry. Her approach to teaching gave students opportunities to analyze real scientific data and write reflective "learning paragraphs"—and she hoped her department would be supportive. "Most senior faculty members don't use that approach, and I wasn't

---

[18] Much of the information in this example comes from an interview with Elizabeth Derryberry, May 3, 2013.

really sure how that would be met or addressed," she says, particularly when it came time for her teaching to be evaluated. To her relief, the reception was much better than she had imagined. Not only was her chair "very supportive," she explains, but he and another colleague attended a summer institute on research-based pedagogy with her, where they "got a chance to see how this approach works and what's effective and how to evaluate somebody using this approach."

Leveraging Reform Through External Groups

Instructors work in contexts that are broader than their department and employing institution. These include their discipline, as represented by disciplinary societies; other associations to which they or their institution belong; the higher education system in their state and in the nation; and public and private agencies and organizations that directly or indirectly influence their work. The following types of external groups are especially influential:

- *Disciplinary societies* and associations of teachers in a particular discipline are important sources of respect and professional interaction for faculty. Their members pass judgment on papers and proposals and critique other professional work (Manduca, 2008). The attitudes of disciplinary peers not only influence the willingness of individual instructors to change how they teach, but also shape research and development of effective approaches to teaching in the discipline. Each of the science and engineering disciplines has a distinct set of values, criteria for excellent work, and behavioral norms (Austin, 2011, p. 7).

- *Higher education associations,* such as the Association of American Universities (AAU), the Association of American Colleges & Universities (AACU), and the American Association of Community Colleges, have undertaken initiatives to improve undergraduate STEM education.

- *Networks and resource centers* offer opportunities for collegial interaction and make available curriculum and other resources to support research-based reforms.

- *Federal agencies,* such as NSF, and some state agencies have provided funding and policy support for reforms of undergraduate STEM education.

- *Nonprofit institutions and foundations* have provided funding, professional development, research and policy support, or other activities to enhance the quality of undergraduate STEM education.

The remainder of this section describes some of the many ways in which external groups can support research-based reforms of undergraduate science and engineering education.

Promoting systemic reform of undergraduate STEM education

AACU, which comprises more than 1,300 member institutions from all sectors of higher education, has joined forces with Project Kaleidoscope (PKAL) to improve the effectiveness of STEM education. For the past two decades, PKAL has researched and implemented strategies to improve STEM curriculum and teaching. The AACU project is developing a framework that campus leaders can use to translate national recommendations for improving student learning and success in STEM into scalable and sustainable actions (Association of American Colleges & Universities, 2014). Up to 12 colleges and universities in California will be selected to test evidence-based strategies for transforming programs, departments, and institutions.

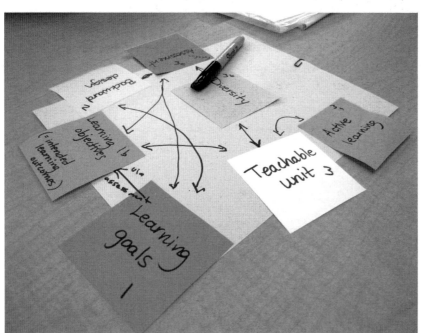

In 2011, AAU launched a five-year undergraduate education STEM initiative to influence the culture of STEM departments at its member institutions, which include leading public and private research universities. An ultimate goal of the initiative is to encourage and support faculty in the use of research-based teaching practices. As described below, the initiative has developed a framework for systemic change in undergraduate STEM teaching and learning and has selected and provided support to eight member institutions to pilot key aspects of the framework.

DESIGNING LEARNING

A National Organization Leverages Systemic Change in STEM Teaching and Learning

AAU has made the improvement of undergraduate STEM education an organizational priority through a five-year initiative that seeks to help higher education institutions align teaching practices with evidence about how students learn best in STEM disciplines. As a national organization, AAU has an advantage of being able to convene crucial stakeholders like university leadership, disciplinary groups, other national organizations, and funding entities, says AAU project director Emily Miller.[a]

The initiative includes the following activities (Association of American Universities, 2013b, n.d.):

- **Framework for systemic change.** AAU developed a framework to guide institutions and faculty as they commit to using research-based practices to improve STEM teaching and learning. The practices promoted by the framework include the kinds of student-centered, active learning pedagogy documented in the 2012 NRC report on DBER. The framework outlines a set of key institutional elements that need to be addressed in order to bring about widespread and sustainable change.

- **Project sites.** With a three-year, $4.7 million grant from the Helmsley Charitable Trust, AAU has provided seed money for pilot projects at eight AAU member universities—both public and private—in various regions of the country. These sites are implementing major undergraduate STEM education reform projects that address the three key elements of the framework: effective pedagogy, scaffolding and support for faculty, and cultural change at the institutional and departmental levels.

- **AAU STEM network.** AAU is developing a network that will enable faculty and administrators at its member institutions to share best practices and promote sustainable change in undergraduate STEM teaching and learning. With seed funding from the Burroughs Wellcome Fund, AAU has developed an online hub to showcase promising programs and practices being implemented at member campuses and to support ongoing interaction among those who are leading reform efforts on their campuses.

---

[a] Interview, November 15, 2013.

- *Metrics and evaluation.* With an NSF grant, AAU is developing metrics to help the project sites, as well as other institutions, assess the current status of STEM teaching and learning at their institutions and track the progress of their reform efforts. The metrics will also be used to evaluate the overall impact of the AAU STEM initiative.

"The initiative has created a platform to bring together individuals on our campuses who have wanted to have a dialogue with each other," says Miller. The eight project sites are taking somewhat different approaches to implementing a common framework and are at different stages of promoting research-based practices.

The initiative has already had an impact (Association of American Universities, 2013a). All AAU member institutions have designated a campus point of contact to serve as a liaison with AAU for the STEM education initiative. In 2013, half of AAU's 62 member institutions participated in a summer workshop focused on creating the AAU STEM network. Even the 23 institutions that applied for but did not receive project grants have been positively affected, notes Miller. As part of their applications, these institutions developed concept papers that examined such factors as department and faculty engagement, institutional commitment, likelihood of sustained organizational change, and commitment to evaluation and assessment. Many of the campuses have successfully advanced these proposed projects with other funding sources.

As a resource for other higher education institutions, AAU is disseminating examples of the innovative efforts to reform STEM teaching and learning that are being implemented by its member campuses (see www.aau.edu/stem).

Setting standards for student outcomes

The accreditation standards adopted in 1996 by ABET, the agency that accredits engineering programs, demonstrate how an external body can influence the quality of teaching and learning in a discipline. These standards—called Engineering Criteria 2000, or EC2000—shifted the basis for accreditation of degree-granting programs from what students are taught to what students have learned. By adopting these standards, the ABET Board intended to increase student learning and to better prepare program graduates to enter the profession.

The standards specify 11 learning outcomes that cover not only students' mathematical, scientific, and technical knowledge, but also other professional skills, such as solving unstructured problems, communicating effectively, and working in teams (ABET, 2009). Programs seeking accreditation must assess and demonstrate their students' achievement in each of those areas, as well as meet additional standards for program faculty and facilities. The standards also stress awareness of ethical and contextual considerations in engineering.

Producing these learning outcomes, which are consistent with findings from research, would require new kinds of teaching. The EC2000 initiative assumed that as engineering programs aligned their curriculum with the standards, faculty would be motivated to revise their instruction and assessment practices accordingly. A study commissioned by ABET of the impact of EC2000 concluded that "the implementation of the EC2000 accreditation criteria has had a positive, and sometimes substantial, impact on engineering programs, student experiences, and student learning" (Lattuca, Terenzini, and Volkwein, 2006, p. 12). Based on comparisons of graduates' self-reported learning outcomes, the study concluded that 2004 graduates were measurably better prepared than their 1994 counterparts in nine learning areas assessed. Findings from the study "strongly suggest that improvements in student learning have indeed resulted from changes in engineering program curricula, teaching methods, faculty practices, and student experiences inside and outside the classroom" (p. 13).

The ABET standards have encouraged frank discussions about curriculum and instructional practices among engineering faculty at many institutions. Faculty involved in the Iron Range Engineering program, described in Chapter 4, considered how to meet the ABET outcomes in the best ways suggested by research, rather than reframing existing curriculum to make it appear that a program already met the ABET outcomes—determining, for example, that "this one week in this one course connects to ethics, so, 'Check!'" says Rebecca Bates,[19]

---

[19] Interview, July 8, 2013.

an engineering professor at Minnesota State University, Mankato, who became involved in the Iron Range program after its founding. With the ABET outcomes as a guide, faculty in the Iron Range program determined that they would teach in a way that drew from research on student motivation, connected technical experiences with issues of value to society, modeled how to solve engineering problems and how to communicate those solutions, and developed students' skills of working in teams, among other components. And while several people agreed that this was what good instruction should look like, "people also said, 'I can't do it at my school,'" Bates recalls. "It's really hard to change a juggernaut's direction. . . . If [the engineering program] is already good, students are already learning. But the question is, are students learning as much as they could, and who is being excluded from engineering education?"

While the ABET standards are unique among accreditation criteria for undergraduate STEM programs, they illustrate how an external group can strongly influence teaching in a discipline.

Sponsoring professional development

Disciplinary societies, professional associations, and other national and regional groups play an important role in sponsoring professional development to improve the teaching skills and knowledge of science and engineering instructors. STEM faculty workshops sponsored by scientific societies often aim "to develop expert competence in teaching, to enhance faculty views of teaching as a scholarly activity, and to promote the use of evidence in evaluating the effectiveness of teaching practices," writes Robert Hilborn, associate executive officer of the American Association of Physics Teachers (Hilborn, 2012, p. 6). Their ultimate goals are to improve student learning and attitudes about STEM education and to attract more students to STEM careers.

Here are some notable, longstanding examples of national professional development efforts sponsored by disciplinary societies, professional associations, and similar groups:

- The *National Effective Teaching Institute,* sponsored by the American Society for Engineering Education, is a three-day workshop established in 1991 to familiarize engineering faculty members with proven, student-centered strategies (Felder and Brent, 2010). Engineering deans may nominate up to two faculty members from their campuses and are expected to pay their nominees' expenses of attending. Past participants in the Institute credited the workshop with increasing their awareness and use of various learner-centered strategies (Felder and Brent, 2010).

- Since 1996, the American Association of Physics Teachers, the American Physical Society, and the American Astronomical Society have sponsored *New Faculty Workshops* for faculty in their first three years of a tenure-track position. More than 1,600 faculty—roughly one-third of all new hires at U.S. institutions awarding a baccalaureate in physics or astronomy—have participated in the workshops since their inception, estimates Ken Krane,[20] an Oregon State University physics professor and longtime workshop leader. At the three-and-a-half-day workshops, participants are introduced to instructional strategies and innovations that "are effective and reasonably easy to adopt," says Hilborn.[21] Roughly half of the workshop time is devoted to small-group sessions in which participants can practice and discuss the techniques they are learning. Department chairs nominate new faculty to attend the workshop, which helps bring the chairs on board with the workshop mission, says Krane, and the involvement of the disciplinary societies carries considerable weight with research universities (which account for more than half of the workshop participants). An evaluation of the New Faculty Workshops found that they have been effective in raising participants' awareness of research-based practices and providing them with an initial experience but are less effective in helping participants implement strategies and stay engaged once they go back to their home institutions (Henderson, 2008).

- *On the Cutting Edge,* a professional development project of the National Association of Geoscience Teachers, has offered workshops for current and future geosciences faculty since 2003 (which are a spinoff of a series of workshops series for new geosciences faculty begun in 1999). On the Cutting Edge also sponsors an integrated website with teaching and learning resources and opportunities for ongoing networking (Manduca, 2011; Manduca et al., 2010). In a survey by McLaughlin and colleagues (2010), faculty who had participated in On the Cutting Edge were more likely than nonparticipants to report adding small-group activities to their teaching; spending less time lecturing and more time using in-class questioning, small-group discussion, and in-class exercises; and making more use of education research. On the Cutting Edge alumni

[20] Interview, December 2, 2013.
[21] Interview, December 3, 2013.

also significantly changed their attitudes about teaching, moving more toward active learning approaches (Macdonald et al., 2005).

- As described in Chapter 2, the National Academies and the Howard Hughes Medical Institute sponsor week-long *Summer Institute* workshops in biology that have reached roughly 1,000 biology instructors since 2004.

As noted in Chapter 2, these types of professional development have generally helped to increase participants' awareness of research-based innovations, but overall their effectiveness in driving changes in practice has been limited. Studies of programs that have shown some success in reforming participants' instruction point to the importance of providing extended follow-up, which is difficult to do. Chapter 2 describes additional components of professional development that tend to be associated with changes in practice.

Providing funding and other support for research-based teaching and learning

External groups can advance improvements in undergraduate science and engineering education through many other means. Funding is one important area. Federal agencies such as NSF, the U.S. Department of Education, and NASA, as well as state agencies and foundations, have provided critical funding for research, innovative programs, materials development, and other activities to improve science and engineering education. "A key for transformation at universities, especially at large research universities, has been federal funding," says Noah Finkelstein of Colorado. At his institution, he notes, "NSF has done tremendous work by supporting institutional transformation in different disciplines at the undergraduate level." Individual practitioners highlighted in this book have also found outside grants to be useful in advancing their research on promising approaches or implementing innovations on a larger scale.

External groups can also contribute to the intellectual and policy foundations of research-based instructional reform. Through its DBER study and other studies of undergraduate science and engineering education, the National Academies, for example, have synthesized and disseminated knowledge about research-based approaches and made policy recommendations.

Establishing collegial networks and sharing materials and information are additional ways in which external groups can be forces for reform. Instructors who are committed to reform but are isolated in their own work environments may find supportive and knowledgeable colleagues outside of their own institution through national or regional networks or professional organizations

(Fairweather, 2008). Often these networks are built around a particular discipline or instructional strategy. For example, instructors who are implementing the Process Oriented Guided Inquiry Learning (POGIL) approach described in Chapter 4 share curriculum materials and expertise, connect through national and regional workshops, and take advantage of expert consultations through The POGIL Project.

Regional and national resource centers also support the use of research-based practices. For example, SERC at Carleton College collects and disseminates curriculum and instructional materials, conducts and publicizes research on teaching and learning, provides guidance and professional development on implementing research-based reforms, and creates opportunities for networking. SERC also serves as a physical and virtual connection point for colleges and universities across the country at which geosciences is taught.

In addition to sponsoring professional development, disciplinary societies and professional associations have advanced effective instructional practices by forming education interest groups within the larger organization, broadening their journals and other publications to highlight research on teaching and learning and effective instructional practices, developing tools to evaluate effective instruction, and scheduling sessions on DBER and effective instruction at their conventions and meetings, to cite just a few examples.

Conclusion

Making meaningful changes in the larger contexts that affect undergraduate science and engineering education requires the effort of faculty and leaders "pulling together to achieve a common goal," write Smith and MacGregor (2000, p. 81). It takes a collegial spirit and a willingness to try new things and learn from them. While individual instructors can do much on their own to improve teaching and learning, a great deal more can be achieved when departments, institutions, and external partners are committed to supporting this process.

Resources and Further Reading

Association of American Universities' Undergraduate STEM Education Initiative
www.aau.edu/stem

Discipline-Based Education Research: Understanding and Improving Learning in Undergraduate Science and Engineering (National Research Council, 2012)
Chapter 8: Translating Research into Teaching Practice: The Influence of Discipline-Based Education Research on Undergraduate Science and Engineering Instruction

Science Education Initiative at the University of Colorado Boulder
http://www.colorado.edu/sei/index.html

Problem-based learning at the University of Delaware
http://www.udel.edu/inst

Epilogue   On Changing Minds

Learning involves changing your thinking. As students progress through the undergraduate years, we not only expect them to change their knowledge and ways of thinking in the disciplines they study, but we also hope they will mature and develop attitudes and behaviors that will prepare them for the next stages of their lives. If you are an instructor, you expect students to undergo conceptual changes that lead to greater understanding of key ideas in your discipline. If you are a higher education leader, you expect your students to grow during their time at your institution in ways that will ready them for graduate education or careers.

A willingness to change your thinking is also integral to the practice of science or engineering. If you test a hypothesis or a prototype and the results differ from what you expected, you need to revise your hypothesis or alter your design—perhaps multiple times. Recognizing the need for change is a strength that produces better outcomes.

So it is, too, with teaching. A compelling body of evidence, drawn from research on how people learn science and engineering, shows that student-centered methods of teaching and learning are more effective than a traditional, passive approach that depends mostly on the instructor delivering information through lectures.

This book makes a case for instructors to hold themselves to the same expectations that they have for their students and to apply the same mindset that they use in their disciplinary research to their roles as teachers. In short, this book advocates that faculty and administrators be open to using research on learning to guide their conceptions about the best way to teach.

The reasons for changing instruction and suggestions for how to do this can be boiled down to these:

- *Effective instruction starts from an understanding of how students learn science and engineering.* Research has yielded insights about how students construct knowledge based on prior understanding, what types of misconceptions students commonly have, how novices differ from experts in their conceptual understanding and problem-solving approaches, and other aspects of learning. These insights provide a blueprint for revising instruction.

- *Changes can be implemented gradually, without taking too much time or causing unnecessary upheaval.* Many expert practitioners started small by incorporating one research-based strategy, such as ConcepTests with Peer Instruction, and then adding other research-based approaches as they became more comfortable with interactive methods. Even partial changes can significantly improve student learning.

  Establishing challenging goals for what students should learn will guide choices of instructional methods and assessments. Setting learning goals that emphasize the comprehension and application of important concepts is an important first step in identifying activities that will help students achieve these goals and the types of assessments that will best measure students' progress.

- *Research-validated instructional strategies and curriculum materials are already available.* Instructors do not have to start from scratch when designing new teaching approaches. The strategies described in this book have been used successfully by numerous practitioners and can be adopted and modified to meet the needs of local students and institutions. Materials are also widely available to help implement these strategies.

- *Research-based strategies can work in a variety of settings, including large introductory courses.* Many of the strategies described in this book have been effectively implemented in classes with hundreds of students as well as small classes; in regular classrooms as well as redesigned learning spaces; and in different types of institutions, from community colleges to large research universities.

- *Challenges to using research-based instructional strategies can be surmounted.* Many of the common reasons people give for why they cannot use student-centered instruction are myths. Genuine challenges, such as concerns about student resistance or the time required to revise your teaching, have been successfully addressed by thoughtful instructors.

- *Assistance with the implementation process is available.* Many expert practitioners eased their jitters about transforming their teaching by participating in professional development, seeking assistance from supportive colleagues, and other strategies.

- *Departments, higher education institutions, and outside organizations can support instructors' efforts to change their teaching.* Examples of such support include making grants to encourage departments to redesign courses, providing professional development, or revamping policies for faculty work schedules, instructor evaluations, and release time, among others. Even if a department or institution is not overtly hospitable to changes in teaching practice, instructors may still receive support from like-minded colleagues inside or outside the institution, disciplinary societies, collegial networks, and other sources.

Change can be uncomfortable, but it can also be exciting and inspiring. Imagine a physics class in which students work in groups to calculate where to place an airbag to safely catch someone shot from a cannon with certain specifications. Or an engineering class in which an undergraduate designs a light board for a disc jockey service as a final project. Or a biology course in which students apply what they have learned about human physiology and data analysis to solve a hypothetical problem about how an alien life-form's kidneys would work.

All of these activities and countless more have been done by practitioners who have successfully implemented research-based instruction. Changing your instruction toward more student-centered approaches can improve your students' learning and stimulate their interest in science or engineering—and inspire you in the process.

References

ABET. (2009). ABET criteria for evaluating engineering programs. Baltimore, MD: ABET.

Abraham, M.R., and Gelder, J.I. (n.d.). Molecular level laboratory experiments (MoLE) Available: http://genchem1.chem.okstate.edu/CCLI/Startup.html.

Abraham, M., Varghese, V., and Tang, H. (2010). Using molecular representations to aid student understanding of stereochemical concepts. *Journal of Chemical Education, 87*(12), 1425–1429.

Ainsworth, S., Prain, V., and Tytler, R. (2011). Drawing to learn science. *Science, 333,* 1096–1097.

Allen, D., and Tanner, K. (2002). Approaches in cell biology teaching. *Cell Biology Education, 1*(1), 3–5.

Amaral, K., Bauer, C., Hanson, D., Hunnicutt, S., Schneider, J., and Yezierski, E. (2005). A white paper for facilitating POGIL activities in large classes. Paper prepared for the POGIL National Meeting, June 13–16, 2005.

American Association for the Advancement of Science. (2011). Vision and change in undergraduate biology education: A call to action. Available: http://visionandchange.org.

American Society for Engineering Education. (n.d.). ASEE Conferences. Available: http://www.asee.org/conferences-and-events/conferences.

Angelo, T.A., and Cross, K.P. (1993). *Classroom assessment technologies,* 2nd ed. San Francisco, CA: Jossey-Bass.

Aronson, E., Blaney, N., Stephin, C., Sikes, J., and Snapp, M. (1978). *The jigsaw classroom.* Beverly Hills, CA: Sage Publishing Company.

Association of American Colleges & Universities. (2014). Project Kaleidoscope (PKAL)—Advancing what works in STEM education. Available: http://www.aacu.org/pkal/educationframework/index.cfm.

Association of American Universities. (2013a, June 25). AAU selects eight campus project sites for Undergraduate STEM Education Initiative. Available: http://www.aau.edu/WorkArea/DownloadAsset.aspx?id=14474.

Association of American Universities. (2013b). Undergraduate STEM Education Initiative: October 2013 update.

Association of American Universities. (n.d.). AAU Framework for systemic change in undergraduate STEM teaching and learning. Available: https://www.aau.edu/WorkArea/DownloadAsset.aspx?id=14357.

Austin, A.E. (2009, September). Cognitive apprenticeship theory and its implications for doctoral education: A case example from a doctoral program in higher and adult education. *International Journal of Academic Development, 14*(3), 173–183.

Austin, A.E. (2011). Promoting evidence-based change in undergraduate science education. Paper presented at the Fourth Committee Meeting on Status, Contributions, and Future Directions of Discipline-Based Education Research, Washington, DC, March 2011. Available: http://sites.nationalacademies.org/DBASSE/BOSE/DBASSE_080124.

Austin, A.E., Connolly, M., and Colbeck, C.L. (2008). Strategies for preparing integrated faculty: The Center for the Integration of Research, Teaching, and Learning. In C.L. Colbeck, K.A. O'Meara, and A.E. Austin (Eds.), *Educating integrated professionals: Theory and practice on preparation for the professoriate. New Directions for Teaching and Learning, Number 113* (pp. 69–81). San Francisco, CA: Jossey-Bass.

Baillie, C., Goodhew, P., and Skryabina, E. (2006). Threshold concepts in engineering education: Exploring potential blocks in student understanding. *International Journal of Engineering Education, 22*(5), 955–962.

Bassok, M., and Novick, L.R. (2012). Problem solving. In K.J. Holyoak and R.G. Morrison (Eds.), *Oxford handbook of thinking and reasoning* (pp. 413–432). New York: Oxford University Press.

Beach, A.L., and Cox, M.D. (2009). The impact of faculty learning communities on teaching and learning. *Learning Communities Journal, 1*(1), 7–27.

Beichner, R.J. (2008). The SCALE-UP Project: A student-centered active learning environment for undergraduate programs. Paper presented at the National Research Council's Workshop on Linking Evidence to Promising Practices in STEM Undergraduate Education. Washington, DC. Available: http://sites.nationalacademies.org/DBASSE/BOSE/DBASSE_080106.

Beichner, R., Saul, J.M., Abbott, D.S., Morse, J., Deardorff, D., Allain, R.J., Bonham, S.W., Dancy, M., and Risley, J. (2007, March). The Student-Centered Activities for Large Enrollment Undergraduate Programs (SCALE-UP) Project. In E.F. Redish and P.J. Cooney (Eds.), *Research-based reform of university physics.* College Park, MD: American Association of Physics Teachers.

Benbow, R., Byrd, D., and Connolly, M.R. (2011). *The Wisconsin longitudinal study of doctoral and postdoctoral teaching development: Key findings.* Available: http://www.cirtl.net/node/7300.

Bhattacharyya, G., and Bodner, G.M. (2005). It gets me to the product: How students propose organic mechanisms. *Journal of Chemical Education, 82*(9), 1402–1407.

Braxton, J., Lucky, W., and Holland, P. (2002). Institutionalizing a broader view of scholarship through Boyer's four domains. In *ASHE-ERIC Higher Education Report, vol. 29, no. 2.* San Francisco, CA: Jossey-Bass/John Wiley & Sons.

Brewe, E., Kramer, L., and O'Brien, G. (2009). Modeling Instruction: Positive attitudinal shifts in introductory physics measured with CLASS. *Physical Review Special Topics—Physics Education Research, 5*(1), 013102-1–013102-5.

Brewe, E., Sawtelle, V., Kramer, L.H., O'Brien, G.E., Rodriguez, I., and Pamelá, P. (2010). Toward equity through participation in Modeling Instruction in introductory university physics. *Physical Review Special Topics—Physics Education Research, 6,* 010106-1–010106-12.

Brewe, E., Traxler, A., de la Garza, J., and Kramer, L.H. (2013). Extending positive CLASS results across multiple instructors and multiple classes of Modeling Instruction. *Physical Review Special Topics—Physics Education Research*, 9(2), 020116.

Brown, A.L., and Campione, J.C. (1994). Guided discovery in a community of learners. In K. McGilly (Ed.), *Classroom lessons: Integrating cognitive theory and classroom practices* (pp. 229–270). Cambridge, MA: MIT Press.

Brownell, S., and Tanner, K. (2012). Barriers to faculty pedagogical change: Lack of training, time, incentives, and . . . tensions with professional identity? *CBE—Life Sciences Education, 11,* 339–346.

Carberry, A.R., and McKenna, A.F. (2014). Exploring student conceptions of modeling and modeling uses in engineering design. *Journal of Engineering Education, 103*(1), 77–91.

Carl Wieman Science Education Initiative. (2009). Learning goals for UBC PHYS 250, Introduction to Modern Physics. Available: http://www.cwsei.ubc.ca/resources/learn_goals.htm.

Catley, K.M., and Novick, L.R. (2008). Seeing the wood for the trees: An analysis of evolutionary diagrams in biology textbooks. BioScience, 58, 976–987.

Catley, K.M., and Novick, L.R. (2009). Digging deep: Exploring college students' knowledge of macroevolutionary time. *Journal of Research in Science Teaching, 46*(3), 311–332.

Center for Scientific Teaching. (2014). Mission statement. Available: http://cst.yale.edu/what-we-do.

Center for the Integration of Research, Teaching, and Learning. (n.d.a). Core ideas. Available: http://www.cirtl.net/files/CIRTL_CoreIdeas.pdf.

Center for the Integration of Research, Teaching, and Learning. (n.d.b). CIRTL network. Available: http://www.cirtl.net.

Cervato, C., and Frodeman, R. (2012). The significance of geologic time: Cultural, educational, and economic frameworks. *Geological Society of America Special Papers, 486*, 19–27.

Chasteen, S.V., Perkins, K.K., Beale, P.D., Pollock, S.J., and Wieman, C.E. (2011). A thoughtful approach to instruction: Course transformation for the rest of us. *Journal of College Science Teaching (40)*4, 70-76.

Chasteen, S.V., Pepper, R.E., Pollock, S.J., and Perkins, K.K. (2012). But does it last?: Sustaining a research-based curriculum in upper-division electricity and magnetism. *Proceedings of the Physics Education Research Conference, 1413*, 139–142. Omaha, NE, August 3–4, 2011. Available: http://www.per-central.org/items/detail.cfm?ID=10321.

Cheek, K.A. (2010). A summary and analysis of twenty-seven years of geoscience conceptions research. *Journal of Geoscience Education, 58*(3), 122–134.

Chen, X., and Ray, R. (n.d.). The story about DNA—Pursuing the big questions in molecular biology. Available: http://biology.wisc.edu/documents/xuchentu.pdf.

Clary, R.M., and Wandersee, J.H. (2007). A mixed methods analysis of the effects of an integrative geobiological study of petrified wood in introductory college geology classrooms. *Journal of Research in Science Teaching, 44*(8), 1011–1035.

Clement, J. (1993). Using bridging analogies and anchoring intuitions to deal with students' preconceptions in physics. *Journal of Research in Science Teaching, 30*(10), 1241–1257.

Clement, J. (2008). The role of explanatory models in teaching for conceptual change. In S. Vosniadou (Ed.), *International handbook of research on conceptual change* (pp. 417–452). New York: Routledge.

Cooper, J.L., MacGregor, J., Smith, K.A., and Robinson, P. (2000). Implementing small-group instruction: Insights from successful practitioners. *New Directions for Teaching and Learning, 81*, 63–76.

Cooper, M., and Klymkowsky, M. (2013). Chemistry, life, the universe, and everything: A new approach to general chemistry and a model for curriculum reform. Journal of Chemical Education, 90(9), 1116–1122.

Cooper, M.M., Cox, Jr., C.T., Nammouz, M., Case, E., and Stevens, R.J. (2008). An assessment of the effect of collaborative groups on students' problem-solving strategies and abilities. *Journal of Chemical Education, 85*(6), 866–872.

Cooper, M.M., Grove, N., Underwood, S.M., and Klymkowsky, M.W. (2010). Lost in Lewis structures: An investigation of student difficulties in developing representational competence. *Journal of Chemical Education, 87*(8), 869–874.

Cooper, M.M., Underwood, S.M., Hilley, C.Z., and Klymkowsky, M.W. (2012). Development and assessment of a molecular structure and properties learning progression. *Journal of Chemical Education, 89*, 1351–1357.

Cross, K.P., and Angelo, T.A. (1988). *Classroom assessment techniques: A handbook for faculty.* Ann Arbor: University of Michigan, National Center for Research to Improve Postsecondary Teaching and Learning.

Crouch, C.H., and Mazur, E. (2001). Peer Instruction: Ten years of experience and results. *American Journal of Physics, 69*, 970–977.

Cummings, K. (2008). The Rensselaer studio model for learning and teaching: What have we learned? Paper presented at the National Research Council's Workshop on Linking Evidence to Promising Practices in Undergraduate Science, Technology, Engineering and Mathematics Education, Washington, DC. Available: http://sites.nationalacademies.org/DBASSE/BOSE/DBASSE_080106.

Dancy, M., and Henderson, C. (2012). Educational transformation in STEM: Why has it been limited and how can it be accelerated? Presentation at the Second Conference on Transforming Research in Undergraduate STEM Education (TRUSE), St. Paul, MN, June 7, 2012. Available: http://www.chem.purdue.edu/towns/TRUSE/TRUSE%20docs/TRUSE%20Talks%202012/Dancy%20Truse%20Talk%20.pdf.

D'Avanzo, C., Anderson, A., Griffith, A., Merrill, J. (n.d.). Thinking like a biologist. Available: http://biodqc.org/node/35.

de Jong, T., and Ferguson-Hessler, M.G.M. (1986). Cognitive structures of good and poor novice problem solvers in physics. *Journal of Educational Psychology, 78*, 279–288.

Deslauriers, L., Schelew, E., and Wieman, C. (2011). Improved learning in a large-enrollment physics class. *Science, 332*(6031), 862–864.

Dickinson College. (2004). Workshop physics overview. Available: http://physics.dickinson.edu/~wp_web/wp_overview.html.

Dirks, C. (2011). The current status and future direction of biology education research. Paper presented at the Second Committee Meeting on the Status, Contributions, and Future Directions of Discipline-Based Education Research, Washington, DC, October 2010. Available: http://sites.nationalacademies.org/DBASSE/BOSE/DBASSE_080124.

Docktor, J.L., and Mestre, J.P. (2011). "A synthesis of discipline-based education research in physics." Paper presented at the Second Committee Meeting on the Status, Contributions, and Future Directions of Discipline-Based Education Research, Washington, DC, October 2010. Available: http://sites.nationalacademies.org/DBASSE/BOSE/DBASSE_080124.

Dodick, J. (2012). Supporting students' cognitive understanding of geological time: A needed "revolution" in science education. *Geological Society of America Special Papers, 486*, 31–33.

Dori, Y.J., and Belcher, J. (2005). How does Technology-Enabled Active Learning affect undergraduate students' understanding of electromagnetism concepts? *Journal of the Learning Sciences, 14*(2), 243–279.

Duch, B.J., Groh, S.E., and Allen, D.E. (Eds.). (2001). *The power of problem-based learning.* Sterling, VA: Stylus Publishing.

Dutrow, B.L. (2007). Visual communication: Do you see what I see? *Elements, 3*, 119–126.

Ebert-May, D., Batzli, J., and Lim, H. (2003). Disciplinary research strategies for assessment of learning. *Bioscience, 53*(12), 1221–1228.

Ebert-May, D., Derting, T.L., Hodder, J., Momsen, J.L., Long, T.M., and Jardeleza, S.E. (2011). What we say is not what we do: Effective evaluation of faculty professional development programs. *Bioscience, 61*(7), 550–558.

Englebrecht, A.C., Mintzes, J.J., Brown, L.M., and Kelso, P.R. (2005). Probing understanding in physical geology using concept maps and clinical interviews. *Journal of Geoscience Education, 53*(3), 263–270.

Fairweather, J. (1996). Faculty work and public trust: Restoring the value of teaching and public service in American academic life. Boston: Allyn & Bacon.

Fairweather, J. (2005). Beyond the rhetoric: Trends in the relative value of teaching and research in faculty salaries. *Journal of Higher Education, 76*, 401–422.

Fairweather, J. (2008). Linking evidence and promising practices in science, technology, engineering, and mathematics (STEM) undergraduate education: A status report. Paper prepared for the National Research Council Board on Science Education Workshop on Evidence on Promising Practices in Undergraduate Science, Technology, Engineering, and Mathematics (STEM) Education, Washington, DC, October 2010. Available: http://sites.nationalacademies.org/DBASSE/BOSE/DBASSE_080106.

Felder, R.M., and Brent, R. (2010). The National Effective Teaching Institute: Assessment of impact and implications for faculty development. *Journal of Engineering Education, 99*(2), 121–134.

Flinn Scientific, Inc. (2014). *POGIL Activities for AP* Biology.* Batavia, IL: Flinn Scientific, Inc. [Permission to reprint copyrighted materials is gratefully acknowledged. Reproduced for one-time use with permission from Flinn Scientific, Inc. All rights reserved.]

Forestell, A., Brissenden, G., Prather, E.E., and Slater, T. (2008). Revisiting Think-Pair-Share: An expanded how-to guide. Center for Astronomy Education. Available: http://astronomy101.jpl.nasa.gov/teachingstrategies/teachingdetails/?StrategyID=23.

Formica, S.P., Easley, J.L., and Spraker, M.C. (2010). Transforming common-sense beliefs into Newtonian thinking through Just-in-Time Teaching. *Physical Review Special Topics—Physics Education Research, 6*(2), 020106-1–020106-7.

Freeman, S., and Parks, J.W. (2010). How accurate is peer grading? *CBE—Life Sciences Education, 9*, 482–488.

Freeman, S., O'Connor, E., Parks, J.W., Cunningham, M., Hurley, D., Haak, D., Dirks, C., and Wenderoth, M.P. (2007). Prescribed active learning increases performance in introductory biology. *CBE—Life Sciences Education, 6*, 132–139.

Freeman, S., Haak, D., and Wenderoth, M.P. (2011). Increased course structure improves performance in introductory biology. *CBE—Life Sciences Education, 10*, 175–186.

Gabel, D., and Bunce, D. (1994). Research on problem solving: Chemistry. In D. Gabel (Ed.), *Handbook of research on science teaching and learning* (pp. 301–326). New York: Macmillan.

Gabel, D.L., Samuel, K.V., and Hunn, D. (1987). Understanding the particulate nature of matter. *Journal of Chemical Education, 64*(8), 695–697.

Gaffney, J.D.H., Richards, E., Kustusch, M.B., Ding, L., and Beichner, R.J. (2008). Scaling up education reform. *Journal of College Science Teaching, 37*(5), 48–53.

Gappa, J.M., Austin, A.E., and Trice, A.G. (2007). *Rethinking faculty work: Higher education's strategic imperative.* San Francisco, CA: Jossey-Bass.

Gillian-Daniel, D. (2008). The impact of future faculty professional development in teaching STEM undergraduate education: A case study about the Delta Program in research, teaching, and learning at the University of Wisconsin–Madison. White paper for the National Academies Workshop on Linking Evidence and Promising Practices in Undergraduate Science, Technology, Engineering and Mathematics Education, October 13–14, 2008.

Gosser, D. (2011). The PLTL boost: A critical review of research. *Progressions, 14*(1), 3–12. Available: http://www.pltl.org.

Haak, D.C., HilleRisLambers, J., Pitre, E., and Freeman, S. (2011). Increased structure and active learning reduce the achievement gap in introductory biology. *Science, 333,* 1213–1216.

Hake, R.R. (1998). Interactive-engagement versus traditional methods: A six-thousand-student survey of mechanics test data for introductory physics courses. *American Journal of Physics, 66*(1), 64–74.

Halloun, I.A., and Hestenes, D. (1985). The initial knowledge state of college physics students. *American Journal of Physics, 53*(11), 1043–1055.

Halloun, I.A., and Hestenes, D. (1987). Modeling instruction in mechanics. *American Journal of Physics, 55*(5), 455–462.

Hancock, G. (2010). Think-Pair-Share lecture. Presentation at the Early Career Geoscience Faculty Workshop Williamsburg, VA. Available: http://serc.carleton.edu/details/files/19471.html.

Handelsman, J., Ebert-May, D., Beichner, R., Bruns, P., Chang, A., DeHaan, R., Gentile, J., Lauffer, S., Stewart, J., Tilghman, S.M., and Wood, W.B. (2004, April 23). Scientific teaching. *Science* (304), 5670.

Hativa, N. (1995). The department-wide approach to improving faculty instruction in higher education: A qualitative evaluation. *Research in Higher Education, 36*(4), 377–413.

Hegarty, M. (2011). The role of spatial thinking in undergraduate science education. Paper presented at the Third Committee Meeting on Status, Contributions, and Future Directions of Discipline-Based Education Research, Irvine, CA, December 2010. Available: http://sites.nationalacademies.org/DBASSE/BOSE/DBASSE_080124.

Hegarty, M., Kriz, S., and Cate, C. (2003). The roles of mental animations and external animations in understanding mechanical systems. *Cognition and Instruction, 21*(4), 209–249.

Hegarty, M., Stieff, M., and Dixon, B.L. (2013). Cognitive change in mental models with experience in the domain of organic chemistry. *Journal of Cognitive Psychology, 25,* 220–228.

Heller, K., and Heller, P. (2010). Cooperative problem solving in physics: A user's manual. Available: http://www.aapt.org/Conferences/newfaculty/upload/Coop-Problem-Solving-Guide.pdf.

Henderson, C. (2008). Promoting instructional change in new faculty: An evaluation of the Physics and Astronomy New Faculty Workshop. *American Journal of Physics, 76*(2), 179–187.

Henderson, C., and Dancy, M. (2011). Increasing the impact and diffusion of STEM education innovations. White paper commissioned for the forum on Characterizing the Impact and Diffusion of Engineering Education Innovations, Washington, DC, February 7–8, 2011.

Henderson, C., Beach, A., and Finkelstein, N.D. (2011). Facilitating change in undergraduate STEM instructional practices: An analytic review of the literature. *Journal of Research in Science Teaching, 48*(8), 952–984.

Henderson, C., Dancy, M., and Niewiadomska-Bugaj, M. (2012). Use of research-based instructional strategies in introductory physics: Where do faculty leave the innovation-decision process? *Physics Education Research, 8*(020104), 1–14.

Heron, P.L, and McDermott, L.C. (1998). Bridging the gap between teaching and learning in geometrical optics. *Optics and Photonics News, 9*(9), 30–36.

Hestenes, D. (1987). Toward a modeling theory of physics instruction. *American Journal of Physics, 55,* 440–454.

Hestenes, D., Wells, M., and Swackhamer, G. (1992). Force Concept Inventory. *The Physics Teacher, 30,* 141–151.

Hilborn, R.C. (2012). Meeting overview. *The role of scientific societies in STEM faculty workshops.* Washington, DC: Council of Scientific Society Presidents.

Howard Hughes Medical Institute. (2011, May 3). HHMI helps summer institute expand to regional sites. *HHMI News.* Available: http://www.hhmi.org/news/hhmi-helps-summer-institute-expand-regional-sites.

Hurley, S.M., and Novick, L.R. (2010). Solving problems using matrix, network, and hierarchy diagrams: The consequences of violating construction conventions. *Quarterly Journal of Experimental Psychology, 63*(2), 275–290.

Jacobson, D., Davis, J., Licklider, B. (1998). Ten myths of cooperative learning in engineering education. Proceedings of the IEEE Frontiers in Education Conference. November 1998, Tempe, AZ.

Johnson, D.W., Johnson, R.T., and Smith, K.A. (1991). *Cooperative learning: Increasing college faculty instructional productivity.* ASHE-ERIC Reports on Higher Education No. 4. Washington, DC: George Washington University School of Education and Human Development.

Johnson, D.W., Johnson, R.T., and Smith K.A. (1998). Cooperative learning returns to college: What evidence is there that it works? *Change, 30,* 26–35.

Johnson, D.W., Johnson. R.T., and Smith, K.A. (2007). The state of cooperative learning in postsecondary and professional settings. *Educational Psychology Review, 19*(1), 15–30.

Johnstone, A.H. (1991). Why is science difficult to learn?: Things are seldom what they seem. *Journal of Computer Assisted Learning, 7,* 75–83.

Kali, Y., and Orion, N. (1996). Spatial abilities of high-school students in the perception of geologic structures. *Journal of Research in Science Teaching, 33*(4), 369–391.

Karpicke, J.D., Butler, A.C., and Roediger, H.L. (2009). Metacognitive strategies in student learning: Do students practice retrieval when they study on their own? *Memory, 17,* 471–479.

Kellman, P.J. (2000). An update on Gestalt psychology. In B. Landau, J. Sabini, J. Jonides, and E. Newport (Eds.), *Perception, cognition, and language: Essays in honor of Henry and Lila Gleitman.* Cambridge, MA: MIT Press.

Kindfield, A.C.H. (1993/1994). Biology diagrams: Tools to think with. *Journal of the Learning Sciences, 3,* 1–36.

Klymkowsky, M., and Cooper, M. (n.d.). Omnis cellula e cellula: Knowledge statements and performance expectations. Available: http://virtuallaboratory.colorado.edu/Cell+Molecular.

Knight, J.K., and Wood, W.B. (2005). Teaching more by lecturing less. *Cell Biology Education, 4*(4), 298–310.

Kortz, K.M., and Smay, J.J. (2012). *Lecture tutorials for introductory geoscience,* 2nd ed. New York: W.H. Freeman and Company.

Kortz, K.M., Smay, J.J., and Murray, D.P. (2008). Increasing learning in introductory geoscience courses using lecture tutorials. *Journal of Geoscience Education, 56*(3), 280–290.

Kozma, R.B., and Russell, J. (1997). Multimedia and understanding: Expert and novice responses to different representations of chemical phenomena. *Journal of Research in Science Teaching, 34*(9), 949–968.

Kraft, K. (2012). Encouraging students to "think" about how they think. *In the Trenches, 2*(1), 6–8.

Kraft, K. (n.d.). Earthquake case study. On the Cutting Edge: Professional development for geoscience faculty. Available: http://serc.carleton.edu/NAGTWorkshops/intro/activities/23588.html.

Krause, S.J., Kelly, J.E., and Baker, D.R. (2012a). Just-in-Time Teaching with Interactive Frequent Formative Feedback (JiTTIFFF or JTF) for cyber learning in core materials courses. Presentation prepared for the American Society of Engineering Education annual conference, 2012. San Antonio, TX, June 2012.

Krause, S.J., Kelly, J.E., and Baker, D.R. (2012b). Strategies and tools for engaging and assessing students with cyber learning by Interactive Frequent Formative Feedback (CLIFF) in core materials classes. ASEE Annual Conference and Exposition, Conference Proceedings, 2012.

Krause, S.J., Baker, D.R., Carberry, A.R., Koretsky, M., Brooks, B.J., Gilbuena, D., Waters, C., and Ankeny, C.J. (2013). Just-in-Time Teaching with Interactive Frequent Formative Feedback (JiTTIFFF or JTF) for cyber learning in core materials courses. Paper prepared for the American Society of Engineering Education annual conference, Atlanta, GA, June 23–26, 2013. Available: http://www.asee.org/public/conferences/20/papers/7863/download.

Larkin, J.H., McDermott, J., Simon, D.P., and Simon, H.A. (1980). Models of competence in solving physics problems. *Cognitive Science, 4*(4), 317–345.

Lattuca, L.R., Terenzini, P.T., and Volkwein, J.F. (2006). *Engineering change: A study of the impact of EC2000: Executive summary.* Available: http://www.abet.org/engineering-change.

Lazry, N., Mazur, E., and Watkins, J. (2008, November). Peer Instruction: From Harvard to the two-year college. *American Journal of Physics, 76*(11), 1066–1069.

Leckie, M. (n.d.). Teaching large introductory geoscience classes. Available: http://serc.carleton.edu/NAGTWorkshops/intro/largeclasses_leckie.html.

Lewis, S.E., and Lewis, J.E. (2005). Departing from lectures: An evaluation of a peer-led guided inquiry alternative. *Journal of Chemical Education, 82*(1), 135–139.

Libarkin, J.C., Kurdziel, J.P., and Anderson, S.W. (2007). College student conceptions of geological time and the disconnect between ordering and scale. *Journal of Geoscience Education, 55*(5), 413–422.

Long, T.M., Dauer, J.R., Kostelnik, K.M., Momsen, J.L., Wyse, S.A., Speth, E.B., and Ebert-May, D. (2014). Fostering ecoliteracy through model-based instruction. *Frontiers in Ecology and the Environment, 12*(2), 138–139.

Loucks-Horsley, S., Hewson, P.W., Love, N., and Stiles, K.E. (2009). *Designing professional development for teachers of science and mathematics,* 3rd ed. Thousand Oaks, CA: Corwin Press.

Luo, W. (2008). Just-in-Time Teaching (JITT) improves students' performance in classes: Adaptation of JITT in four geography courses. *Journal of Geoscience Education, 56*(2), 166–171.

Lyman, F. (1981). The responsive classroom discussion. In A.S. Anderson (Ed.), *Mainstreaming digest.* College Park, MD: University of Maryland College of Education.

Macdonald, R.H., Manduca, C.A., Mogk, D.W., and Tewksbury, B.J. (2005). Teaching Methods in Undergraduate Geoscience Courses: Results of the 2004 On the Cutting Edge Survey of US Faculty. *Journal of Geoscience Education, 53*(3), 237.

Manduca, C.A. (2008). Working with the discipline—Developing a supportive environment for education. Paper commissioned for the National Research Council's Workshop on Evidence on Promising Practices in Undergraduate Science, Technology, Engineering, and Mathematics (STEM) Education, Washington, DC. Available: http://sites.nationalacademies.org/DBASSE/BOSE/DBASSE_080106.

Manduca, C.A. (2011). Improving undergraduate geoscience education—A community endeavor., *GSA Today, 21*(9), 12–14.

Manduca, C.A., Mogk, D.A., Tewksbury, B., Macdonald, R.H., Fox, S.P., Iverson, E.R., Kirk, K., McDaris, J., Ormand, C., and Bruckner, M. (2010). SPORE: Science Prize for Online Resources in Education: On the Cutting Edge: Teaching help for geoscience faculty. *Science, 327*(5969), 1095–1096.

Marrs, K.A., and Novak, G. (2004). Just-in-Time Teaching in biology: Creating an active learner classroom using the Internet. *Cell Biology Education, 3*(1), 049–061.

Massey, W.F., Wilger, A.K., and Colbeck, C. (1994). Overcoming "hallowed" collegiality. *Change, 26,* 11–20.

Mayer, R.E., and Wittrock, M. (2006). Problem solving. In P.A. Alexander and P.H. Winne (Eds.), *Handbook of educational psychology,* 2nd ed. (pp. 287–303). Mahway, NJ: Lawrence Erlbaum.

Mazur, E. (1997). *Peer Instruction: A user's manual.* Upper Saddle River, NJ: Prentice Hall.

Mazzella, D. (2013). A year of women in STEM: Michelle Withers. *West Virginia University Magazine.* Available: http://wvumag.wvu.edu/a-year-of-women-in-stem/michelle-withers.

McConnell, D., and Steer, D. (2014). *The good Earth: Introduction to earth science,* 3rd ed. New York: McGraw-Hill.

McConnell, D., and Steer, D. (n.d.). ConcepTest: Determining numbers of plates. Available: http://serc.carleton.edu/introgeo/conceptests/examples/numbers.html.

McConnell, D.A., and van der Hoeven Kraft, K.J. (2011). Affective domain and student learning in the Geosciences. *Journal of Geoscience Education, 59*, 106–110.

McConnell, D., Steer, D.N., Owens, K.D., Knott, J.R., Van Horn, S., Borowski, W., Dick, J., et al. (2006). Using ConcepTests to assess and improve student conceptual understanding in introductory geoscience courses. *Journal of Geoscience Education, 54*(1), 61-68.

McDermott, L.C., and Shaffer, P.S. (2002). *Tutorials in introductory physics,* 1st ed. Upper Saddle River, NJ: Prentice Hall.

McLaughlin, J., Iverson, E., Kirkendall, R., Bruckner, M., and Manduca, C.A. (2010). Evaluation report of On the Cutting Edge. Available: http://serc.carleton.edu/files/NAGTWorkshops/2009_cutting_edge_evaluation_1265409435.pdf.

Mestre, J.P. (2008). Learning goals in undergraduate STEM education and evidence for achieving them. Commissioned paper for the National Research Council Workshop on Evidence on Promising Practices in Undergraduate Science, Technology, Engineering, and Mathematics (STEM) Education, Washington, DC, June 30, 2008.

Michigan State University. (2011, December 12). MSU program trains researchers in the finer points of teaching. *MSU Today.* Available: http://msutoday.msu.edu/news/2011/msu-program-trains-researchers-the-finer-points-of-teaching/#sthash.gsvENcDF.IXNL7RmO.dpuf.

Minnesota State University, Mankato. (2013). Iron Range engineering. Available: http://cset.mnsu.edu/ie.

Moog, R.S., Creegan, F.J., Hanson, D.M., Spencer, J.N., and Straumanis, A.R. (2006). Process Oriented Guided Inquiry Learning: POGIL and The POGIL Project. *Metropolitan Universities, 17*(4), 41–52.

Moretto, K. (2011). Assessment of the impact of the Lilly Teaching Fellowship: Summary 1991–2004, 2004–2009 cohorts. Available: http://fod.msu.edu/sites/default/files/3%20Assessment%20of%20the%20Impact%20of%20the%20Lilly%20Teaching%20Fellowship-%20Summary%201991-2004%202004-09%20Cohorts.pdf.

Nachshon, I. (1985). Directional preferences in perception of visual stimuli. *International Journal of Behavioral Neuroscience, 25*, 161–174.

Nakhleh, M.B., and Mitchell, R.C. (1993). Concept learning versus problem solving: There is a difference. *Journal of Chemical Education, 70*(3), 190–192.

National Academies. (n.d.). Summer institutes. Available: http://www.academiessummerinstitute.org.

National Academy of Sciences, National Academy of Engineering, and Institute of Medicine. (2005). *Facilitating interdisciplinary research.* Committee on Facilitating Interdisciplinary Research. Committee on Science, Engineering, and Public Policy. Washington, DC: The National Academies Press.

National Academy of Sciences, National Academy of Engineering, and Institute of Medicine. (2011). *Expanding underrepresented minority representation: America's science and technology talent at the crossroads.* Committee on Underrepresented Groups and the Expansion of the Science and Engineering Workforce Pipeline. Committee on Science, Engineering, and Public Policy and Policy and Global Affairs. Washington, DC: The National Academies Press.

National Research Council. (1999). *How people learn: Bridging research and practice.* M.S. Donovan, J.D. Bransford, and J.W. Pellegrino (Eds.), Committee on Learning Research and Educational Practice, Commission on Behavioral and Social Sciences and Education. Washington, DC: National Academy Press.

National Research Council. (2000). *How people learn: Brain, mind, experience, and school: Expanded edition.* J.D. Bransford, A.L. Brown, and R.R. Cocking (Eds.), Committee on Developments in the Science of Learning and Committee on Learning Research and Educational Practice, Commission on Behavioral and Social Sciences and Education, National Research Council. Washington, DC: National Academy Press.

National Research Council. (2001). *Knowing what students know: The science and design of educational assessment.* J.W. Pellegrino, N. Chudowsky, and R. Glaser (Eds.). Washington, DC: National Academy Press.

National Research Council. (2003). *Evaluating and improving undergraduate teaching in science, technology, engineering, and mathematics.* M.A. Fox and N. Hackerman (Eds.), Committee on Recognizing, Evaluating, Rewarding, and Developing Excellence in Teaching of Undergraduate Science, Mathematics, Engineering, and Technology. Washington, DC: The National Academies Press.

National Research Council. (2007). *Taking science to school: Learning and teaching science in grades K–8.* R.A. Duschl, H.A. Schweingruber, and A.W. Shouse (Eds.), Committee on Science Learning, Kindergarten Through Eighth Grade, Board on Science Education, Center for Education, Division of Behavioral and Social Sciences and Education. Washington, DC: The National Academies Press.

National Research Council. (2011). *Promising practices in undergraduate science, technology, engineering, and mathematics education: Summary of two workshops.* N. Nielsen, Rapporteur. Planning Committee on Evidence on Selected Innovations in Undergraduate STEM Education. Board on Science Education, Division of Behavioral and Social Sciences and Education. Washington, DC: The National Academies Press.

National Research Council. (2012). *Discipline-based education research: Understanding and improving learning in undergraduate science and engineering.* S.R. Singer, N.R. Nielsen, and H.A. Schweingruber (Eds.), Committee on the Status, Contributions, and Future Directions of Discipline-Based Education Research, Board on Science Education. Washington, DC: The National Academies Press.

Novak, G.M. (1999). *Just-in-Time Teaching: Blending active learning with Web technology.* Upper Saddle River, NJ: Prentice Hall.

Novick, L.R., and Catley, K.M. (2007). Understanding phylogenies in biology: The influence of a gestalt perceptual principle. *Journal of Experimental Psychology: Applied, 13*(4), 197–223.

Novick, L.R., Catley, K.M., and Funk, D.J. (2010). Characters are key: The effect of synapomorphies on cladogram comprehension. *Evolution: Education and Outreach, 3,* 539–547.

Novick, L.R., Stull, A.T., and Catley, K.M. (2012). Reading phylogenetic trees: Effects of tree orientation and text processing on comprehension. *BioScience, 62,* 757–764.

Pelaez, N.J., Boyd, D.D., Rojas, J.B., and Hoover, M.A. (2005). Prevalence of blood circulation misconceptions among prospective elementary teachers. *Advances in Physiology Education, 29*(3), 172–181.

Pfund, C., Miller, S., Brenner, K., Bruns, P., Chang, A., Ebert-May, D., Fagen, A.P., Gentile, J., Gossens, S., Khan, I.M., Labov, J.B., Pribbenow, C.M., Susman, M., Tong, L., Wright, R., Yuan, R.T., Wood, W.B., and Handelsman, J. (2009). Summer institute to improve university science teaching. *Science, 324,* 470–471.

Pfund, C., Mathieu, R., Austin, A., Connolly, M., Manske, B., and Moore, K. (2012, November/ December). Advancing STEM undergraduate learning: Preparing the nation's future faculty. *Change,* 64–72.

Piburn, M., Kraft, K., and Pacheco, H. (2011). A new century for geoscience education research. Paper presented at the Second Committee Meeting on the Status, Contributions, and Future Directions of Discipline-Based Education Research, Washington, DC, October 2010. Available: http://sites.nationalacademies.org/DBASSE/BOSE/DBASSE_080124.

Pollock, S., Pepper, R., Chasteen, S., and Perkins, K. (2011). Multiple roles of assessment in upper-division physics course reforms. *AIP Conference Proceedings, 1413,* 307–310.

Porter, L., Bailey-Lee, C., and Simon, B. (2013). Halving fail rates using Peer Instruction: A study of four computer science courses. Paper prepared for the SIGCSE 2013 conference, Denver, CO, March 6–9, 2013.

Prather, E. (2010). *When students are not learning, are you really teaching?* Center for Astronomy Education. Available: http://cetalweb.utep.edu/docs/Prather_Aug%202010_UTEP_ Implementation%20of%20Interactive%20Teaching.pdf.

Prather, E.E., and Brissenden, G. (2008). Development and application of a situated apprenticeship approach to professional development of astronomy instructors. *Astronomy Education Review, 7*(2), 1-17.

Prather, E.E., Slater, T.F., Adams, J., and Brissenden, B. (2007). *Lecture-tutorials for introductory astronomy,* 2nd ed. New York: Prentice Hall.

President's Council of Advisors on Science and Technology. (2012). *Engage to excel: Producing one million additional college graduates with degrees in science, technology, engineering, and mathematics*. Washington, DC: Executive Office of the President.

Price, E., Tsui, S., Hart, A., and Saucedo, L. (2011). Don't erase that whiteboard!: Archiving student work on a photo-sharing website. *The Physics Teacher, 49*, 426.

Price, E., Goldberg, F., Robinson, S.J., Harlow, D., McKean, M., Keene, S., and Czarnocki, K. (2013a). Development and evaluation of a large-enrollment, active-learning physics curriculum. Physics Education Research Conference series, 285–288. Available: http://www.per-central.org/items/detail.cfm?ID=13183.

Price, E., Goldberg, F., Patterson, S., and Heft, P. (2013b). Supporting scientific writing and evaluation in a conceptual physics course with calibrated peer review. *2012 Physics Education Research Conference: AIP Conference Proceedings, 1513*, 318–321.

Process Oriented Guided Inquiry Learning. (2014a). What is POGIL? Available: https://pogil.org/about.

Process Oriented Guided Inquiry Learning (2014b). Sample HSPl activities. Enzymes and cellular regulation. Available: https://pogil.org/high-school/hspi/activities/sample-activities.

Rebich, S., and Gautier, C. (2005). Concept mapping to reveal prior knowledge and conceptual change in a mock summit course on global climate change. *Journal of Geoscience Education, 53*(4), 355–365.

Rice, R.E., Sorcinelli, M.D., and Austin, A.E. (2000). *Heeding new voices: Academic careers for a new generation*. Washington, DC: American Association of Higher Education.

Richardson, C.T., and O'Shea, B.W. (2013). Assessing gender differences in response system questions for an introductory physics course. *American Journal of Physics, 81*, 231.

Rogers, E.M. (2003). *Diffusion of innovations*, 5th ed. New York: Free Press.

Rosengrant, D., Etkina, E., and Van Heuvelen, A. (2007). An overview of recent research on multiple representations. *AIP Conference Proceedings, 883*, 149–152.

Sandi-Urena, S., Cooper, M.M., and Stevens, R.H. (2011). Enhancement of metacognition use and awareness by means of a collaborative intervention. *International Journal of Science Education, 33*(3), 323–340.

Sandi-Urena, S., Cooper, M., Gatlin, T., and Bhattacharyya, G. (2011). Students' experience in a general chemistry cooperative problem-based laboratory. *Chemistry Education Research and Practice, 12*, 434–442.

Schuster, J.H., and Finkelstein, M.J. (2006). *The American faculty: The restructuring of academic work and careers*. Baltimore, MD: Johns Hopkins University Press.

Schwartz, D., and Bransford, J.D. (1998). A time for telling. *Cognition and Instruction, 16*(4), 475–522.

Schwartz, D.L., Lin, X., Brophy, S., and Bransford, J.D. (1999). Toward the development of flexibly adaptive instructional designs. In C.M. Reigelut (Ed.), *Instructional design theories and models, volume II* (pp. 183–213). Hillsdale, NJ: Erlbaum.

Science Education Resource Center. (2013). How to teach with Google Earth. Available: http://serc.carleton.edu/sp/library/google_earth/how.html.

Science Education Resource Center. (n.d.). ConcepTest examples. Available: http://serc.carleton.edu/introgeo/interactive/ctestexm.html.

Seidel, S.B., and Tanner, K. D. (2013). "What if students revolt?"—Considering student resistance: Origins, options, and opportunities for investigation. *CBE—Life Sciences Education, 12*, 586–595.

Seymour, E., and Hewitt, N.M. (1997). *Talking about leaving: Why undergraduates leave the science*. Boulder, CO: Westview Press.

Silverthorn, D.U. (2006). Teaching and learning in the interactive classroom. *American Journal of Physiology—Advances in Physiology Education, 30*(4), 135–140.

Simon, B., and Taylor, J. (2009). What is the value of course-specific learning goals? *Journal of College Science Teaching, 39*(2), 53–57.

Smith, K.A. (1998). Grading cooperative projects. *New Directions for Teaching and Learning, 74*, 59–67.

Smith, K.A. (2000). Going deeper: Formal small-group learning in large classes. *New Directions for Teaching and Learning, 81,* 25–46.

Smith, K.A. (2011). Cooperative learning: Lessons and insights from thirty years of championing a research-based innovative practice. Paper prepared for the 41st ASEE/IEEE Frontiers in Education Conference, Rapid City, SD, October 12–15, 2011.

Smith, K.A., and MacGregor, J. (2000). Making small-group learning and learning communities a widespread reality. *New Directions for Teaching and Learning, 81,* 77–88.

Smith, M.K., and Perkins, K.K. (2010, March). "At the end of my course, students should be able to ...": The benefits of creating and using effective learning goals. *Molecular Biology Australia,* 35–37.

Smith, M.K., Wood, W.B., Adams, W.K., Wieman, C., Knight, J.K., Guild, N., and Su, T.T. (2009). Why peer discussion improves student performance on in-class concept questions. *Science, 323*(5910), 122–124.

Smith, M.U. (1992). Expertise and the organization of knowledge: Unexpected differences among genetic counselors, faculty, and students on problem categorization tasks. *Journal of Research in Science Teaching, 29,* 179–205.

Sokoloff, D.R., and Thornton, R.K. (1997). Using interactive lecture demonstrations to create an active learning environment. *The Physics Teacher, 35*(6), 340–347.

Sokoloff, D.R., and Thornton R.K. (2004). *Interactive lecture demonstrations: Active learning in introductory physics.* New York: John Wiley & Sons.

Sorby, S.A. (2009). Educational research in developing 3-D spatial skills for engineering students. *International Journal of Science Education, 31*(3), 459–480.

Sorcinelli, M.D., Austin, A.E., Eddy, P., and Beach, A. (2006). *Creating the future of faculty development: Learning from the past, understanding the present.* Bolton, MA: Anker Press.

Sözbilir, M. (2004). What makes physical chemistry difficult?: Perceptions of Turkish chemistry undergraduates and lecturers. *Journal of Chemical Education, 81*(4), 573–578.

Streveler, R.A., Smith, K.A., and Pilotte, M. (2012). Aligning course content, assessment, and delivery: Creating a context for outcome-based education. In K.M. Yusof, N.A. Azli, A.N. Kosnin, S.K.S. Yusof, and Y.M. Yusof (Eds.), *Outcome-based science, technology, engineering, and mathematics education: Innovative practices.* Hershey, PA: IGI Global.

Svinicki, M. (2011). Synthesis of the research on teaching and learning in engineering since the implementation of ABET Engineering Criteria 2000. Paper presented at the Second Committee Meeting on the Status, Contributions, and Future Directions of Discipline-Based Education Research, Washington, DC, October 2010. Available: http://sites.nationalacademies.org/DBASSE/BOSE/DBASSE_080124.

Talanquer, V. (2012). Chemical thinking. Prezi presentation. Available: http://prezi.com/ds5j9zjqnf3x/c21.

Talanquer, V., and Pollard, J. (2010). Let's teach how we think instead of what we know. *Chemistry Education Research and Practice, 11,* 43–47.

Talanquer, V., and Pollard, J. (2012). Chemical thinking. Pilot online textbook for General Chemistry I. Available: http://www.chem.arizona.edu/tpp/chemthink (Password: chem21).

Tewksbury, B.J., and Macdonald, R.H. (2007). A practical strategy for designing effective and innovative courses. In K. Karukstis and T. Elgren (Eds.), *Developing and sustaining a research-supportive curriculum: A compendium of successful practices* (pp. 127–136). Washington, DC: Council on Undergraduate Research. Available: http://serc.carleton.edu/NAGTWorkshops/coursedesign/tutorial/index.html.

Titus, S., and Horsman, E. (2009). Characterizing and improving spatial visualization skills. *Journal of Geoscience Education. 57*(4), 242–254.

Towns, M., and Kraft, A. (2011). Review and synthesis of research in chemical education from 2000–2010. Paper presented at the Second Committee Meeting on the Status, Contributions, and Future Directions of Discipline-Based Education Research, Washington, DC, October 2010. Available: http://sites.nationalacademies.org/DBASSE/BOSE/DBASSE_080124.

Tversky, B., Zacks, J., Lee, P.U., and Heiser, J. (2000). Lines, blobs, crosses, and arrows. In M. Anderson, P. Cheng, and V. Haarslev (Eds.), *Theory and Application of Diagrams* (pp. 221–230). Berlin, Heidelberg: Springer-Verlag.

University of British Columbia. (n.d.). Carl Wieman Science Education Initiative: Tools. Available: http://www.cwsei.ubc.ca/resources/tools.htm.

University of Colorado Boulder. (2013). PhET interactive simulations. Available: http://phet.colorado.edu.

University of Georgia. (2007). Bylaws and peer evaluation form. Document provided by Michelle Momany, professor and head of the Department of Plant Biology at the University of Georgia.

van der Hoeven, Kraft, K.J., Srogi, L.A., Husman, J., Semken, S., and Fuhrman, M. (2011). Engaging students to learn through the affective domain: A new framework for teaching in the geosciences. *Journal of Geoscience Education, 59*, 71–84.

Van Heuvelen, A. (1991). Learning to think like a physicist: A review of research-based instructional strategies. *American Journal of Physics, 59*(10), 891–897.

Vergara C.E., Campa, H., Cheruvelil, K., Ebert-May, D., Fata-Hartley, C., Johnston, K., and Urban-Lurain, M. (2013). FAST-Future Academic Scholars in Teaching: A high-engagement development program for future STEM faculty. *Innovative Higher Education, 39*(2), 93-107.

Vygotsky, L.S. (1978). *Mind in society: The development of higher psychological processes.* Cambridge, MA: Harvard University Press.

Weinstein, C.E., Husman, J., and Dierking, D.R. (2000). Self-regulation interventions with a focus on learning strategies. In B. Monique, R.P. Paul, M. Zeidner, M. Boekaerts, and P.R. Pintrich (Eds.), *Handbook of self-regulation* (pp. 727–747). San Diego, CA: Academic Press.

Wieman, C., and Perkins, K. (2005). Transforming physics education. *Physics Today, 58*(11), 36.

Wieman, C., Perkins, K., Gilbert, S., Benay, F., Kennedy, S., Semsar, K., Knight, J., Shi, J., Smith, M., Kelly, T., Taylor, J., Yurk, H., Birol, G., Langdon, L., Pentecost, T., Stewart, J., Arthurs, L., Bair, A., Stempien, J., Gilley, B., Jones, F., Kennedy, B., Chasteen, S., and Simon, B. (2008). *Clicker resource guide: An instructor's guide to the effective use of personal response systems (clickers) in teaching.* Vancouver, BC, Canada: University of British Columbia. Available: http://www.cwsei.ubc.ca/resources/clickers.htm.

Wieman, C., Perkins, K., and Gilbert, S. (2010). Transforming science education at large research universities: A case study in progress. *Change: The Magazine of Higher Learning, 42*(2), 6–14. Available: http://www.changemag.org/Archives/Back%20Issues/March-April%202010/transforming-science-full.html.

Wieman, C., Deslauriers, L., and Gilley, B. (2013). Use of research-based instructional strategies: How to avoid faculty quitting. *Physical Review Special Topics: Physics Education Research, 9*, 023102.

Wiggins, G., and McTighe, J. (2005). *Understanding by design,* 2nd ed. Alexandria, VA: Association for Supervision and Curriculum Development.

Wilson, S.M. (2011, May). Effective STEM teacher preparation, instruction, and professional development. Paper presented at the workshop of the National Research Council's Committee on Highly Successful Schools or Programs for K–12 STEM Education, Washington, DC, May 2011. Available: http://sites.nationalacademies.org/DBASSE/BOSE/DBASSE_080128.

Wirth, K.R. (2003, November). Using an M&M® magma chamber to illustrate magmatic differentiation. In *Annual Meeting of the Geological Society of America, Abstracts with Programs, 34*, 250.

Wirth, K.R. (n.d.). Using an M&M® magma chamber to illustrate magmatic differentiation: background and notes for instructors. Available: http://www.macalester.edu/geology/wirth/CourseMaterials.html.

Wirth, K.R., and Perkins, D. (2008). Learning to learn. Available: http://www.macalester.edu/academics/geology/wirth/learning.pdf.

Wlodkowski, R.J. (1999). *Enhancing adult motivation to learn: A guide to improving instruction and increasing learner achievement,* revised edition. San Francisco, CA: Jossey-Bass.

Wood, D., Bruner, J.S., and Ross, G. (1976). The role of tutoring in problem solving. *Journal of Child Psychology and Psychiatry, 17*(2), 89–100.

Yezierski, E.J., and Birk, J.P. (2006). Misconceptions about the particulate nature of matter. Using animations to close the gender gap. *Journal of Chemical Education, 83*(6), 954–960.

Yuretich, R.F. (2003). Encouraging critical thinking: Measuring skills in large introductory classes. *Journal of College Science Teaching, 33*(3), 40–45.

Yuretich, R.F., Khan, S.A., Leckie, R.M., and Clement, J.J. (2001). Active-learning methods to improve student performance and scientific interest in a large introductory oceanography course. *Journal of Geoscience Education, 49*(2), 111–119.

List of Interviewees

We are deeply grateful to the following individuals who participated in interviews for this book conducted by Nancy Kober between March 2013 and March 2014. Their knowledge and insights have enriched this book in countless ways.

Deborah Allen, University of Delaware
Hyunsoo Bak, student, University of Washington
Maria Balajadia, student, University of Washington
Rebecca Bates, Minnesota State University, Mankato
Robert Beichner, North Carolina State University
John Belcher, Massachusetts Institute of Technology
Michael Blum, student, North Carolina State University
Cynthia Brame, Vanderbilt University
Eric Brewe, Florida International University
Derek Bruff, Vanderbilt University
Henry "Rique" Campa, Michigan State University
Stephanie Castañeda, student, Florida International University
Courtney Collingwood, student, University of Arizona
Melanie Cooper, Michigan State University
Elizabeth Derryberry, Tulane University
Clarissa Dirks, Evergreen State College
Erin Dolan, University of Georgia
Fernando Dossantos, student, Florida International University
Diane Ebert-May, Michigan State University
James Fairweather, Michigan State University
Noah Finkelstein, University of Colorado Boulder
Scott Freeman, University of Washington
Don Gillian-Daniels, University of Wisconsin–Madison
David Gosser, City College of New York
Molly Greenshields, student, University of Minnesota
Paula Heron, University of Washington
Robert Hilborn, American Association of Physics Teachers
Karen Kortz, Community College of Rhode Island
Kaatje van der Hoeven Kraft, Mesa Community College, Arizona
Ken Krane, Oregon State University
Stephen Krause, Arizona State University
Priscilla Laws, Dickinson College
Mark Leckie, University of Massachusetts Amherst
Kaitlyn Lestak, student, University of Washington

Roland Maio, student, City College of New York
Cathy Manduca, Carleton College
Eric Mazur, Harvard University
David McConnell, North Carolina State University
Lillian McDermott, University of Washington
Emily Miller, Association of American Universities
Richard Moog, Franklin & Marshall College
Carol Ormand, Carleton College
Valerie Otero, University of Colorado Boulder
Laura Palma, student, Florida International University
Kathy Perkins, University of Colorado Boulder
John Pollard, University of Arizona
Steve Pollock, University of Colorado Boulder
Edward Prather, University of Arizona
Edward Price, California State University San Marcos
Hannah Reisner, student, University of Minnesota
Chris Richardson, Elon University
Allison Rober, Ball State University
Alex Rudolph, California State Polytechnic University, Pomona
Carly Schnoebelen, student, University of Arizona
Dee Silverthorn, University of Texas
Beth Simon, University of California, San Diego
Jessica Smay, San Jose Community College
Bethany Smith, student, Arizona State University
Jacob Smith, student, California State Polytechnic University, Pomona
David Sokoloff, University of Oregon
Christian Strong, student, North Carolina State University
Charles Sukenik, Old Dominion University
Chris Swan, Tufts University
Vicente Talanquer, University of Arizona
Valerie Taraborelli, student, University of Arizona
Barbara Tewksbury, Hamilton College
Mackenzie Tilley, student, North Carolina State University
Cindy Waters, North Carolina Agricultural and Technical State University
Ashea West, student, City College of New York
Carl Wieman, Stanford University
Karl Wirth, Macalester College
William Wood, University of Colorado Boulder
Robin Wright, University of Minnesota
Natalie Yeo, student, Community College of Rhode Island
Richard Yuretich, University of Massachusetts Amherst

Biographical Sketches of Consulting Experts

ANN E. AUSTIN is a professor of higher, adult, and lifelong education at Michigan State University, where she also served as the inaugural Dr. Mildred B. Erickson Distinguished Chair. Dr. Austin's research interests, within the United States and international contexts, concern faculty careers, roles, and professional development; the academic workplace; organizational change and transformation in higher education; doctoral education; science, technology, engineering, and mathematics (STEM) education; and the improvement of teaching and learning processes in higher education. She is co–principal investigator of the Center for the Integration of Research, Teaching, and Learning and serves on the council of the American Educational Research Association (AERA). She has served as a Fulbright fellow in South Africa and as president of the Association for the Study of Higher Education. In recognition of her substantial contributions to educational research, she also was named as an AERA fellow. Dr. Austin has written several books and served as a consultant for a number of universities and colleges; her international higher education work has taken her to several countries in Europe, Asia, and the Middle East. Dr. Austin received a B.A. in history from Bates College, an M.A. in American culture from the University of Michigan, and a Ph.D. from the University of Michigan.

MELANIE COOPER is the Lappan-Phillips Professor of Science Education and a professor of chemistry at Michigan State University. Her initial appointment at Clemson University was one of the first tenure track appointments in chemistry education in a chemistry department. Her research has focused on improving teaching and learning in large enrollment introductory chemistry courses, including general and organic chemistry. She has worked on how students learn to construct and use representations, problem solving, conceptual understanding, and the development of practices such as argumentation and metacognition. An outgrowth of this research is the development and assessment of evidence-driven, research-based curricula. She was a member of the National Research Council's Committee on Status, Contributions, and Future Directions of Discipline-Based Education Research. She is a fellow of the American Association for the Advancement of Science and has received a number of awards for excellence in teaching. She holds a B.S., an M.S., and a Ph.D. from the University of Manchester (England).

HEATHER MACDONALD has been teaching in the Department of Geology at the College of William and Mary since 1983. She was dean of Undergraduate Studies in Arts and Science from 1994 to 1996; during that time she also served as the chief transfer officer at the college. She has been chair of the Geology Department and is currently co-director of the Marine Science Minor Program. Her awards include the Thomas Jefferson Teaching Award given by the College of William and Mary, an Outstanding Faculty Award given by the State Council of Higher Education for Virginia, the Biggs Award for Excellence in Earth Science Teaching given by the Geological Society of America, and the Neil Miner Award given by the National Association of Geoscience Teachers.

KARL SMITH is Cooperative Learning Professor of engineering education, School of Engineering Education, at Purdue University, West Lafayette, and is in phased retirement as a Morse-Alumni Distinguished Teaching Professor and professor of civil engineering at the University of Minnesota. His research and development interests include building rigorous research capabilities in engineering education; the role of cooperation in learning and design; problem formulation, modeling, and knowledge engineering; and project and knowledge management. He is a fellow of the American Society for Engineering Education and past chair of the Educational Research and Methods Division. He has served as primary investigator and co–primary investigator on several National Science Foundation (NSF)-funded projects, including two NSF Centers for Learning and Teaching and a dissemination project on course, curriculum, and laboratory improvement. He was a member of the National Research Council's Committee on the Status, Contributions, and Future Directions of Discipline-Based Education Research. He holds a B.S. and an M.S. in metallurgical engineering from Michigan Technological University and a Ph.D. in educational psychology from the University of Minnesota.

CARL WIEMAN holds a joint appointment as Professor of Physics and in the Graduate School of Education at Stanford University. He was associate director for science in the White House Office of Science and Technology Policy. Before joining the White House, he founded the Carl Wieman Science Education Initiative at the University of British Columbia, and he was a President's Teaching Scholar and Distinguished Professor of Physics at the University of Colorado Boulder. Dr. Wieman has carried out research in a variety of areas of atomic physics and laser spectroscopy. His research has been recognized with numerous awards, including the Nobel Prize in Physics in 2001. Dr. Wieman's discipline-based education research has examined a variety of innovations in teaching physics to a broad range of students, as well as students' problem-solving skills and their beliefs about physics. The collaborative initiatives he founded are aimed at achieving departmental-wide sustainable change in undergraduate science education. He served as founding chair of the National Research Council's Board on Science Education. He is a member of the National Academy of Sciences and the National Academy of Education. Dr. Wieman received a B.S. from the Massachusetts Institute of Technology and a Ph.D. from Stanford University.

WILLIAM B. WOOD is Distinguished Professor of Molecular, Cellular, and Developmental Biology, Emeritus, at the University of Colorado Boulder. He began his career at the California Institute of Technology, moving to the University of Colorado Boulder in 1977 as professor and chair of molecular, cellular and developmental biology. He was one of the youngest members inducted into the National Academy of Sciences in recognition of his pioneering research on the assembly of complex viruses that infect bacteria. His research interests more recently have included genetic control and molecular biology of axis formation, pattern formation, and sex determination in development of the nematode *Caenorhabditis elegans*, as well as biology education. Dr. Wood has won several awards for his scientific achievements, as well as the Bruce Alberts Award for Excellence in Science Education from the American Society for Cell Biology. He co-chaired the National Research Council (NRC) committee that created the Summer Institute on Undergraduate Biology Education and now serves as co-director of this Summer Institute. Previous National Academies appointments include the Committee on Programs for Advanced Study of Mathematics and Science in American High Schools, which authored the report *Learning and Understanding*; the Committee on Developmental Toxicology; and the Howard Hughes Medical Institute Predoctoral Fellowships Panel on Genetics and Molecular Biology. He also served as a member of the NRC Committee on Evidence on Selected Innovations in Undergraduate Science, Technology, Engineering, and Mathematics (STEM) Education and was a member of the Board on Science Education. Dr. Wood received his Ph.D. in biochemistry from Stanford University.

About the Author

NANCY KOBER is an editorial consultant at the George Washington University, where she edits and writes reports, articles, and other publications for the Graduate School of Education and Human Resources and writes, edits, and conducts policy analysis and research for the Center on Education Policy. At the time she wrote this book, Kober was a freelance writer, editor, and consultant specializing in education, with extensive experience translating research findings into plain language. Her numerous publications include dozens of reports for the Center on Education Policy, a chapter in *Narrowing the Achievement Gap* published by the Harvard Education Press, a book on family literacy issued by the Center for the Book at the Library of Congress, and reports for the U.S. Department of Education. She assisted in editing and writing reports for the Board on Testing and Assessment of the National Research Council (NRC) and for several NRC committees, including the Committee on Developments in the Science of Learning. Kober has taught writing to federal executives, including senior researchers and leaders at federal science mission agencies. Previously she served as a legislative specialist for a U.S. House of Representatives subcommittee on education. She has a bachelor's degree from Cornell University and a master's degree in writing from the University of Virginia.

Index

Association of American Universities, 201, 202, 203-204, 210
Astronomy examples, 46, 52, 65, 97, 170-171
Austin, Ann, 177, 182

B

Backward design, 33
Bak, Hyunsoo, 25
Ball State University, 44, 197
Bates, Rebecca, 31, 36, 119, 132, 205-206
Beichner, Robert, 113, 150-151, 173, 190-191
Belcher, John, 136, 137, 190-191
Biology examples, 21, 22-24, 27, 29, 33, 34-35, 46, 47-49, 61, 63-64, 74, 82, 85, 86-87, 97, 109, 113, 118, 131, 133-134, 151, 161, 163-164, 165, 166-167, 188, 190, 197, 213
Blackboard® software, 68
Brame, Cynthia, 42, 154
Brewe, Eric, 33-34, 43, 113-115, 126, 127, 148-149, 156
Brownell, Sara, 31
Bruff, Derek, 144, 158, 187, 188, 192-193
Burroughs Wellcome Fund, 203

C

Calibrated Peer Review, 141
California State Polytechnic University, Pomona, 46, 142, 143-144, 153, 191
California State University San Marcos, 122, 138, 139-140, 164
Campa, Henry "Rique" III, 196, 197
Carl Wieman Science Education Initiative, 16, 35, 155, 158
Carleton College, 30, 175, 205
Carnegie Academy for the Scholarship of Teaching and Learning, 168-169
Castañeda, Stephanie, 115, 130
CCNY (see City College of New York)
Center for Astronomy Education, 46, 121, 169
Center for Peer-Led Team Learning, 18-19, 128
Center for the Integration of Research, Teaching, and Learning network, 31, 32, 52, 136, 195, 198, 199

Chemistry examples, 14, 18-19, 60, 61, 64, 65-66, 76, 79, 80-81, 82, 83, 84, 85, 91, 92-94, 110, 111, 124-125, 131, 134-135, 145, 148, 184, 191
CIRTL (see Center for the Integration of Research, Teaching, and Learning)
City College of New York, 18-19, 118, 191
Cladograms, 82
Classroom Observation Protocol for Undergraduate STEM, 195
Classrooms (see Learning spaces)
Clickers and clicker questions, 21, 22-24, 27, 37, 38, 41, 52, 66, 98, 99, 100, 103, 110, 121, 122, 126, 128, 130, 138, 139-141, 142-144, 147, 149, 166, 190, 194-195, 197
Collaborative learning, 10, 15, 17, 19, 20, 25, 37, 41, 55, 62-63, 77, 89, 96-98, 103, 104-105, 108-115, 126, 131-132, 133, 147, 148, 150, 165, 184-185, 197
Collingwood, Courtney, 148
Colorado (see University of Colorado Boulder)
Community College of Rhode Island, 28, 51, 108
Concept Warehouse system, 68, 102
ConcepTests, 3, 37, 38-39, 40, 41, 66, 98, 99-100, 101-102, 103, 113, 121, 122, 126, 128, 129, 168, 180, 212
Conceptual understanding
  assessing, 23, 25-26, 27, 66, 128-129
  DBER studies, 63
  deep time example, 65
  fundamental concepts of disciplines, 63-72
  instructional strategies, 69-72
  misconceptions and, 2, 23, 25-26, 27, 39, 52, 53, 57, 64-66
  "muddiest points" reflection, 66, 67-68, 101-102, 129
  Newton's laws example, 71
  scaffolding, 70, 76, 95, 121
Cooper, Melanie, 80-81
Cooperative learning, 15, 49, 95-96, 104-105, 108-115, 131, 132-133
COPUS (see Classroom Observation Protocol for Undergraduate STEM)
CPR (see Calibrated Peer Review)
Cross, Patricia, 66
Crouch, Catherine, 58-59
CSUSM (see California State University San Marcos)

D

DBER (*see* Discipline-based education research)
Deep (geologic) time concept, 65
Delta Program in Research, Teaching, and Learning, 158-159, 197-198
Derryberry, Elizabeth, 42, 200-201
Designing instruction
    "bookended" approach, 96
    case studies, 92-94, 100-101, 106-107, 109, 114-115, 119
    "flipped classroom" approach, 96, 102
    formative feedback, 101-103
    group work, 108-115
    interactive exercises, 103
    jigsaw approach, 7, 52, 105-108
    learning goals, 90-91
    lectures, 96-103
    Peer Instruction and ConcepTests, 98-103
    practice-based and authentic experiences, 117-120
    student-centered instruction, 91-96
    student-to-student interaction, 104-117
    Think-Pair-Share activities, 24, 96-98
    tutorials, 116-117
Dickinson College, 69, 148, 163, 187-188
Diffusion of innovation theory, 20
Dirks, Clarissa, 47-49
Disciplinary societies, 44, 46, 172, 176, 201, 206, 207, 209, 213 (*see also specific organizations*)
Discipline-based education research
    assessment of students' conceptual understanding as, 33-34
    on faculty decisions about teaching practices, 20-27
    faculty expertise in, 188
    how DBER can help, 12-17
    and importance of improving instruction, 10-12
    on learning, 57, 61, 63, 64, 69-72, 73, 77, 79, 85, 95
    on lecturing, 17-20
    measuring effectiveness of student-centered instruction, 13-15, 48-49, 64
    scientific or engineering mindset for applying DBER, 16-17
    teaching impacts of, 2-10, 51
    theories of learning and, 13
Dolan, Erin, 131, 188
Dori, Yehudit Judy, 136
Duch, Barbara, 184

E

Ebert-May, Diane, 86, 87, 133
Elon University, 32, 197
Engineering examples, 15, 16, 35, 41-42, 46, 60, 66, 67-68, 75, 77, 79, 83, 84, 90, 100, 102, 113, 118, 119, 120, 132, 158, 160, 164, 205-207, 213
Engineering Criteria 2000 or EC2000, 205
Engineers Without Borders, 120
Evergreen State College, 47
External organizations
    accreditation standard setting, 205-206
    funding reform, 208-209
    promoting systemic reform, 202-204
    sponsoring professional development, 206-208
    types of influential organizations, 201-202

F

Facebook groups, 148
Faculty development (*see also* Professional development)
    hiring expert instructors, 188
    peer-evaluation process, 194
    promotion, tenure, and salaries, 191-195
    recognition of teaching excellence, 182, 183, 194, 195
    training assistants, 189
Faculty Institutes for Reforming Science Teaching, 38, 49, 200
Fairweather, James, 29, 177
FAST (*see* Future Academic Scholars in Teaching)
FCI (*see* Force Concept Inventory)
Finkelstein, Noah, 30, 31, 45, 180, 190, 208
FIPSE (*see* Fund for the Improvement of Postsecondary Education)
FIRST (*see* Faculty Institutes for Reforming Science Teaching)
FIU (*see* Florida International University)
Flickr, 140-141
Florida International University, 34, 43, 113, 114-115, 126, 127, 148-149, 156
Force and Motion Conceptual Evaluation, 70
Force Concept Inventory, 2, 99, 129
Formative assessment, 14, 55, 95, 101-103, 123, 124-125, 126, 128, 129-131, 135, 143, 194
Franklin & Marshall College, 45, 110, 112, 123
Freeman, Scott, 21, 22-27, 149

Fund for the Improvement of Postsecondary Education program, 150
Future Academic Scholars in Teaching fellows program, 44, 196-197, 199

G

GARNET (*see* Geoscience Affective Research NETwork)
GCI (*see* Geoscience Concept Inventory)
Gelder, John, 145
Geoscience Affective Research NETwork project, 9, 40, 135
Geoscience Concept Inventory, 40, 52, 126
Geosciences examples, 4, 33, 38-40, 44, 51-52, 65, 72, 83, 84, 97, 99, 103, 105, 106-108, 117, 121, 126, 132, 148, 155, 164, 195, 207-208, 209
Gillian-Daniel, Don, 158-159, 198
Google Earth, 106, 148
Gosser, David, 17, 18-19, 191
Group worksheets, 25-26

H

Haak, David, 24
Halloun, Ibrahim, 2
Hamilton College, 105, 106, 174
Handelsman, Jo, 16, 20, 33
Harvard University, 2, 98
Helmsley Charitable Trust, 203
Heron, Paula, 16, 117, 191
Hestenes, David, 2
Hilborn, Robert, 206, 207
Howard Hughes Medical Institute, 46, 47, 208

I

ILDs (*see* Interactive Lecture Demonstrations)
Implementing instructional reform
    acclimating students, 162-167
    assessments and evidence of effectiveness, 33-34
    challenges, 20-27, 154-157
    changing practices and influencing others, 48
    collaboration with colleagues, 10, 17, 21, 30, 39, 41, 42-43, 168, 179, 184, 187, 195, 196, 197
    content coverage, 160-162
    departmental context, 172-174, 177, 178-182
    evaluations of impacts, 48-49
    faculty development, 187-189
    first steps, 29-30
    funding/fellowships, 172, 187-188
    institutional context, 177, 182-186
    learning goals (curriculum and instruction), 34-41, 186-189
    mindset change about teaching, 30-32
    out-of-class activities, 40, 96, 161
    peer influence and, 172-174
    phasing in reforms, 41-42
    professional development, 43-44, 45-51, 168-171
    resources for, 44-45, 172
    scheduling classes, 190-191
    teaching as research, 32-34
    time allocation for, 157-159, 189-191
    workshops on, 4, 8, 10, 30, 33, 44, 46, 47-49, 51, 52, 105, 135, 188, 194, 207-208
Interactive Lecture Demonstrations, 69, 70, 71, 103, 145
Iron Range Engineering program, 118, 119, 205-206
Itasca Community College, 119

J

Jigsaw approach, 7, 52, 105-108
JiTT (*see* Just-in-Time Teaching)
JiTTIL (*see* Just-in-Time Teaching with Interactive Learning)
Just-in-Time Teaching, 101-103
Just-in-Time Teaching with Interactive Learning, 68, 101-103

K

Kortz, Karen, 28, 51-52, 108, 117, 121
Kraft, Kaatje van der Hoeven, 5, 6-10, 135, 193
Krane, Ken, 207
Krause, Stephen, 46, 66, 67-68, 101-103, 164

National Association of Geoscience Teachers, 8, 51, 207
National Effective Teaching Institute, 206-207
National Science Foundation, 4, 16, 19, 24, 32, 46, 49, 92, 135, 150, 171, 172, 185, 195, 196, 200, 201, 204, 208
NC State (*see* North Carolina State University)
New Faculty Workshops, 207
North Carolina State University, 36, 37, 99, 113, 149, 150, 151, 163, 173, 190-191
Notebooks, 6, 7, 9
NSF (*see* National Science Foundation)

O

Old Dominion University, 149
On the Cutting Edge, 8, 33, 44, 51, 52, 105, 135, 207-208
Oregon State University, 207
Otero, Valerie, 168-169, 189

P

Pedagogy in Action Web portal, 89
Peer Instruction, 3, 4, 16-17, 28, 98-103, 126, 212
    and ConcepTests, 98-103
Peer-Led Team Learning, 17-20, 110, 191
Perkins, Dexter, 55
Perkins, Kathy, 34, 146, 147, 178, 179-180, 182
PhET (Physics Education Technology) simulations, 145, 146-147, 152
Physics examples, 2-3, 14, 35, 38, 45, 60, 64, 66, 69-70, 74, 75-76, 79, 85, 95-96, 98, 101-103, 112-115, 116, 117, 118, 121-122, 126, 127, 128, 129, 134, 136, 139-141, 143-144, 145, 146-147, 148, 149, 150-151, 152, 160, 163, 173, 180, 190-191, 197, 213
Pilotte, Mary, 16
PKAL (*see* Project Kaleidoscope)
PLTL (*see* Peer-Led Team Learning)
Pollard, John, 91, 92-94, 95, 148, 189
Pollock, Steven, 128, 168, 169
Practice-based instruction, 86-87, 117-120
Prather, Ed, 130, 153, 169, 170-171

President's Council of Advisors on Science and Technology, 11
Price, Edward, 121-122, 138, 139-141, 142, 164, 165
Problem solving
    cooperative, 20, 77, 99, 103, 110-111
    expert versus novice, 58-59, 72-73, 79
    focus on principles, 73-75
    instruction strategies, 3, 60, 76-77, 84, 92, 93, 96, 103, 110, 212
    metacognitive strategies and, 60, 134-135
    representations and, 78
    working forward, 75-76
Problem-based learning, 112
Process Oriented Guided Inquiry Learning (POGIL) Project, 45, 92, 108-109, 110, 123, 124-125, 209
Professional development (*see also* Faculty development)
    in active learning, 47-48, 49, 51, 107, 130, 169, 170, 189, 196, 207-208
    centers for teaching, 189
    discussion opportunities, 187
    external organizations and associations, 206-208
    FAST program, 44, 196-197, 199
    fellowships, 46, 172, 187, 188
    grants, 172, 187-188
    in implementing reforms, 43-44, 45-51, 168-171
    institutional support for, 195-201
    On the Cutting Edge program, 8, 33, 44, 51, 52, 105, 135, 207-208
    prospective faculty, 12, 199
    workshops, 4, 8, 10, 30, 33, 44, 46, 47-49, 51, 52, 105, 135, 188, 194, 207-208
Project Kaleidoscope, 202
Purdue University, 16

R

Randomized calling, 24-25
Reading reflections, 9, 55, 129
Real Time Physics, 69
Reflective learning, 6-9, 200
Relevant learning, 51, 59, 61, 74, 76, 118
Rensselaer Polytechnic Institute, 149
Representations, visual and mathematical
    animations and simulations, 84-85, 145, 146-147, 152
    assessing use of, 127

V

W

Y

Photo and Illustration Credits